*CLASSIC RAF BATTLES*

*Editor in Chief Michael Armitage*

# CLASSIC RAF BATTLES
## *from World War One to the Present*

BROCKHAMPTON PRESS
LONDON

**Arms and Armour Press**
An Imprint of the Cassell Group
Wellington House, 125 Strand, London WC2R 0BB


This edition published 1999 by Brockhampton Press
an imprint of the Caxton Publishing Group
Reprint 2002
ISBN 1 86019 897X

British Library Cataloguing-in-Publication Data: a catalogue
record for this book is available from the British Library



Cartography by Cilla Eurich

Designed and edited by DAG Publications Ltd.
Designed by David Gibbons; edited by Philip Jarrett;

Printed and bound by Oriental Press, Dubai

# Contents

THE ROYAL FLYING CORPS BEGAN THE FIRST WORLD War by deploying to France in August 1914 with the maximum strength that it could muster. This amounted to 105 officers, 755 men, 95 transport vehicles and 63 aircraft. Today there are about 70,000 people in the uniform of its successor Service, the Royal Air Force, and just over 600 aircraft in the front line. Between those two points lies the unique history of the first independent air force in the world. It is a story of pioneering aviation, of challenges in peace and war, and, above all, it is a story of combat action and of other flying operations across the world.

In the seven decades of its existence, the RAF has seen tremendous technical change; indeed, it has led the world in many of those changes, such as the development and exploitation of the jet engine and the introduction of many pioneering developments in electronic warfare, not least in the introduction of radar. The passing years have also seen electronic systems replace many of the earlier mechanical ones; more capabilities are packed into a single aircraft than the early military fliers could have dreamed of; weapon accuracies have improved so much that a raid that might have needed the dispatch of hundreds of bombers during the Second World War can now be carried out by a mere handful of aircraft.

Yet though the equipment has changed so greatly over the years, most of the basic roles of the RAF have remained constant. Reconnaissance, one of the very first missions of military aircraft, still forms a vital part of the repertoire of today's Service, as do the roles of attack against land and sea targets, tactical and strategic transport, air combat against enemy fighters and the interception of hostile aircraft. The basic operational tasks carried out by the crews of today's Tornados would be easily recognised by the earliest military aviators flying their wood and fabric machines, though

they would be astonished at the complexities of today's aircraft and at the skills needed to operate them.

So we find in the story of the RAF a long process of technical development, from the very first viable fighting machines right up to the supersonic marvels of today; and we find a Service that has consistently performed a remarkably wide range of roles. It is also a Service that, to a unique extent, has taken part in operations world-wide. Widespread deployments began even before the Royal Flying Corps and the Royal Naval Air Service combined to form the RAF. For example, RNAS squadrons were operating over Gallipoli in 1915, and RFC squadrons were active on the Northwest Frontier of India at about the same time. Imperial commitments between the wars meant that some squadrons were permanently stationed overseas, in India, Iraq, Aden, Egypt or Singapore. During the Second World War and in the years immediately after, RAF operations extended even further, with deployments in Burma, West Africa, the Dutch East Indies and over the waters off Korea. Then, for almost three decades, there were various and often extensive operations in Malaya, Aden, Egypt, Korea and Borneo, as Britain sought to hand over former colonies and dependent territories to democratic elements rather than to governments that were communist-inclined.

This period was followed by an era in which, while RAF units prepared for an all-out war between East and West, the essential business of training continued, exercises being held in such widely scattered places as the deserts of the American Middle West, the Far East, northern Norway and Australia. The pattern was broken in 1982, when the Falklands conflict brought about a commitment in the South Atlantic that continues to the present day. Then, in 1990, the war in the Gulf was fought, a campaign that saw every operational type of aircraft in RAF service involved in one way or

# Introduction

*Michael Armitage*

another. More recently, the crisis in former Yugoslavia has meant the deployment of several aircraft types to southern Europe, including Tornados, Jaguars, E-3A Sentrys and Hercules among others. Meanwhile, humanitarian tasks continue to crop up, from Nepal to Ethiopia, Somalia and Central Africa. At the time of writing, about 100 RAF aircraft are going about their business outside the United Kingdom, and every operational type is either on operations or on standby for operations. We are seeing the continuation of a long tradition of activity of the kind represented within these pages.

With such a rich seam of past experience from which to draw, there are clearly more stories of the RAF to be told than any library could possibly hold. Some of the exploits in this colourful past will be familiar to many readers through written histories, films and photographs, all of which help to bring parts of the story to life. But there is a fourth medium that makes it possible both to capture the detail of events and to convey something of the atmosphere in which they took place. This is the window opened for us by the artist, with the artist's unique ability to capture war in the air by his portrayal of a single instant.

There have, of course, been other books of military aviation paintings. Most of them have dealt with the subject as a whole, and therefore include illustrations of basic training aircraft, peacetime exercises, air displays, first flights and so on. However, there seemed to be none that dealt exclusively with what is, after all, the whole point of an air force; military aircraft purely on operations, whether warlike, in the case of fighting units, or performing the equally vital business of transport and support.

The editors of the present publication therefore decided to concentrate on this particular aspect of the history of the Service, the RAF in action. The book brings together 40 such works by prominent aviation artists. We were particularly anxious to reproduce paintings to which the general public has little or no access. Many such paintings are in private collections, some are held by the squadron that took part in the action portrayed, and others are held by the RAF College at Cranwell, the RAF Staff College at Bracknell, or by the RAF Museum at Hendon. One thing seemed certain to the editors; such a wide diversity of paintings had never been brought together in one gallery, but it might be possible to put a selection of them between the covers of a book. This is the result.

Knowing that some striking works of aviation art grace the walls of, for example, various RAF officers' messes, we wrote to every RAF flying station, as well as to several other likely sources, such as the RAF Club. This produced some very interesting paintings, most of which have not before been reproduced for a public readership. But we did not confine ourselves to these so-far hidden treasures. There are other paintings which are very well known, but without their inclusion we would not have been able to create a reasonable balance of aircraft types, of campaigns and of the several periods of RAF history. Having said that, it is quite clear that all aspects of the RAF's operational story cannot be covered by a selection of only 40 paintings. Many other paintings had to be put to one side, and doubtless there are still many other worthy works of art that have yet to be brought into public view.

As to the collection that has been assembled here, each painting shows the RAF in action. Together, the paintings cover as wide a selection as we could manage of events in a long and colourful past. They range, for example, from air fighting during the First World War, represented by Michael Turner's depiction of one of McCudden's dogfights and Crosby's painting of Lieutenant Warneford's aircraft bringing down a Zeppelin, through Johnny Johnson's Wing in action in 1944 to three paintings of actions during the Gulf War of 1990. Many of them, like Warneford's action or Geoff Lea's painting of combat between a Halifax and an Fw 190, depict the heat of air-to-air combat. Others show bombing attacks, like that famously carried out by Guy Gibson over the Ruhr dams and depicted here by Maurice Gardner, or the daylight raid to Augsburg painted by Chris Stothard. Still others tell of less hazardous but equally important operations.

One of these, by John Young, is of Operation 'Manna' over Holland, during which many tons of supplies were dropped to thousands of Dutch civilians who might otherwise have perished in the winter weather of early 1945. Another, by Michael Rondot, depicts Wessex helicopters in their key mission of supporting the army in Northern Ireland. At least one painting, that by Jim Mitchell, is sheer nostalgia, showing the last operational flight by the last Spitfire in RAF service. It is depicted over Malaya, offering another reminder of the ubiquitous past of many of the squadrons of the RAF.

Most of the paintings are of very specific actions. 'Pheonix over Rangoon' by Mark Postlethwaite, for instance, is a study of one particular and well-researched mission by the Thunderbolt fighters of 30 Squadron on a specific day during the campaign in Burma. Jim Mitchell's 'The High Fighter' and Philip West's 'Corporate Prelude – Black Buck' are other examples, the latter showing a Vulcan heading in to its target, Stanley airfield, during the Falklands conflict.

Other paintings are more general, and are included because they are representative of broad campaigns or phases in various conflicts. Geoff Lea's 'Tempest and the Flying Bomb' is one; Michael Turner's 'Malta Gladiators' is another. They do not claim to represent a specific event. But whether a painting is specific or what I have called here 'representative', each of them is accompanied by a descriptive narrative from the pen of a well-known authority on military aviation. Some of these writers have a strong Service background. Ron Dick, for example, is a retired air vice-marshal with very wide experience of many types of aircraft; Tony Mason is another retired air vice-marshal, internationally known for his work on the history of air power. Other writers are universally recognised authorities on military aircraft and military aviation history, like Ray Sturtivant; Jack Bruce, one of the best-known names among aviation historians of the First World War; and Peter Kilduff, who is rapidly becoming an acknowledged expert on Von Richthofen.

In the cases of specific missions, these writers have researched the incident depicted in the painting so as to give details of the particular aircraft concerned, the performance characteristics of that aircraft type, the squadron's task on that particular day, perhaps the name of the pilot involved, the significance of the mission being flown, its success or otherwise, and so on.

Where the painting has been included to represent a type of operation, Mark Postlethwaite's 'Wapitis over Kurdistan' being a good example, the written description mixes hard fact about the aircraft depicted, when it entered service, and so on, with deductions and assumptions about the mission being undertaken. This information has resulted from research into squadron records to find out what the squadron concerned was doing in the period depicted, the nature of the terrain over which they operated, the height at which the Wapiti was flying, and the like. Critics might refer to this as 'faction', but what is said is based on research and on the writer's own experience of military aviation in general. Each of our distinguished writers hopes in this way to bring another, though more modest, dimension to the story told by the paintings, and to add in as authentic a way as possible to the interest of the events captured by the artists.

# The Artists

**Maurice Gardner** has had a keen interest in art since his schooldays and, having been brought up during the Second World War, has combined this interest with aviation subjects of that period. His art has won several awards, and fine art prints have been published of some of his works, the originals of which hang in private collections world-wide. An Associate Member of the Guild of Aviation Artists, he has studied commercial art and technical illustrating, and he seeks the advice of former aircrew to ensure the accuracy in his paintings.

**Air Vice-Marshal N. E. Hoad,** CVO CBE AFC* was commissioned into the Royal Air Force in May 1943 and joined 61 Squadron as a Lancaster pilot in 1944. He has always been interested in the visual arts, but it was not until the early 1950s that Service life permitted him the opportunity to give practical expression to this interest. By studying part-time at the York College of Art he gained the start which now permits him to pursue this interest full time. A Founder Member of The Guild of Aviation Artists, he was Chairman of The Society of Equestrian Artists for seven years, and is now fully occupied in meeting demands from his military patrons and those from the world of the horse.

**Geoff Lea** first took up oil painting while serving as a radio officer in the Merchant Navy, to make good use of his off-duty time, and became more interested in aviation art over the years. Most of his works are commissioned by military and business customers, although some have been produced for international private collections. They have also appeared as fine art prints, calendars, greetings cards and on book covers. Geoff Lea's distinctive style is also evident in the landscape, portrait and historical period pieces he creates when not working on military subjects.

**Jim Mitchell,** Dip AD, ATD, was born in Stoke-on-Trent in 1947 and is a nephew of the late Reginald Mitchell, the famous designer of the Spitfire and other Supermarine aircraft. Jim has exhibited widely, his paintings having been displayed in the London galleries, Derby City Gallery, Manchester Museum Gallery and galleries in the USA and Australia. He also teaches art to degree students. The hallmark of Jim Mitchell's work is his attention to detail, authenticity and interpretation of mood. Jim paints a wide variety of subjects in varying media. He has had many commissions for his original watercolours, and is equally happy painting in oils, in which medium he is well known for his aviation works.

**Mark Postlethwaite** is a professional artist painting exclusively aeronautical subjects. Born in Leicestershire in 1964, he spent ten years as a photographer before becoming a full-time artist in January 1992. Mark started painting aircraft at the age of 18 and, in 1978, he became the first Artist in Residence at the RAF Museum, Hendon, in what was the first major exhibition of his work. One-man exhibitions in the north of England and the Midlands followed shortly afterwards, and then, in 1991, he was elected to full membership of the Guild of Aviation Artists, thereby becoming the youngest artist ever to receive this distinction. In recent years, Mark's work has won him an outstanding reputation within the RAF and other armed services around the world, and more than 75 per cent of his work now comes from military commissions. The remaining 25 per cent is mainly concerned with producing original paintings for limited-edition prints, including the highly successful 'Famous Fighter' series published by Skyscapes Aviation Art.

**Michael Rondot** has gained an international reputation for his paintings of modern combat aircraft in powerful atmospheric settings. During his career as an RAF pilot he has flown many of his subject aircraft, culminating with the Jaguar single-seat fighter-bomber in the tactical-reconnaissance and ground-attack roles. He became a Founder Associate Member of the Guild of Aviation Artists in 1971, and published his first limited-edition print in 1980.

**David Shepherd** As a small boy, David Shepherd had only one ambition, to be a game warden, but his early career was 'a series of disasters'. Having left school in 1949 and been rejected by the Slade School of Fine Art as having 'no talent whatsoever', he owes much of his success to a chance meeting and much assistance from Robin Goodwin. He started his career as an aviation artist with many commissions from the RAF, and is also known for his landscape paintings, his portraits and his many military paintings.

David soon became active in conservation, and is now regarded by many as one of the world's leading wildlife artists. Because of the enormous debt that he says he owes wildlife for what it has done for him, he is also known internationally as a leading conservationist. One of the first major fund-raising successes was with the painting 'Tiger Fire', which raised £127,000 for Operation Tiger in 1973, and in 1984 the David Shepherd Conservation Foundation was set up to focus David's own conservation efforts and to increase awareness and funds for wildlife conservation both in this country and abroad.

David is also well known for his love of steam locomotives, and in 1967 he purchased the *Black Prince* and *Green Knight* and founded the East Somerset Railway, in Cranmore, Somerset. He intends to bring a South African Railways Class 15F locomotive to the East Somerset Railway in 1995.

His life story was featured in the BBC documentary 'The Man who Loves Giants', and he has featured in other films for Harlech TV, the BBC, Thames Television and Central Television. Many books of his paintings have been published.

David Shepherd was awarded an Honorary Degree of Fine Arts by the Pratt Institute in New York in 1971, and the Order of the Golden Ark in 1973 by HRH the Prince of the Netherlands for his services to conservation. He was made a Member of Honour of the World Wide Fund for Nature in 1979, and received the Order of the British Empire for his services to wildlife conservation. In 1986 David was elected a Fellow of the Royal Society of Arts, and in 1988 President Kenneth Kaunda of Zambia awarded him the Order of Distinguished Service. He was made a Fellow of the Royal Geographical Society in 1989, and he was awarded an Honorary Doctorate of Science by Hatfield Polytechnic in 1990.

**Christopher James Stothard** lives in Wainfleet, Lincolnshire, where he has worked as a design draughtsman and has been a retained fire fighter with the Lincolnshire Fire Brigade since 1983. He has always been interested in aviation and art, and became a member of the Guild of Aviation Artists in 1981. He has a daughter and one grandson, and his other interest is playing drums in a local group.

**Michael Turner** was born in Harrow, Middlesex, in 1934. Raised in the suburbs of London during the Second World War, he was inspired by the exploits of the RAF and developed an early talent for aircraft recognition, drawing aeroplanes in his school exercise books to the chagrin of his teachers. The enthusiasm for aviation found a parallel passion in the thrill of motor racing.

His formal education completed, Michael spent a year at Art College followed by two years National Service with the Royal Electrical & Mechanical Engineers.

Three years in advertising studios in London provided valuable experience, and in 1967 he went freelance.

With a strong belief that there is no substitute for first hand-involvement in order to be able to portray such demanding subjects with authority and feeling, Michael has travelled extensively to the world's major race tracks to satisfy his need for authenticity, and he continues to visit several Grands Prix and major Sports Car races each year. To the same end, he has flown in many service aircraft, from Tiger Moth and Lancaster to Harrier and Tornado, plus aerobatic sorties with the Red Arrows, to gain first-hand impressions for his aviation paintings. A Founder Member of The Guild of Aviation Artists, of which he has been twice Chairman and is now President, Michael also holds a Private Pilot's Licence and flies his own Chipmunk aircraft.

His clients include many racing drivers, teams, sponsors, pilots, motor and aircraft manufacturers, RAF and Army messes, museums, and private collections worldwide, and he has held one-man exhibitions in London, New York, Australia and the USA, as well as participating in specialist shows in the UK and Europe.

To date, Michael has had four books of his paintings published - one featuring aircraft of the Royal Air Force, one on Formula One motor racing, one on aircraft of the Luftwaffe, and a new book of his aviation art that appeared in autumn 1994.

Michael married his wife, Helen, in 1960, and they have two daughters, Alison and Suzanne, and a son, Graham.

**Tiro Vorster,** undoubtedly South Africa's best-known painter of aircraft and aviation scenes, showed his talent while still at school. Joining the South African Air Force in 1963, he spent much of his service life flying Shackletons on maritime patrols, and during this time perfected his artistic technique. His early work earned him recruitment as official artist for the *Air Force Safety Magazine*, which is held in high esteem by air forces around the world. In recognition of his work in aviation safety, chiefly through this magazine, he was awarded the Gold Aviation Safety Award. He is an artist member of the American Society of Aviation Artists, and was recently selected for exhibition by the Society at American Airlines' C. R. Smith Museum in Dallas, USA.

**Philip West** has an individual and original style, born not from formal art school training but from practical, practised and intuitive self-teaching. Love of art and subject matter helps immensely, and his natural enthusiasm is clearly evident in his work. Born in 1956, Philip was educated in Salisbury, Wiltshire. He is married to Alice (herself a noted artist), and he is a family man. Before taking up art full time, he worked in the business markets. Philip's original artwork is much prized, and his fine art limited-edition prints are being purchased by collectors world-wide.

**Brian Withams** has been a professional freelance artist for the past twenty years, initially working mainly as an aviation artist and book cover illustrator, and is one of the founder members of the Guild of Aviation Artists.

Before going freelance Brian worked for many years as a chief draughtsman and technical illustrator, skills he has used to striking effect in his paintings.

Brian has exhibited his work and sold commissions worldwide, especially in the Americas and in the UK. He has exhibited work at the RAF Museum, Hendon, the Fleet Air Arm Museum, Yeovilton, and annually for the past twenty years at the Guild of Aviation Artists.

**Frank Wootton** is one of the most celebrated names in aviation art, with numerous exhibitions in venues such as the Smithsonian Institution in Washington, DC, and the Royal Air Force Museum in London to his credit. Frank was educated at the Eastbourne College of Art, and he was an Official War Artist for the Royal Air Force between 1939-1946. His work hangs in national air force museums in Britain, the USA and Canada. His awards include Companionship of the Royal Aeronautical Society, and he is currently President of the Guild of Aviation Artists.

**John Young** was born in 1930 and educated in Buckinghamshire, at the Royal Grammar School and the School of Art in High Wycombe. A lifelong love affair

with aviation was inspired by a visit of Sir Alan Cobham's National Aviation Day air display to a site near his home, and he has developed a style of painting which portrays technical subjects in natural, atmospheric situations. Having established a career in illustration, working for many aviation manufacturers, airlines, air forces and publishers, John went freelance in the early 1960s to expand his capabilities and move toward the world of fine art. To this end he exhibited in the inaugural and subsequent exhibitions of the Society of Aviation Artists, later to become the Guild of Aviation Artists. A founder member of the Guild, John recently completed a term as its Chairman. John has taken the opportunity to fly in over 60 different types of aircraft, both military and civilian, giving his artwork an 'I was there' flavour. His accuracy in painting aircraft is a noted feature. He was awarded the Guild of Aviation Artists' Medal in 1983, was the first member of the Guild to receive the *Flight International* trophy for the Best Professional Aviation Artist three times, and has countless other professional awards and tributes to his credit. In addition to numerous private and corporate collections in the USA and UK, the Royal Air Force Museum at Hendon displays a collection of 45 of John's original paintings.

# The Authors

**Air Chief Marshal Sir Michael Armitage,** KCB, CBE joined the Royal Air Force as an Apprentice at Halton at the age of sixteen. Commissioned from Cranwell in 1953, he then served as a fighter pilot with 28 Squadron in Hong Kong for three years. After that tour he held a wide range of flying, command, staff and academic posts, including appointments as station commander at RAF Luqa in Malta, Deputy Commander RAF Germany, Air Member for Supply and Organisation on the Board of the Royal Air Force, Chief of Defence Intelligence in the Ministry of Defence, and, finally, Commandant of the Royal College of Defence Studies in London. During his RAF service Sir Michael amassed over 4,000 first-pilot flying hours, mainly on jet aircraft. He served in the Far East, the Mediterranean and three times in Germany, and visited over 60 countries world-wide during a career lasting 43 years.

**J. M. Bruce,** ISO, MA, FRAeS, FRHistS was educated at Perth Academy and the University of Edinburgh, where he was a founder member of that university's Air Squadron. After commissioned service in the RAF from 1942 to 1946 he became known chiefly for his published work on aircraft of the First World War and before, and for his seventeen-year service at the Royal Air Force Museum, Hendon. He was Lindbergh Professor of Aerospace History at the National Air and Space Museum, Washington, DC, from 1983 to 1984. Jack Bruce has been writing on aviation history for over forty years, and is widely regarded as one of the leading experts on the 1914–18 air war.

**Michael Burns,** MA was born in Aberdeen, educated in Edinburgh and read Modern History at Oxford. After graduating in 1975 he entered publishing, first with Gordon & Gotch, then with Orbis (Wings) and latterly as military editor for Blandford Press and Arms &

Armour Press. In 1987 he became a freelance editor, author and lecturer, and settled with his family in Lincolnshire. Michael has published poems, aviation and military articles and numerous books, including *The Windless Orchard* (1975), *Bader – The Man and His Men* (1990/94), and *'Cobber' Kain* (1992). He is also a faggot-oven master baker.

**Peter G. Cooksley,** ARHistS was born in Andover, Hampshire. He has spent the greater part of his life connected with aviation and writing about it. He entered full-time aviation journalism when he was invited to illustrate British and United States magazines on the subject, although he had previously been contributing to model-aviation publications since the age of sixteen. He now has a large number of aviation books to his credit and is engaged on a major book for Arms & Armour Press. After several years' experience in the Royal Observer Corps, Peter finally left that service as a full-time training officer. He is now a life member of the Society of Friends of the RAF Museum and a member of the Executive Committee of the Croydon Airport Society, the journal of which he edits. He was formerly the London Meetings Organiser of Cross & Cockade, the Society of World War One aviation historians, and until recently was a Vice-President of that organisation.

**Ken Delve** graduated with honours in Ancient History and Archaeology from the University of Birmingham. He maintained his interests throughout his RAF career, serving as field officer of the RAF Archaeological Society and conducting excavations in Cyprus. Qualifying as a navigator in 1977, he had an extended first tour of six years flying Canberra PR.9s with 39 Squadron. This was followed by a one-year attachment to the RAF Museum to assist with the Bomber Command Museum Appeal. His next operational tour was with IX

Squadron, the first Tornado unit. During this period he became a lecturer in air power studies for the RAF, a role which has since expanded to encompass regular lectures at various defence colleges. In 1985 he moved to Finningley to become a navigation instructor, and during a six-year spell he achieved A1 status as a ground instructor and A2 as an air instructor, acquiring over 1,000 hours of instructional experience on the Dominie teaching low-level techniques and radar navigation. January 1991 saw a return to the front line with II (AC) Squadron and the reconnaissance Tornado at RAF Marham. Having amassed almost 3,500 flying hours, Ken Delve retired from the RAF in 1994 to become editor of the aviation magazine *Flypast*. A prolific writer on all aspects of aviation history, he has eight major books and numerous articles to his credit.

**Air Vice-Marshal Ron Dick,** CB, FRAeS began his Royal Air Force career at the RAF College in January 1950, and was commissioned in July 1952. He joined 64 Squadron at RAF Duxford, flying Meteor 8 day fighters, and during this tour of duty he became a member of the aerobatics display team which represented the RAF for the 1953/54 seasons. On leaving 64 Squadron he converted to the Jet Provost and the Vampire, and in 1955/56 he won both the Clarkson and Wright Jubilee individual aerobatic trophies while flying these aircraft. In an unusually varied flying career he became a flying instructor, an examiner, an exchange flight commander with the USAF at Craig AFB, Alabama, a flight commander on a nuclear strike squadron, and a Vulcan squadron commander in Cyprus. From 1978-80 he commanded the Buccaneer low-level-strike wing at RAF Honington, and led RAF detachments taking part in the Red Flag and Maple Flag exercises in Nevada and Alberta. In more recent years Air Vice-Marshal Dick has been involved with historic aircraft, and has flown the

T-6, P-40 and P-51 with the Confederate Air Force. In 1983 he flew a restored Boeing B-17G from California to England for the RAF Museum, and 1989 he advised on the aerial sequences for the movie 'Memphis Belle'. He has flown more than 5,000 hours in over 60 types of aircraft. During the latter part of his career Air Marshal Dick was Air Attaché and then Defence Attaché at the British Embassy in Washington, DC. He retired from the RAF in August 1988, and was a Smithsonian International Fellow at the National Air and Space Museum in Washington, DC, until 1991. He now writes and lectures generally on military and aviation history, and is a Visiting Lecturer at the USAF's Air University at Maxwell AFB, Alabama.

**Michael J. Gething,** AMRAeS is currently the editor of *Jane's Defence Systems Modernisation*. He has been an aviation journalist since 1973. He was assistant editor of the Royal Aeronautical Society's magazine *Aerospace* from 1973 to 1976, and from 1976-93 he worked on the international journal *Defence*, being its editor for eight years. His many books include *Sky Guardians – RAF Air Defence 1918-93*, *Air Power 2000*, *Tornado*, *Harrier*, *Jaguar*, *NATO Air Power Today* and *Soviet Air Power Today* (Arms & Armour Press), *Test Pilots* and *F-15 Eagle*. A former RAFVR(T) officer with 2211 (Bracknell) Squadron, Air Training Corps, Michael is also a member of the Aviation & Space Writers Association, Air-Britain and the International Plastic Modeller's Society. Born in Bridlington, East Yorkshire, in 1949, he is married with two children and lives in Cowfold, West Sussex.

**Squadron Leader Peter Jacobs** was born in 1958 and educated near Southampton. He joined the Royal Air Force in 1977 as a Technician Apprentice at RAF Halton. On completion of training he was posted to Brize

Norton before being accepted for officer training at the RAF College Cranwell. After being commissioned he was posted to fly the F.4 Phantom at Coningsby. Having completed his first tour with 29 Squadron, during which time he served with 23 Squadron in the Falkland Islands, he was posted back to Finningley as a navigator instructor. In 1990 Peter returned to Coningsby as an instructor with the Tornado F.3 Operational Conversion Unit. On completion of his tour with 56 Squadron, in 1993, he became the Air Defence Advisor to the Defence Research Agency at Farnborough. Married, and with two young children, Peter is a keen RAF historian and has numerous articles to his credit.

**Peter Kilduff,** an American historian, is the author of seven aviation books, the last two for Arms & Armour Press, and in the past 25 years he has also written numerous articles for magazines and historical journals in the USA and Europe. Peter is a founding member and the immediate past president of The League of World War I Aviation Historians, and former managing editor of and a regular contributor to its quarterly journal, *Over the Front*. To date, the journal's readers have voted him four annual editorial excellence awards. Also active in German-American cultural exchange programmes, in 1987 Peter Kilduff was awarded the Cross of the Order of Merit of the Federal Republic of Germany.

**Air Vice-Marshal R. A. Mason,** CB, CBE, MA has been the Leverhulme Air Power Research Director for the UK-based Foundation for International Security since his retirement from the Royal Air Force in 1989. Over a period of 20 years he has written several books and many articles on air power, including *Air Power in the Nuclear Age* with Sir Michael Armitage, *The Soviet*

*Air Force* with J. W. R. Taylor, and *To Inherit the Skies: Britain's Air Defences.* His most recent book, *Air Power: a Centennial Appraisal*, was published by Brassey's in November 1994. Air Vice-Marshal Mason lectures on air power to military colleges and universities worldwide, and is a frequent defence analyst for the BBC. He is a Senior Visiting Fellow to the post-graduate School of International Security Studies at the University of Birmingham and to the Mosher Defence Institute, Texas, and he is a Senior Research Fellow at the Conflict Studies Centre, Sandhurst.

**John Maynard** was educated at Charterhouse and in 1949 joined the de Havilland Aircraft Company for engineering training. After commissioned service in the Royal Air Force he returned to Hatfield and remained in the aircraft industry until 1972, by which time he was working for BAC at Weybridge. He then joined Reed International, rising to become managing director of part of that company's papermaking interests. He retired in 1990 and now writes regularly for Aeroplane

Monthly, including his monthly 'Crosswind' column. He is a passionate supporter of all aspects of British aviation.

**Dr John Ray** is a member of the Society of Authors, the Crime Writers' Association and the RAF Historical Society. He has written 36 books, mostly on history for young people. His most recent book, *The Battle of Britain: New Perspectives*, is a detailed study which has been well received. Now a retired schoolmaster, he lived under the battle and subsequent night Blitz as a schoolboy, and witnessed many actions similar to those portrayed in these paintings. In his view, the bravery of the wartime Service and civilian defences in 1940-41 should never be forgotten.

**Mike Spick** is a full-time author/consultant with an international reputation. To date he has over 25 aviation books to his credit, many of which have been translated into other languages. An acknowledged authority on air combat, both fixed- and rotary-wing, between 1988 and

1991 he was the adviser on operational usage of the Swiss-based Project Atlas, with which he is still associated. Currently he is a consultant to *AirForces Monthly* and a frequent contributor to *Air International* and *Air Enthusiast*, and most recently he edited the official programme for Farnborough International '94.

**Ray Sturtivant,** ISO over the last forty years has written numerous articles and books on various aspects of British military aviation. His talent for searching out and assembling facts and figures has resulted in much historical information being pieced together which would otherwise have been lost to posterity. He has a particular interest in naval aviation, and his standard work *The Squadrons of the Fleet Air Arm* received general acclaim and is now in its much revised second edition. The results of his researches into the lesser-known RAF units, published from time to time in *Aviation News*, have also filled a gap in the recorded history of that Service.

# Lieutenant Warneford's Great Exploit

*Painting by Gordon Crosby*
*Text by Peter Kilduff*

WHEN KAISER WILHELM II OF GERMANY authorised the aerial bombardment of Britain on 9 January 1915, his military leaders were confident that they had the ideal weapons delivery system in their growing fleet of lighter-than-air craft. In May, the arrival of the new Zeppelin-built army airships LZ 37 and LZ 38 at forward bases in Belgium set the stage for what were intended to be unprecedented terror raids.

'Gott strafe England!' (May God punish England!) the German monarch had thundered, and the 536ft-long, four-engined rigid airships were to be the airborne instruments of retribution. Since 29 April LZ 38, commanded by Hauptmann (Captain) Erich Linnarz, had shown the airship's promise with a series of raids from Germany to British coastal cities. The great range and height of the new Zeppelins seemed to make them invulnerable to air attacks, and the closer proximity of a Belgian base would make more frequent raids possible. But the one million cubic feet of hydrogen gas that gave the airships their great lifting capacity also made them flying bombs that could themselves be destroyed, along with their crews.

As seen in Gordon Crosby's painting, the right combination of bravery, determination, skill and luck could bring down the biggest of Germany's aerial terror weapons. Early on the morning of Thursday 7 June 1915, Flight Sub-Lieutenant Reginald A. J. Warneford struggled to bring his Morane-Saulnier L monoplane above the airship LZ 37 and, in his ensuing attack, became the first British airman to cause the destruction of a Zeppelin in the air.

Pre-war flights aboard the civilian Zeppelin airship *Viktoria Luise* by advisors to Britain's Committee of Imperial Defence had alerted military planners to the potential value of the huge airships. Accordingly, early in the war, British aircraft were deployed to neutralise the threat of 'Zeppelins', as German airships of all manufac-

ture came to be known. Royal Naval Air Service aircraft slipped across the German border on 22 September 1914 and dropped bombs, without success, on airship sheds in Cologne and Düsseldorf. On 8 October, however, RNAS aircraft destroyed the German army airship Z IX in its shed in Düsseldorf. A few months later, following the initial success of LZ 38 over Bury St Edmunds, Southend and Ramsgate, 1 Wing RNAS at Dunkirk stepped up efforts to attack German airships within their operational area. They achieved modest success in the early dawn of 17 May, when LZ 39 was spotted near Dunkirk by two RNAS aircraft on patrol. They were joined immediately by seven other assorted aircraft.

Two Nieuports flew up under the airship. Squadron Commander Spenser D. A. Grey was in one, and Flight Sub-Lieutenant Warneford and his gunner, Leading Mechanic G. E. Meddis, were in the other. They opened up with machine-gun and rifle fire. LZ 39's commander ordered ballast to be dumped, immediately raised the airship and climbed away from his attackers, lest a stray bullet strike some metal object and cause a spark. While the hydrogen was stored securely in rubberised cotton cells, gas loss occurred and, in the air, produced a highly volatile mixture. The framework was made of aluminium to save weight, but Zeppelin crewmen always wore felt boots over their working shoes as a precaution against striking sparks while in among any of the airship's steel parts.

Flight Commander A. W. Bigsworth in an Avro 504B followed LZ 39 and got above it long enough to make one pass and drop four 20lb bombs along the flat top decking. Bigsworth saw smoke issuing from the Zeppelin, but his joy turned to disgust when he saw LZ 39 continue to head for Belgium, apparently little harmed by his bombs.

On the evening of Sunday 6 June 1915, a four-Zeppelin raid against London was launched. The

army airships LZ 37, LZ 38 and LZ 39 were joined by the naval Zeppelin L 9, commanded by Kapitänleutnant (naval Lieutenant) Heinrich Mathy. L 9 bombed coastal cities, but heavy fog made further attacks useless and Mathy headed back out to sea. Meanwhile, engine trouble stalled LZ 38 shortly after leaving her base, and she was forced to return. At just after 0200 on 7 June, two RNAS Henri Farman biplanes from Dunkirk bombed the Belgian airship base at Evère and destroyed LZ 38 in her shed.

In the hope of heading off the remaining raiders, two other RNAS aircraft had been despatched to bomb the Zeppelin sheds at Berchem St Agathe, in Belgium. One aeroplane suffered mechanical difficulties shortly after take-off and was forced to land. The pilot of the other, Flight Sub-Lieutenant Reginald Warneford, spotted the unmistakable outline of a Zeppelin off in the distance near Ostend. He headed his Morane-Saulnier L parasol monoplane for it, and caught up with the giant airship at about 0150, over Bruges.

Warneford's target was the army airship LZ 37, commanded by 28-year-old Oberleutnant (First Lieutenant) Otto van der Haegen. As soon as Warneford's aeroplane came within range it was warded off by a stream of machine-gun fire from one of the Zeppelin's gondolas. The British pilot knew from previous experience that his own machine-gun fire was likely to have little effect against the German airship, so he withdrew to gain the higher altitude needed to drop his six 20lb Hales bombs.

Inexplicably, van der Haegen turned away from the homeward course that offered him relief from the determined RNAS pilot. In an act that must have seemed like a crow going after a bothersome gnat, LZ 37 turned towards the small monoplane, keeping it under constant machine-gun fire. For the next twenty minutes Warneford eluded the hail of bullets and rose

steadily above the airship to about 11,000ft altitude. He pulled ahead of the slower-moving craft, then turned, headed for the Zeppelin and dived on it, making a fore-to-aft pass along the airship's spine some 150ft above it. One by one, Warneford released the bombs from a crude rack beneath his fuselage. They fell along the Zeppelin's full length.

The 23-year-old RNAS pilot looked back, at first disappointed at seeing nothing in the darkness

and fog. Then an explosion tore open the airship's forward section, followed by other flashes of flame as the released hydrogen was ignited. The explosions were so powerful that Warneford's small monoplane was thrown over on its back and hurled upward for 200ft. Then, as depicted in the painting, the RNAS pilot nose-dived the Morane to regain control while the stricken airship went down in a column of flame and smoke.

Seconds later Warneford looked around for his opponent, only to see, as he later reported, that 'the Zeppelin was on the ground in flames and ... that there were pieces of something burning in the air all the way down'. LZ 37 had come down at tremendous speed (falling 6,000ft in about seven seconds according to one source) and smashed on to a convent just outside Ghent. Two nuns, a man and a child in the convent died under the flaming, twisted wreckage. One member of the airship's crew, coxswain Alfred Mühler, survived; when the forward gondola came through the convent roof he was pitched on to a bed, completely uninjured.

Meanwhile, far above the wreckage, Warneford had regained control of his aeroplane only to have the engine cut out. He made a forced landing within German lines and found that a fuel line had been ruptured by the force of the explosion. After repairing it he restarted the Morane's engine, took off, and made his way back through the fog to the RNAS aerodrome at Furnes.

Two German airships had been accounted for by No. 1 Wing RNAS early that day, but Warneford's feat was the event that made international news. He received personal congratulations from King George V, and was officially notified that he would receive Britain's highest award for valour, the Victoria Cross. The French Secretary of War proposed Warneford for the rank of Knight of the Legion of Honour.

The young pilot lived to see only the French award. Following the presentation ceremony in Paris on 17 June, Warneford used the occasion to go to nearby Buc aerodrome to pick up a new Henri Farman biplane for his unit. He was making a short orientation flight with an American journalist when both of the aeroplane's right wings collapsed. The aircraft broke up in the air and both men fell from the wreckage. The pilot was still alive when help arrived, but he died en route to Versailles Hospital.

Flight Sub-Lieutenant Reginald A. J. Warneford, the first British airman to destroy a Zeppelin in the air and the second aviation recipient of the VC, was buried with full military honours in London on 22 June 1915, two weeks and one day after his great triumph.

# The Last Flight of Werner Voss

*Painting by Michael Turner*
*Text by J. M. Bruce*

BY SEPTEMBER 1917 THE BITTER FIGHTING OF THE Battles of Ypres of that year had been raging for a month; a month in which the rainfall had been more than twice the normal. The land on which that rain had fallen had had its natural surface drainage destroyed by an artillery bombardment that in ten days had poured 65,000 tons of shells on to the stricken area. Despite the weather, aerial forces had been participating on a large scale, not merely in reconnaissance and artillery spotting, but also in strategic bombing and ground attack. In September the immediate run-up to the offensive that became identified as the Battle of the Menin Road Ridge (20-25 September 1917) saw no fewer than 26 Royal Flying Corps and Royal Naval Air Service squadrons thus engaged. One of these units was No. 56 Squadron RFC, equipped with S.E.5a fighters and based at Estrée Blanche.

Leutnant Werner Voss had become one of Germany's most successful fighter pilots, building up a substantial tally of victories over a period of ten months. Late in July 1917, at the request of Rittmeister Manfred, Baron von Richthofen, commander of Jagdgeschwader 1, Voss had been posted to the command of Jagdstaffel 10. An Albatros D.V was made available to him, but late in August one of the pre-production Fokker triplanes, an F.1 Nr 103/17, was sent to Jasta 10, and he immediately found it to be an aircraft of exceptional manoeuvrability and responsiveness, one that might have been created specifically to suit his fighting skill and methods. Flying the triplane, he added nine more victories to his score in the space of just three weeks in that September of 1917.

On the morning of Sunday, 23 September, Voss shot down the D.H.4 A7643 of No. 57 Squadron, RFC. It was his 48th combat success. The evening of that day was overcast, with heavy cloud at 10,000ft and broken cloud lower down. Just after 1800, Voss took off in his triplane, leading a mixed formation of Albatros D.Vs and Pfalz D.IIIs, flying in two Ketten, each of three aircraft.

From Estrée Blanche two Flights of No. 56 Squadron had taken off at 1700, six S.E.5as of 'B' Flight led by Captain J. T. B. McCudden, and five of 'C' Flight, led by Captain G. H. Bowman. A little over an hour later McCudden, with clinical efficiency, destroyed a DFW two-seater over Houthem. It was his 13th combat success. McCudden's Deputy Flight Leader was Lieutenant A. P. F. Rhys Davids, whose score at the time was reckoned to be 19.

A few miles further north, two Flights of No. 60 Squadron (also flying S.E.5as) were returning from patrol. Lieutenant H. A. Hamersley, although aware of the near presence of a large formation of Albatros D.V fighters, went to the aid of what he thought was a Nieuport Scout being attacked by an Albatros, only to find, to his cost, that the 'Nieuport' was Voss's Fokker triplane, then a new and unfamiliar shape on the Western Front. Hamersley fired at the triplane, but to no avail, and Voss riposted with a burst of fire that so disabled the S.E.5a that Hamersley had to withdraw from the combat.

Captain R. L. Chidlaw-Roberts, Hamersley's Flight Commander, managed to fire a few rounds at Voss, but the Fokker's extraordinary manoeuvrability gave Voss a decisive advantage that he exploited to the full. In an instant he was on Chidlaw-Roberts' tail and had virtually shot away the S.E.5a's rudder bar, rendering it incapable of continuing to fight. By then the S.E.5as of No. 56 Squadron's 'B' Flight had joined the fray.

The ensuing fight was one of the most outstanding combats of the aerial war, and made a profound impression on the British pilots; their admiration for the courage and skill of Werner Voss was immense. He

was flying an aircraft that was tiny, compact, and outstandingly responsive: its wing span was only 22ft net, or 23ft 5in over the aileron balance areas that extended beyond the wingtips. The opposing S.E.5as had a span of 26ft 7.4in, and were powered by the 200hp Hispano-Suiza engine, a water-cooled V-8 with a frontal radiator, whereas Voss's Fokker had a captured Le Rhône 9J of 110hp, an air-cooled nine-cylinder rotary. The Le Rhône, at 268lb dry, was less than half the weight of the Hispano-Suiza, which weighed 515lb dry plus the weight of the radiator, water, plumbing and exhaust pipes. Significantly, the size and shape of the rotary engine enabled the Fokker's main masses (engine, fuel, armament and pilot) to be concentrated in a short, manoeuvrability-enhancing length of about 7ft 3in, whereas in the S.E.5a the corresponding dimension was about 12ft 6in. Fully loaded, the Fokker weighed 1,290lb, the S.E.5a 2,048lb. At an altitude of 4,000m (13,120ft) the triplane's speed was 165km/hr (102.5mph), some 18mph slower than that of the S.E.5a; yet its phenomenal agility amply compensated for lack of speed in combat. The Fokker's disadvantage was that it had little hope of being able to break off combat and escape, should that be dictated by circumstances.

It was in this disadvantageous situation that Voss found himself. Although none of his opponents had a victory score approaching his, the S.E. pilots were all seasoned men. Bowman's Flight had arrived to join the battle, and his tally was then 16, McCudden's 13, Rhys David's 19, Maybery's 17, Hoidge's 24 and Muspratt's 5. These pilots sustained the fight with Voss, who seemed undaunted by being so heavily outnumbered. He had twin belt-fed guns on his triplane, whereas each S.E.5a had one belt-fed Vickers gun firing through the propeller arc and a magazine-fed Lewis gun on the upper wing. This magazine had to be changed every 97 rounds, not an easy operation at the best of times, and a perilous exercise in the heat of combat.

Werner Voss was born on 13 April 1987, the youngest of three sons of Max Voss of Crefeld. His was a comfortable German middle-class family, but instead of going into his father's business Werner joined the 2nd Westphalian Hussars in April 1914, when he was barely 17. Although ordered to the Eastern Front when war broke out, he found that there was little practical use for cavalry and applied for a transfer to the Fliegertruppe. This was granted on 1 August 1915, and after flying training he flew two-seaters during the summer of 1916. Commissioned as a Leutnant der Reserve on 9 September, he was posted to a fighter unit, Jagdstaffel 2, on 21 November 1916. Here he found his *métier* as a fighter pilot. After several changes of unit, and an impressive sequence of combat successes, he was given command of Jasta 10 in the newly formed Jagdgeschwader 1 on 30 July 1917. Voss was a somewhat unruly spirit, and found difficulty in conforming to military convention. In the air he was an aggressive and resourceful fighter, second only to Manfred von Richthofen in the reckoning of combat victories.

James McCudden, the second son of a serving solider, Corporal William McCudden, and his wife Amelie Byford, was born on 28 March 1895. In April 1910 James McCudden enlisted in the Royal Engineers at Sheerness, became a bugler, and was posted to Gibraltar on 24 February 1911. By then his elder brother, Sapper W. T. J. McCudden, was with the Royal Engineers Balloon School at Farnborough, and went on to qualify as an aeroplane pilot in August 1912. James returned to England in September 1912, applied for transfer to the Royal Flying Corps, was accepted, and reported to the RFC Depot at Farnborough on 9 May 1913. In No. 3 Squadron he proved to be a highly competent and conscientious mechanic, a talent that was to serve him well

in his operational career. With the squadron in France he flew as an observer, having several combats. McCudden's flying training began on 22 February 1916, and he was posted to No. 20 Squadron on 8 July, to fly F.E.2d two-seaters. A month later he was transferred to No. 29 Squadron, a D.H.2 unit, thus becoming a scout pilot for the first time. His first combat victory was won on 6 September 1916, when he shot down a German two-seater. After a spell as a fighting instructor he flew Sopwith Pups for a few weeks with No. 66 Squadron before securing a posting to No. 56 Squadron in mid-August 1917.

Arthur Rhys Davids was a little younger than McCudden, and had had a different kind of life. Born on 26 September 1897 into a family of distinguished scholars, he won a King's Scholarship to Eton in 1911. There he excelled both in the classroom and on the sports field, and was Captain of that school in 1915-16. In March 1916 he won the Newcastle Scholarship to Balliol College, Oxford, but in August 1916, a month short of his 19th birthday, he joined the RFC, and was commissioned that month. He was picked by Captain Albert Ball for the new No. 56 Squadron, and went to France with them on 7 April 1917. His first combat success was won on the evening of 23 May 1917, when he sent down an Albatros scout out of control. Next day he destroyed a two-seater and sent another down out of control.

Rhys Davids was then under 20 years of age, and indeed was still three days away from his 20th birthday when he played a leading part in the defeat of Werner Voss. Several of the British pilots in the fight later wrote about it, commenting on Voss's astonishing mastery of his aircraft. McCudden was to write:

'By now the German Triplane was in the middle of our formation and its handling was wonderful to behold. The pilot seemed to be firing at all of us simultaneously, and although I got behind him a second time I could hardly stay there for a second. His movements were so quick and uncertain that none of us could hold him in sight at all for any decisive time.'

Lieutenant V. P. Cronyn recounted, of Voss's flying, how '...he whipped round in an extraordinary way, using no bank at all, but just throwing his tail behind him.'

Clearly, the S.E.5a's control responses could not match the quicksilver agility of the Fokker triplane, but there could be only one end to such an uneven contest of one against seven. Something that seems to have gone virtually unremarked, or at least unaccounted for, is the seemingly curious fact that for much of the fight Voss was alone, apart from being 'later joined by a red-nosed Albatros fighter', according to the official historian. He had, after all, left his base accompanied not only by Leutnant Bellen and Vizefeldwebel Rudenberg as his wing men, but also by Oberleutnant Wiegand in his Albatros D.V and Leutnants Bender and Kuhn in Pfalz D.IIIs. Perhaps the red-nosed Albatros was Wiegand's, but the other four German pilots have not been mentioned, and it appears that the 'large formation of enemy aircraft, about 25 Albatros D.Vs' mentioned by Lieutenant Hamersley in his account made no attempt to intervene.

Rhys Davids described what proved to be the *coup de grâce* in his combat report:

'Eventually I got east and slightly above the triplane and made for it, getting in a whole Lewis drum and a corresponding number of Vickers into him. He made no attempt to turn, until I was so close to him I was certain we would collide. He passed my right-hand wing by inches and went down. I zoomed. I saw him next with his engine apparently off, gliding west. I dived again and got one shot out of my Vickers; however, I reloaded and kept in the dive. I got in another good burst and the triplane did a slight right-hand turn, still going down. I had now overshot him (this was at 1,000 feet), zoomed, but never saw him again. Immediately afterwards I met the red-nosed scout, who was a very short way south-east of me. I started firing at 100 yards. The E.A. [enemy aircraft] then turned and fired at me. At 30 yards range I finished a Lewis drum and my Vickers stopped, so I dived underneath him and zoomed. When I looked again, I saw the E.A. spiralling down steeply out of control.'

McCudden and Bowman saw Voss's triplane crash about half a mile north of the ruins of Frezenberg. Voss was buried where he fell, but the grave was soon lost, merging anonymously into a war-ravaged landscape. His resting-place remains unknown and unmarked.

McCudden was later to write, in his account of the combat:

'As long as I live I shall never forget my admiration for that German pilot, who, single-handed, fought seven of us for ten minutes, and also put some bullets through all of our machines. His flying was wonderful, his courage magnificent, and, in my opinion, he was the bravest German airman whom it has been my privilege to see fight.'

Rhys Davids' only response to the subsequent congratulations of his squadron-mates was to say: 'Oh, if only I could have brought him down alive'. Tragically, he had little time left to live with his regrets, for he himself was shot down and killed on 27 October 1917, little more than a month later. He was only a few months younger than Voss, both of them being under

21 years of age when they died. Rhys Davids' grave, like that of Voss, is unknown.

Although McCudden did not meet his death in combat, he did not survive the war. With his victory score at 57, he died on 9 July 1918 following a take-off accident at Auxi-le-Château, while he was flying out to assume command of No. 60 Squadron, RAF. He was 23 years old, and now lies in the British war cemetery at Wavans. They were all so young.

So, too, were the many hundreds who were slain in that Battle of the Menin Road Ridge, which continued for two more days after Voss's death. The total casualties sustained by the 26 RFC and RNAS squadrons that participated in it were 62 pilots and observers killed, wounded or missing.

*They carry back bright to the coiner the mintage of man,*
*The lads that will die in their glory and never be old.*

wrote A. E. Housman some twenty years earlier. The poet could not have foreseen how much of that bright mintage might have been returned to his allegorical coiner in that war of 1914-18; its price would have been, as it proved to be, too dreadful to contemplate.

*The artist writes:* This was painted for a book by Christopher Shores entitled *Fighter Aces* and was also included in a book of my paintings of Luftwaffe aircraft published in 1985. In composing the picture I felt it important to get 'as close as possible' to the principal combatants in order to convey the eyeball-to-eyeball confrontations, which were in the nature of aerial combat during those early years

# The Flying Sword: Fokker D.VII Dogfight

*Painting by Mark Postlethwaite*
*Text by Peter Kilduff*

HIGH OVER THE SOMME RIVER VALLEY, THE HEAVY cloud cover was pierced by a flight of square-nosed Fokker D.VII biplanes. The German fighters rose above the rain and the grey pall below to gain the advantage of height. When opportune targets appeared through holes in the clouds, the Fokkers would streak down in swift, determined attacks. The fire from their twin Spandau machine-guns could tear apart many less sturdy enemy aircraft.

Angular and sinister-looking, the steel- framed D.VIIs were fast, rugged killing machines. The last of the famed Fokker fighter series to see service in appreciable numbers in the First World War, they were so effective that they became the only air weapon specifically denied to the Germans under the terms of the Armistice.

Intended to restore in 1918 the aerial superiority that Germany had enjoyed a year earlier, the D.VII was a formidable fighter, but Britain's equally angular and sturdy Royal Aircraft Factory S.E.5a generally held its own against the Fokker. The many aerial victories scored by such top RFC/RAF aces (and S.E.5a pilots) as Major Edward 'Mick' Mannock, Lieutenant Colonel William 'Billy' Bishop and Major James McCudden proved the point.

Mark Postlethwaite's painting shows a typical scene in which prowling Fokkers are challenged by S.E.5as high over the battlefront. In this summer view, the blue and red Fokkers of Jagdstaffel 18 are led by Germany's sixth highest scoring fighter ace of the First World War, Hauptmann (Captain) Rudolf Berthold. The aircraft in the foreground bears his white winged sword insignia on the fuselage. Berthold was very much a man to put his own stamp on things, and his Staffel colours came from the uniform of his pre-war army unit, Infanterie-Regiment Nr 20 'Graf Tauentzien', with its dark blue overcoat and red collar and cuffs.

A skilled fighter pilot and a tenacious opponent, Rudolf Berthold had 44 confirmed aerial victories to his credit in a comparatively long air combat career, from 2 February 1916 to 10 August 1918. A collision with his 44th victim then left him so badly injured that he was out of action for the rest of the war.

A native of Ditterswind in northern Bavaria, Rudolf Berthold joined a regiment in the neighbouring Kingdom of Saxony after he entered the army in 1909. Fiercely patriotic, he felt that he could best serve the unified German nation as a career army officer. Later he applied for flying training, and in January 1914 he qualified as an observer. At the time the German Army was very class-conscious, and assigned only officers as observers; piloting skills were of secondary importance, and were left primarily to enlisted men, who were often regarded as aerial 'drivers'.

Social convention meant little to Berthold, whose singleminded determination earned him the nickname 'the unbending Franconian'. He wanted to fight in the skies, and, when he went to war in 1914 with Feldflieger-Abteilung 23, he pursued his new calling with his usual zeal. He carried out many long-range reconnaissance flights during the German advance to the Marne, undaunted even by bad weather. On 4 October 1914 his efforts were recognised when he received the Iron Cross 1st Class from the hand of Prince August Wilhelm of Prussia, a son of the Kaiser.

The following month Berthold started pilot training and, in January 1915, he began flying over the Front. He felt secure at the controls of a big twin-engined AEG G.I, protected by three machine-guns, but on 15 September his slow-moving aeroplane became an easy target for a daring French fighter pilot. Before Berthold and his crew could respond, the hostile aircraft dived on them, shot up the AEG and flew off to bring down a German reconnais-

sance aircraft a short distance away. The AEG fell, but Berthold made a 'controlled crash' and the crew walked away from the wreck.

Feldflieger-Abteilung 23 was a general-aviation unit, equipped with several aircraft types. Though Berthold continued to fly the awkward AEG G.Is, he was more interested in the unit's fast and manoeuvrable single-seat fighters. By this time the air combat successes of Oswald Boelcke and Max Immelmann were widely discussed throughout the German air service. Both had started as reconnaissance fliers and graduated to single-seaters, a fact that encouraged Berthold to pursue the same end.

He was assigned to fly Fokkers in January 1916, the same month in which Boelcke and Immelmann became the first two aviators to receive the decoration Pour le Mérite. Prussia's highest award for bravery, the decoration was bestowed in recognition of each ace's having downed eight enemy aircraft. On 2 February Berthold claimed his first victory when he shot down a French Voisin two-seater over Chaulnes. Aerial victories were still sufficiently unusual to warrant special attention, and Berthold began to be rewarded for his achievements. Following his second 'kill', Berthold's home state of Bavaria awarded him its Military Merit Order 4th Class with Swords on 29 February.

During the Battle of Verdun, the general-aviation units formed specialised single-seat fighter Kampfein-

sitzer-Kommandos, and Berthold flew with Feldfl.-Abt 23's KEK Vaux, located at Chateau Vaux. While there, he was presented with Saxony's Knight's Cross of the Military St Henry Order on 8 April. He scored his fifth victory on 17 April, three days after his close friend and former squadron colleague Oberleutnant (First Lieu-

tenant) Hans-Joachim Buddecke became the third aviation recipient of the Pour le Mérite.

A week later Berthold crashed at Vaux airfield while flying a Pfalz monoplane. He suffered a severe skull injury, brain concussion, and a broken nose, thigh and pelvis. It seemed that Berthold's flying career was over, and he was sent home to convalesce. But, with typ-

ical stubbornness, he refused to go, saying: 'No power in the world will make me go back home. I will fly again – even if I have to be carried to the aeroplane.'

True to his word, Oberleutnant Berthold was back at the Front in four months, and scored his sixth aerial victory on 24 August. Under the strict rules then in force, he did not receive credit for aircraft shot down on 22 and 24 September. It was not until his eighth confirmed victory, on 26 September, that he became eligible for the Pour le Mérite.

The high Prussian award was approved on 12 October 1916. Within a year the hard-driving Berthold had become leader of Jagdstaffel 14 and then of Jagdstaffel 18. His score stood at 28 confirmed victories. While he was striving to achieve his 29th, Berthold's upper right arm was shattered by a burst of machine-gun fire, and this time he had to accept convalescent leave in Germany. With his right arm hanging limply at this side, totally beyond medical treatment, Berthold taught himself to write left-handed. 'If I can write, then I can fight,' he told his doctor, and when asking to be approved for return to front-line service.

Rudolf Berthold's indomitable will prevailed again and, on 1 March 1918, he returned to the Western Front in advance of Germany's last great offensive. Two weeks later, Bavarian fighter ace Hauptmann Adolf Ritter von Tutschek was killed in combat, and Berthold was appointed his successor as Kommandeur of the fighter wing Jagdgeschwader 2, composed of Jagdstaffeln 12, 13, 15 and 19. He was a brave but very demanding leader, showing by example that any obstacle could be overcome. Because of his useless right arm, his aeroplane was modified to allow the controls and guns to be operated with his left hand. For all his tenacity, however, he suffered severe pain from his arm injuries, which had not healed completely, and bone fragments continued to protrude painfully through his wounds. On 19 June 1918 Berthold wrote of his wounds: 'The pains are just maddening. During my aerial combat of yesterday, in which I shot down two British single-seaters in flames, my 35th and 36th victories, I cried out loudly in pain.'

Those victories were a pair of S.E.5s, encountered in a scene much like that in the painting by Mark Postlethwaite. Despite continued excruciating pain, Berthold shot down eight more aircraft until his final crash on 10 August. By the time he was ready to return to the Front, the war was over.

In the chaotic postwar period, communists attempted to seize political power in Germany, and ex-soldiers formed themselves into paramilitary groups to battle the reds in the streets. These groups were known as Freikorps, and one of them was the Eiserne Schar (Iron Band), led by Rudolf Berthold. He fought the communists with the same fervour that he had directed against British and French aeroplanes, no quarter being asked or given.

Finally, outnumbered and defeated in the town of Harburg, on the Elbe, Berthold was forced to surrender on the morning of 20 March 1920. He was leaving under a promise of free passage when he was attacked by the reds and beaten to the ground with rifle butts. According to one account, he was strangled with the silver-threaded ribbon of the Pour le Mérite he always wore. Four days later, on his 29th birthday, Hauptmann Rudolf Berthold was given a hero's funeral in Berlin.

*The artist writes:* When I was commissioned to do this painting I was concerned by my lack of knowledge of the subject. My basic knowledge of the First World War air war was enough to know that there was an immense amount of variation, not only in markings but also in individual aircraft modifications. Undaunted, however, I dug out everything I could on the subject and actually found that I had more on my bookshelf than I realised. The advantage of painting First World War aircraft lies in the variety of bold colour schemes that you can choose from, this being especially true of the German units.

One thing I hadn't realised was the considerable altitudes at which some of the combats took place. I therefore decided to do a high-altitude scene instead of doing the obvious 'over the trenches' view. With all of this in hand, I really enjoyed producing this painting, and I now have several ideas for future paintings that would be based upon these early beginnings of air warfare.

# *Wapitis over Kurdistan*

*Painting by Mark Postlethwaite*
*Text by Michael Armitage*

KURDISTAN! BETWEEN THE TWO WORLD WARS IT was a region known only to the most intrepid travellers, and to its wild inhabitants; yet during those years it was also the scene of regular activity by several squadrons of the RAF. This came about because, in the peace settlement at the end of the First World War, Britain had been given a League of Nations mandate over what was renamed Iraq in 1922. Britain had two very important interests in the region: oil, and its strategic position astride the route from Egypt to the Far East.

But the whole area was very turbulent. Local tribes fought each other both in the desert regions of the south and in the mountainous north-east; and up until 1926 Turkey sought the return of Mosul province with its oil reserves, from which she had been forced to withdraw in 1918 without having been militarily defeated there. Policing this huge territory conventionally, using the army, involved very large numbers of troops. In 1919, for example, the garrison comprised 25,000 British and 80,000 Indian troops. Despite the high priority given to Iraq, an impoverished Britain could ill afford such high costs.

During Winston Churchill's time in office as Secretary of State for both War and Air, the RAF had achieved a notable success in British Somaliland when a single squadron of aircraft had suppressed a tribal uprising in just three weeks. This experience led Churchill, when he was Colonial Secretary in 1921, to encourage Air Marshal Trenchard to propose a plan for similarly controlling Iraq. The eventual outcome was Cabinet agreement that the RAF should assume responsibility for Iraq, with an Air Vice-Marshal as C-in-C. This decision was implemented on 1 October 1922, and the forces to garrison Iraq were settled at eight RAF squadrons backed by nine British and Indian Battalions and some local levies, together with six companies of RAF armoured cars and various support services.

Trenchard's confidence proved to be fully justified. Using three main bases and numerous forward landing grounds, air power could be brought to bear anywhere in the country within a few hours, and it could be kept up for weeks if need be. It overcame most of the enormous difficulties involved in conventional campaigning across an inhospitable and hostile region, often without usable roads. Experience had shown that, for the army to mount an incursion into such territory, troops had to be assembled, a mass of transport vehicles and pack animals had to be gathered together, and supplies for the whole column amassed before a start could be made. The expedition itself then moved out at only a marching pace, hampered by the forbidding terrain, by the extremes of temperature between day and night, and very often by sickness. Its lines of communication, which became progressively extended, also had to be protected, and once the army had withdrawn from their territory, the tribesmen knew only too well that it would be many months before the manoeuvre could be repeated, during which they could make full use of the respite.

Two of the squadrons sent to Iraq were equipped with Vickers Vernon transport aircraft, two of the others flew Bristol Fighters and four more, including No. 30 Squadron, operated Airco D.H.9As. The Westland Wapiti, which first flew in 1927, was another two-seat general-purpose machine. It was selected to replace the D.H.9A after a competition with several other types at Martlesham Heath, in Sussex. In Iraq, the Wapiti Mk IIA, with either the 480hp Bristol Jupiter VIII radial engine or, in some squadrons, the later Jupiter XFa of 550hp, equipped Nos. 30, 55 and 84 Squadrons. The Wapiti had a top speed of 135mph, a cruising speed of 110mph and a range of 360 miles. Its initial rate of climb was 1,140ft/min, and it could reach 10,000ft in just under ten minutes. As armament, the Wapiti carried one fixed Vickers machine-gun firing forward

through a huge 11ft 6in-diameter propeller, and a Lewis gun mounted on a Scarff ring in the rear cockpit. A 500lb bomb load could be carried on underwing mountings, made up, for example, of four 112lb and four 20lb bombs. Altogether, about 500 Wapitis were built; about 80 were still flying with the RAF in India as late as 1939, and a handful were still operating as target tugs until 1943.

The painting by Mark Postlethwaite shows Wapitis of No. 30 Squadron over Kurdistan in northern Iraq during the 1930s. The nearest machine, K1389, was delivered from the manufacturer in December 1930 and shipped out to Basra in Iraq, arriving in July 1931. It was then taken to the nearby RAF airfield at Shaibah to be uncrated and assembled before being flown up to No. 30 Squadron at Mosul. As far as can be determined from the existing records, it remained with that unit until 1935, when No. 30 Squadron re-equipped with Hawker Hardys. In 1938 K1389 was at Karachi in India, and it was finally struck off charge on 31 July 1940 and scrapped, when just ten years old.

In the background of the painting are shown the mountains along the Iraqi border with Turkey, which lie to the north. Some rise to well over 12,000ft and are often snow-covered. In the foreground are the arid sandstone cliffs and gorges of the Cha-e-Chirin mountains in the Barzan area of Kurdistan. This landscape, and the position of the shadows, tells us that the Wapitis are flying in a roughly easterly direction, probably on a reconnaissance patrol in the late afternoon. Ahead of the formation will be the Zagros mountains that lie on the Iraqi border with Persia (now Iran), and the aircraft will be climbing to avoid the severe turbulence to be expected over the mountains in the heat of the late afternoon. In another fifteen minutes or so the formation will be approaching the border with Persia, and it will then probably turn starboard on to a south-westerly heading to return to the squadron base at Mosul, some 200 miles up the Tigris from Baghdad. The crews would be aiming to reach Mosul, by then 45min flying time away, before dusk, so that the aircraft could land in daylight, an important consideration because the night landing aids of the time were very rudimentary.

The two crew members were the pilot in the front cockpit, usually a commissioned officer, and one of the squadron ground crew in the rear cockpit. Under this curious arrangement, which was in force in most overseas squadrons at the time, the duties of rear gunner *cum* observer and, later in the decade, sometimes radio operator, were part-time roles carried out by volunteers; usually, but not always, armament tradesmen. No formal training was given, but these airmen were paid an 'aircrew supplement' of a few pence per day, and they wore the then coveted air gunner's badge, a winged brass cartridge. Both members of the crew would be carrying weapons with which to defend themselves in the event of a forced landing in this remote area, and several other precautions would have been taken for survival on the ground. Stowed inside the fuselage would be such items as engine covers, screw pickets, ropes, tools, rations, bedrolls and groundsheets. Not least, the crew would carry money in the form of gold coins, and so-called 'gooliechits'. These were leaflets written in the local languages, promising substantial rewards to the tribesmen for the safe return of crew members rescued from the desert.

At this time, the officers and men of No. 30 Squadron would have known Iraq well. During the interwar years, overseas postings lasted for at least five years, and the squadron itself built up a very wide experience of the country in the 24 years that it eventually spent there. The unit had been formed in Egypt on 24 March 1915, and flew in defence of the Suez Canal until 26 November of that year, when it moved to Mesopotamia. It then saw action against Turkish forces in all parts of the country until their surrender in 1918, in the roles of reconnaissance, bombing, fighter and army co-operation and, in June 1916, even air supply for two weeks in the desperate attempt to relieve Kut-el-Amara during its siege by the Turks. After the war the squadron remained in Mesopotamia, which was renamed Iraq in 1922, and was initially based at Baghdad West, with detachments operating from Kirkuk, Mosul and various advanced landing grounds, until it moved to Mosul as a complete unit.

In August 1939 the squadron re-equipped with Blenheims and moved to Ismailia in the Suez Canal Zone. After seeing action in the North African and Greek campaigns, No. 30 Squadron returned to Egypt, re-roled as a fighter squadron equipped with Hawker Hurricanes, and sailed for Ceylon embarked on the aircraft carrier HMS *Indomitable*. The aircraft flew off to land at Colombo in time to take part in the defence of the island against Japanese air attack in April 1942. The squadron remained in the Burma/India theatre for the rest of the war, operating in the fighter/bomber role and flying American-built Republic Thunderbolts in the later stages of the campaign. Today, No. 30 Squadron operates Lockheed Hercules C.1P and C.3P transport aircraft from RAF Lyneham in Wiltshire.

*The artist writes:* This was a very simple painting, produced on behalf of 30 Squadron Association, RAF, to commemorate their use of the Wapiti in the 1930s. Although I had very little information from which to work, I did manage to talk to one pilot who was on the squadron at the time, and who flew this distinctive aircraft. He told me some highly amusing tales concerning the operations that they undertook with the Wapiti, and described its characteristic flying habits.

The terrain in the area was very inhospitable, as were many of the inhabitants(!), and I've tried to show this in the painting. My only regret is not having had time to produce a larger, more detailed picture which I feel the Wapiti deserves. One day, I hope I can find time to fulfil this promise.

# Gladiators Over Malta

*Painting by Michael Turner*
*Text by Peter Cooksley*

SINCE 1814 THE ISLAND OF MALTA, ONLY 80 MILES south of Sicily, had occupied a strategic position for Britain in the eastern Mediterranean Sea. Its importance was renewed by Italy's entry into the Second World War and the opening of hostilities against the British Isles and France on Monday 10 June 1940. It seemed clear, however, that adequate defence measures against this anticipated threat had already been taken, for Hal Far, Luqa and Ta'Qali, the island's military airfields, had all been earmarked as prospective bases for the four squadrons of Hawker Hurricanes promised for Malta's protection. These decisions had, however, been taken in the light of military experience gained by strategists in France 22 years earlier, during the First World War. As it seemed likely that the scenario of a war of attrition would be repeated, the most active immediate step taken was the dispatch of HMS *Terror* to augment Malta's anti-aircraft defences.

History now records that attrition was not to be the case. The Nazi blitzkrieg of 1940 carried all before it, the British Expeditionary Force was miraculously plucked from the Dunkirk beaches, and the enemy was then poised to strike a death blow at the Motherland itself, making its defence the overriding priority.

Britain had also fared badly in the campaign in Norway. In May, Gloster Gladiator biplane fighters had been taken there in the carrier HMS *Glorious*, which had been ordered to weigh anchor with so few preliminaries that she had left crated fighters behind for later collection. These were to lie idle when the carrier failed to return, having been sent to the bottom by the *Scharnhorst* and *Gneisenau* when British forces were forced to evacuate from the Scandinavian campaign in June.

These apparently unrelated events were to have an effect even as far away as the 122 square miles of almost treeless islands in the Mediterranean. The summer of that historic year was to see the unexpected spectacle of the last of the RAF's biplane fighters flung into combat against such trimotor bombers as the dark green, brown and hazel-camouflaged Savoia Marchetti S-79 Sparviero bombers of Facist Italy's Regia Aeronautica, the earliest sorties of which were flown from the Sicilian bases of 30° Stormo BT. Few of the RAF defenders bore individual markings except for N5519's single letter 'R' aft of its fuselage cockade, and it was not long before even the spinners of the wooden two-bladed propellers vanished in a concession to swifter servicing. The Italians certainly showed no reluctance to bomb Malta into submission, for only a matter of hours after their dictator had declared war the little island was hit by two attacks that cost the lives of 35 civilians and six British soldiers. The extraordinary defence measures and the way in which subsequent events came about have been the subject of much fiction, legend and romance. The truth is every bit as exciting.

The Gloster Gladiator was no relic from an earlier age of air fighting, although to the layman its biplane configuration harked back to First World War fighter design. In fact it had entered RAF service only 30 months before, and during that period had formed the equipment of 24 squadrons at home and overseas. But so swift had been the march of technology that liquid-cooled engines had replaced air-cooled radials (in Britain, at least), armament had doubled and new methods of construction had ushered in monoplanes capable of greater speeds. For example, the 245mph maximum of which the Sea Gladiator, first accepted in May 1939, was capable, was topped by more than 70mph in the Hurricane. Not that biplane fighters were by any means confined to the British services. A contemporary existed in Italy's Fiat C.R.42, which, with a lighter but heavier-calibre armament could better the Gladiator's maximum speed by over 20mph. This type frequently escorted Mussolini's

bombers, bent on pounding into submission the island fortress which Malta quickly became.

Fable clouded fact regarding the crated Gladiators' procurement, some sources claiming that they were 'discovered', and others stating that between eight and twelve Sea Gladiators, dismantled and crated, were ordered to be assembled by Higher Command, which was well aware of their existence. Whatever the truth might be, it is certain that the containers had been at Kalafrana since 1939, an appropriate site when the process of erection was contemplated, as this RAF seaplane base, located on the bay at the south of the island, housed the Aircraft Repair Section. Although there was no airfield attached, land-planes being taken a mile down the road to Hal Far for test flying, the station had large workshops and stores.

During May work was begun on the assembly of four of the Sea Gladiators, N5519, N5520, N5524 and N5531. They were to form a Station Fighter Flight, with volunteers, none of whom were versed in fighter tactics, to fly them. The maritime origins of the aircraft were evident; the fairings for a collapsible dinghy were still in place beneath their bellies; and housings for deck-landing arrester hooks remained under their rear fuselages. As April drew to a close the quartet was ready, but the men who had laboured to erect them were thunderstruck by an order to dismantle the aircraft and crate them again, ready for transportation by sea to Alexandria. An entry in the Hal Far Operations Book for the afternoon of the 29th states: 'Station Fighter Flight temporarily disbanded and Sea Gladiators dismantled and returned to Kalafrana.'

The work was finished before lunch the following day, only for the men involved to be told that, as a result of the direct intervention of the New

Zealand-born AOC, Air Commodore F. H. M. Maynard, AFC, authority had been granted to retain the Gladiators. They began the weary job of uncrating and reassembly.

Although there were four aircraft, it is very likely that only three were serviceable at any one time. This, coupled with the sight of them operating in the conventional 'vic' formation, gave strength to the leg-

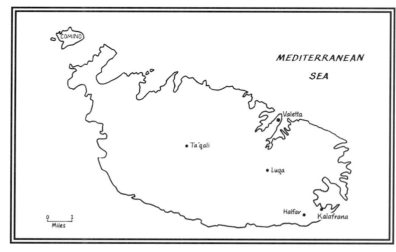

end that only a trio existed, and the formation earned a variety of names. Some called them Freeman, Hardy and Willis, others recalled Churchill's words Blood, Tears and Sweat, while those of a humorous inclination referred to Pip, Squeak and Wilfred – three strip-cartoon characters in the *Daily Mirror*. But the names by which the three Gladiators have become famous are those which seemed appropriate for that time of trial, and which, originating with St Paul, made a strong appeal to the firm religious basis of Maltese life: Faith, Hope and Charity.

It is fruitless to attempt to determine to which machine each name was allocated. This was never done; it was a general and indivisible title, and was conse-

quently still in use after N5519 was seriously damaged during the first week in June, only to have the fourth aircraft step in to take its place. Matters took a graver turn when N5520 was damaged during the following week. Two more Gladiators, N5523 and N5529, had been erected and tested by 14 June.

There were now four fighters again, but as they still operated as a triumvirate the appellation held. This situation still prevailed on 22 June, by which date the damaged N5519 was returned to service, having undergone an important change. Its 840hp Bristol Mercury VIIIA was now replaced by a fresh 920hp Mercury XV from a Bristol Blenheim, driving a Hamilton three-bladed variable-pitch propeller, at first fitted with a spinner. However, owing to the unit's practice of persistently flying with the throttle 'through the gate', the engine was doomed to be short-lived, and it was mechanical failure that caused the machine's loss on 24 June. To this was added the loss of another Gladiator on 26 June, two days before the addition of four extra Hurricanes to Malta's defences.

During the days when Faith, Hope and Charity were establishing a place in RAF and also in world history, their pilots seemed to enjoy almost charmed lives. A contributory factor might have been the order to avoid, if possible, actual combat with the enemy's fighter escorts and not to pursue Italian bombers setting course for home, but instead to dive through formations of enemy aircraft making a bombing run in an attempt to spoil the bombardiers' aim – a desperate tactic calling for a very high degree of courage. This was stiffened and supported by the supreme RAF training, and also by the quality of their aircraft, for whatever the Gladiators lacked in comparison with their sleeker contemporaries, they possessed the ability to turn sharply. Coupled with their comparatively slow speed, this made them difficult targets for the faster enemy fighters.

During the eleven days when Faith, Hope and Charity were adding to the traditions of the RAF and using a strange combination of tactics involving bluff and aggression, some equally uncommon demands were being made on the British pilots in combat. For example, it was sometimes necessary to out-think their opposite numbers in the Regia Aeronautica if an Italian machine happened to get on a Gladiator's tail. More than one enemy pilot found his aircraft in a spin after attempting to keep the biplane in his sights, a condition which quickly changed him from hunter to hunted. However, despite the diversionary diving tactic on which the trio's pilots were expected to rely, there were few occasions when the ammunition belts of the Gladiators' Browning guns were returned with no expenditures.

All the time, the hard-pressed ground crews had to work on the defending aircraft regardless of the attentions of the enemy. The three which they managed to keep serviceable at any one time were heavily reliant on parts from other unassembled or unserviceable airframes, for the aircraft were maintained in first-class condition, or as near to this as humanly possible once the engines began to show the results of continuous high revolutions. It was this which triggered the search for alternative power units that led to the adoption of Mercurys intended for Bristol Blenheims. The decision called for much more than a straight transfer of engines, since those intended for the bombers had been designed to drive a wide variety of auxiliary services, and several

modifications were called for, demanding all of the groundcrew's skills.

By the end of October the sole remaining Gladiator flying from Malta seemed something of an anachronism alongside the more modern interceptors, so more than one eyebrow was raised at the appearance of a second at the end of the month. This had been slowly refurbished from a virtual wreck, and held a second surprise for the curious who examined it at close quarters, for it sported not four, but six machine-guns, the extra pair being mounted over the upper wings after the manner of some fighters over the Western Front 22 years previously. This was strictly a local modification, and was quickly forgotten, as was the sight of the three Gladiators which had seemed so symbolic in the sunny Mediterranean sky that they were given the names which have passed into history. Not all men forgot them, however, for on the afternoon of Friday 3 September 1943 a strange ceremony formed the centre of interest for the people of Malta's capital, Valetta. It took place in the presence of the new AOC, Air Vice-Marshal Sir Keith Park, who had commanded No.11 Group of Fighter Command in the UK during the Battle of Britain, and Sir George Borg, the Island's Chief Justice, together with a Guard of Honour and the band of the Royal Malta Artillery.

The focal point was the skeletal fuselage of a Gloster Gladiator about to be presented to the people of Malta, who now exhibit it in The Fort St Elmo War Museum. Whether it was one of those which made up part of the historic 'threesome' is uncertain, since it was salvaged from the rubbish at Kalafrana. Its true identity

is also unknown, as at some time the serial numbers were sanded off the components, although the fabric covering later added – initially confined to the rear fuselage – has been marked 'N5520'. In common with an inscription under the windscreen on the port side, a nearby plaque declares: 'This is "Faith"'. Since the name was never applied to any individual machine, who can say that the claim is inappropriate? In 1974 the Gladiator fuselage was painstakingly restored to immaculate condition by volunteer tradesmen from RAF Luqa.

As the 20th century draws to its close, Malta's wartime RAF stations present a very different picture. Hal Far is now the only military base on the island, while Luqa dominates the south-centre with a modern airport boasting a 10,000ft main runway. Some of the former wartime Nissen huts and service buildings survive at Luqa and Ta'Qali, which is a craft centre. The old seaplane base at Kalafrana has become Malta's second port, capable of handling tankers and container ships.

*The artist writes:* Painted for a paperback book jacket, this picture was subsequently used as one of a series of 189 picture cards portraying aircraft of the Royal Air Force. Just prior to producing the painting I had visited RAF Malta, during which I had opportunities to fly over the island, gathering useful reference for future use. the coastline below the aircraft shows Marsaxlokk Bay, to the left of which is Hal Far airfield, smoking from hits by the Italian SM79 bombers. Knowledge of background settings and locations is always worth the effort of collecting against the possibility of future use, no matter how small or large a contribution they can make.

# Sailor Malan, 1940

*Painting by Tiro Vorster*
*Text by Michael Burns*

THIS IMPRESSIVE PAINTING WOULD WELL ILLUSTRATE any one of the desperate days of summer 1940. Above the white cliffs and green fields of south-east England a dogfight rages, marked by the twisting vapour trails of opposing fighters. Away from the main action, a Spitfire turns round on to the tail of a Luftwaffe Messerschmitt. But this is no imaginary scene; Tiro Vorster has captured a precise moment during a freak clash of arms between two of the most influential and experienced pilots flying in the Battle of Britain.

In the opinion of many of their peers, 'Sailor' Malan and ' Vati' Moelders were the finest fighter pilots of their generation. Both developed important tactics and led fighters with ruthless success. There were many parallels in their careers, and as the Battle of Britain began they met in combat. Both were commissioned and posted to fighters in 1936 after being assessed as exceptional pilots during training. Adolph Gysbert Malan joined a Gloster Gauntlet unit, No. 74 Squadron RAF at Hornchurch in Essex, while Werner Moelders learned his trade flying the Luftwaffe's Arado Ar 68 and Heinkel He 61 biplanes. Both swiftly won recognition and by 1938 were junior commanders. Within months of Malan becoming Flight Commander of his squadron's 'A' Flight it won the Sir Philip Sassoon Trophy through his efficiency and leadership. Moelders took command of the Luftwaffe approximation of a Flight, a Staffel.

Moelders' strong friendship with First World War ace Ernst Udet had a major impact on his career. Believing that the close vic of three aircraft inhibited the fighter's manoeuvrability and aggression, they agreed that a loose pair, the Rotte, would be more flexible. Two spaced pairs, the Schwarm, would be superbly defensive and offensive. Such a formation covered a large volume of sky, allowed pilots to watch different sectors, and split an enemy attack, yet its pilots could counter or attack with co-ordination.

Upon Udet's recommendation in mid-1938, Moelders was sent to develop tactics under combat conditions in Spain, commanding III Staffel of JG 88 flying the new Messerschmitt Bf 109B-2. The new fighters and new tactics allowed proportionately larger areas to be patrolled for the same resources, and swiftly won air superiority. With 14 kills and great tactical experience to his credit, Moelders returned to Germany to revolutionise fighter warfare. His serious approach earned him the nickname ' Vati' ('Daddy').

When the Second World War began, No. 74 Squadron RAF was operational on the Spitfire. Malan saw little action during the 'Phoney War', but Moelders, commanding III Gruppe JG 53 with the Bf 109E-1 on the Western Front, was frequently in action. Opposing 'aces' rarely met, though Moelders shot down Flying Officer E. J. Kain – twice! The day the Blitzkreig began, 10 May, he claimed his tenth victory in France.

In late May, when No. 74 Squadron was among the home-based units committed to defend the Dunkirk evacuation, Malan commanded his Flight skilfully. On 21 May he claimed his first victory, a Junkers Ju 88. More claims followed. The 24th was particularly tough, Malan's Spitfire being shot up and the squadron losing four pilots. Three days later he claimed his first fighter, a Bf 109. On 28 May, after a week of constant action and attrition, the squadron withdrew to Leconfield. Malan had technically become an ace in a week, and he was awarded the DFC for offensive patrols over France.

On 29 May, Moelders was awarded the Knights Cross, but was shot down and captured by the French on 5 June. With 25 victories, he was the top-scoring Luftwaffe pilot.

On 6 June, No. 74 Squadron returned to Hornchurch, and Malan became the first RAF single-seat pilot to destroy a bomber at night when he shot down two He 111s held by searchlights over Essex

soon after midnight on 19 June. It was his first attempt, and the feat won a bar to his DFC.

Early in July a month of Luftwaffe attacks on coastal shipping and ports began. To protect convoys, No. 74 Squadron detached Flights to Manston Forward Landing Ground. Malan's pilots engaged several formations before the Spitfire's main opponents became fighters as the threat to the Channel ports intensified in the last week of July. His Flight fought tough combats, with steady losses. A principal opponent was JG 51.

Released after France surrendered, Moelders remained inactive until he was appointed Kommodore of JG 51 on 27 July. Flying the Bf 109E-4, I and II Gruppen were based at Wissant and III Gruppe at St Omer, Pas de Calais. The youngest Kommodore succeeded the second oldest, 48-year-old Osterkamp, but it was experienced leadership, not rank, that made a Geschwader of 60 to 80 fighters an effective fighting force. Moelders was keen to make up for lost time, not only to better the scores of Galland and Wick, but also to persuade the German High Command to use fighters offensively, especially as bomber escorts. The British fighter defence was of a far higher calibre than the Germans had met in Spain, Poland and France, and The Battle was only now warming up.

Early on the afternoon of Sunday 28 July, No. 74 Squadron was ordered off from Manston to cover Hurricanes which were intercepting bombers attacking shipping off Dover. The Spitfires, as usual, were to deal with the Bf 109 escort. Flight Lieutenant Malan led the squadron at the head of 'A' Flight, Red and Yellow Sections, while Flight Lieutenant D. P. D. Kelly led 'B' Flight, Blue and Green Sections, using three-fighter sections. Malan's wingmen were Pilot Officers Peter Stevenson (Red 2) and Peter St John (Red 3).

Over the Straits of Dover they ascended through loose cloud that filled the lower sky after the previous

day's storm and came into clear blue sky. Malan worked round to put the strong high sun behind them. At 1355 No. 74 Squadron found Bf 109Es at 18,000ft approaching Dover, coming in south-south-west sunward. They were four staffeln of I and II Gruppen JG 51, led from the front in his Stab Flight by Moelders. They had formed up at 15,000ft and set out in a steady climb from Pas de Calais ten minutes earlier, and their orders were to protect the bombers and engage RAF fighters in 'free chase'.

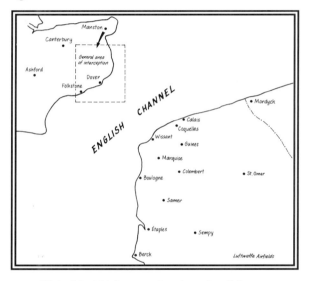

This, his 129th operational sortie of the war, was Moelders' first as JG 51's Kommodore. He had not had time to remould its formations and tactics, or to weld its Gruppen, brought together from other Geschwadern, into an entity. The 36 Bf 109Es were in loose formations over a wide and deep area. The leading formation was some eight strong, in two groups.

In a perfect bounce, Malan turned his Spitfires in behind the Bf 109Es, coming in from the glare of the sun without being seen. Leaving Green and Yellow Sections led by Pilot Officers H. R. Gunn and John Freeborn

above as top cover, he led Red and Blue Sections into the attack in line astern. They fanned out to pick targets.

Selecting a Bf 109 in the leading flight, Malan fired a two-second burst from 250 down to 100 yards. The German slowed in a gentle starboard turn, crippled. Malan left it and looked for further trade. Kelly had committed Blue Section behind Malan's attack, but diverted to a group of Bf 109s that dived into the fray, destroying one and damaging another. But Malan's two wingmen had stayed with him.

St John damaged a Bf 109E on the right of the leading formation, but had to escape a four-fighter onslaught as the Germans behind him reacted. Stevenson damaged a Bf 109 on the left of Malan's target and squirted at another. But as he tried to hold one more in his sight he was attacked by Moelders, who had not been engaged as the assault began and had turned fast in a wide circle to the left – an instinctive fighting reaction – on to Stevenson's tail. Moelders riddled the Spitfire.

Leaving Stevenson, Moelders hunted for another target. He found Malan and fell on his tail. Malan turned to face the attack in a classic counter-manoeuvre. His Spitfire could out-turn a Bf 109 at this height. He kept turning hard until he got Moelders in his sight, and with full deflection raked the Bf 109 for three seconds. Moelders spiralled down, his best escape, but Malan's ammunition was almost spent. Isolated in a sky full of Messerschmitts, he broke for home.

High overhead, another fight raged. Top-cover leaders Gunn and Freeborn had led the six Yellow and Green Spitfires in a full-boost climb to attack 50 Bf 109s from JG 26 and 51 that threatened Red and Blue Sections. Fighting courageously, they suffered badly but the leaders each claimed victories, and they covered their comrades' escape.

As isolated Spitfires made for home, the victims fell away from the fight. Moelders headed for Wissant.

His fighter was badly damaged and he was wounded in the leg. It was an inglorious first day as Geschwaderkommodore. With superior numbers, JG 51 had come out worst. Both Gruppen lost a pilot killed. Moelder's fighter and another from each Gruppen crashed at Wissant. Three pilots, including Moelders, claimed a victory, but Oberstleutnant Leppla claimed the Spitfire that shot up Moelders, and Moelders' claim – Stevenson's aircraft – was repaired and not struck off.

The pilots of No. 74 Squadron claimed four Bf 109s destroyed and five damaged. They lost two Spitfires, Pilot Officer J. H. R. Young being killed and Sergeant E. A. Mould wounded. Two Spitfires were damaged. Contrasting claims plus crash-landings on both sides account for many controversies over attrition in combat. Malan had taken a leading tactician and Kommodore out of combat at a critical point: the strategic assault on Britain. It delayed Moelders' welding of JG 51's disparate Gruppen and his instruction of the unit in his tactics.

This combat demonstrates the principles Malan later condified in 'Ten of My Rules for Air Fighting', widely displayed at fighter and training airfields and summarised as: 'Go in quickly – Punch hard – Get out!'

On 8 August, as the main assault began, Malan became No. 74 Squadron's commanding officer. He made powerful interceptions as the Luftwaffe fell on airfields and aircraft factories. Malan withdrew his squadron to the Midlands on 14 August, as Moelders returned to combat and gained swift distinction as a leader.

Quiet authority came easily to Malan from his days as a Merchant Navy officer (hence his nickname) and pre-war Regular service. Malan was a disciplinarian who was determined that his men would share his goal of destroying as many Germans as they could. He believed that tight teamwork would win the fighter war

and save lives. His strong, open face and friendly smile belied the intensity of his hatred of the Germans. He believed that damaging bombers so that they limped home to crash-land with blood and death aboard had more effect on Luftwaffe morale than simply shooting them down as statistics.

The battle had a fortnight to run when Malan took his squadron south again, to Biggin Hill, on 14 October. The measure of his success as commander is his squadron's tally of 86 victories, the seventh highest in Fighter Command, during the Battle of Britain. Malan had precisely ten per cent. He was the most influential of those who tested new defensive tactics.

On 13 December Malan became the first South African of the war to be admitted to the Distinguished Service Order. He was in the vanguard of the growing Commonwealth fraternity in the RAF. In March 1941 he assumed command of the Biggin Hill Wing. Fighter Command began an intensive campaign of daylight sweeps into France and Belgium to provoke and destroy the Jagdgeschwadern, doing what they had attempted to do in 1940.

Leading a wing on the ground and in the air was a terrific emotional and physical strain. Malan sometimes led three sweeps a day during that spring and summer, and there were many clashes with Bf 109s. In five days in June, Malan destroyed seven. Having mastered defensive tactics, he now developed offensive tactics. He did not adopt the 'finger-four' formation by now adopted by many wings, preferring a loose line of fighters.

Moelder's JG 51 frequently met the RAF challenge over France until it was transferred East to spearhead the German assault on Russia, Barbarossa, launched on 22 June. At the end of June his Geschwader became the first to score 1,000 victories, and within two weeks Moelders was the first Luftwaffe pilot with 100 victories. In August he was appointed Inspector

General of Fighters. Although he was an outstanding fighter pilot, leader and teacher, 'his abilities and ambitions,' wrote Adolf Galland, 'lay in tactics and administration'. But he had only three months to exploit his new influence. He died in an air crash when being flown to the funeral of his mentor, Udet.

At about the time Moelders claimed his 115th and last victory, Malan, too, claimed his last, a Bf 109 on 6 July, followed by a last 'damaged' on the 23rd. He recognised combat fatigue in himself, and with immense courage asked to be relieved of his command on the grounds that he would endanger his men's lives by being stale. He retired from operations to use his experience in instruction, especially in gunnery, and tactical development. He later commanded the Central Gunnery School. Soon after leaving his Wing, Malan was awarded a Bar to his DSO, for conspicuous leadership. The citation credited him with 32 confirmed victories, six probables and 20 damaged, most achieved in defensive warfare. This made him the RAF's top-scoring fighter pilot, a position he retained until the summer of 1944, when he was overtaken by J. E. Johnson, by whom this painting was commissioned.

*The artist writes:* During 1990 Tiro Vorster was given his first overseas commission. After a chance meeting with Air Vice-Marshal Johnny Johnson, who was much impressed by the artist's studio of paintings, he commissioned Vorster directly to paint a dogfight depicting the famous South African fighter pilot Adolph 'Sailor' Malan. For political reasons Malan had never been afforded full official recognition by his home country for his exploits over Britain, and the painting was duly presented by Air Vice-Marshal Johnson to the South African Ambassador in London. The painting, and a framed pencil sketch of Malan, enjoy pride of place at the South African Embassy in London.

# 'Pinocchio' – Learoyd's Hampden

*Painting by Philip West*
*Text by Ron Dick*

PHILIP WEST'S PAINTING DEPICTS A HANDLEY PAGE Hampden making a daring low-level night attack on a German aqueduct in August 1940. The Hampden, one of several twin-engined monoplane bombers brought into service in the late 1930s, was not one of the RAF's most memorable aircraft. Its life as a front-line bomber was short, and it is not generally associated with dramatic achievements such as the one captured by Philip West. It is true that the Hampdens and the other new prewar twins were markedly better than the biplane 'cloth bombers' they replaced, but for the most part, with the possible exception of the Vickers Wellington, they proved to be less than impressive performers when put to the test. Their shortcomings were to be ruthlessly exposed in the early months of the Second World War.

When the war began, Bomber Command's front-line aircraft were almost all twin-engined types: Blenheims, Whitleys, Wellingtons and Hampdens. These were the instruments with which the RAF was to put into practice the as yet untried theories about strategic air power. According to the air power prophets, bombers were supposed to revolutionise warfare by leaping over intervening armies and navies and delivering crushing, war-winning blows directly against the heartland of an enemy nation. As became only too obvious after September 1939, this task was beyond the capabilities of air forces at the time.

For strategic air power theory to work as originally conceived, a bomber force first had to be allowed to operate without restriction against an enemy nation. Bombers then needed to be able both to find their targets and to bomb them accurately, and they had to be capable of defending themselves effectively against enemy opposition. The strategic theory had been used to great effect as one of the principal arguments for maintaining the independence of the RAF in the 1920s, but unfortunately the development of the means with which to fulfil the prophecies of the theoreticians had not been nearly so successful.

By the late 1930s, as the descent into war gained momentum, the RAF remained wedded to the belief that the bomber was potentially a war-winning weapon, but at least some of the RAF's leaders doubted whether Bomber Command could meet its commitments. At the end of 1937 Air Chief Marshal Sir Edgar Ludlow-Hewitt, C-in-C Bomber Command, startled the Air Ministry by reporting that his command was 'entirely unprepared for war, unable to operate except in fair weather, and extremely vulnerable both in the air and on the ground'. At the time it was hoped that the most worrying problems would be overcome with the introduction of the new twin-engined monoplanes, a process which had begun with the Whitley in 1937 and continued with the first of the Wellingtons and Hampdens in 1938. However, although these aircraft were undoubtedly superior to their biplane predecessors, there were still very serious limitations in both the bombers and the training of their crews which were not fully appreciated, and would not be until the harsh reality of combat had been experienced.

In the early months of the war it quickly became apparent that none of the requirements essential for the success of a strategic bombing campaign could be met. Political restraints initially limited Bomber Command to leaflet dropping, or to bombing targets where the risk of civilian casualties was minimal. Those sorties which were flown revealed that bomber formations operating in daylight were extremely vulnerable to attacks by modern fighters, and daylight bombing was effectively stopped early in 1940. By August 1941, when the political gloves had long been off and targets inside Germany had been subjected to frequent attacks by night, the Butt Report, a scientific study of the bomber offensive, confirmed growing fears by stating that less than 30 per cent of the

RAF's bombers had been getting within five miles of their intended targets in the first two years of war.

Given the equipment with which they were operating and the nature of the job they were being asked to do, it is hardly surprising that Bomber Command's squadrons had not accomplished what many of their prewar leaders expected of them by crippling German resistance and bringing the war rapidly to an end. The Hampden was typical of the problem. Even before it entered service, at least some of the limitations of the Hampden and its twin-engined cousins were being acknowledged by the air staff planners. Tacit recognition that they would be interim aircraft was contained in the specifications for four-engined bombers laid down as early as 1936. The first Hampdens were delivered to the RAF two years later, in August 1938, and by the outbreak of war there were ten squadrons of them in the front line. By the standards of the time the Hampden was considered a complex aircraft, an all-metal, metal-skinned monoplane, which to an air force that was only now relinquishing its fabric-covered open-cockpit biplanes was almost revolutionary in concept. However, it was by no means the mighty engine of destruction needed at the heart of the strategic air offensive.

The Hampden was powered by two 1,000hp Bristol Pegasus radials which were supposedly capable of giving it a maximum speed of 265mph at 15,000ft, but which normally allowed it a cruising speed of only about 155mph. With a radius of action of 600 miles, it could carry up to 4,000lb of bombs, although 2,000lb was a more usual load. At the outbreak of war, many Hampden crews were apprehensive about their first mission, principally because none of them had ever taken off with an operational bomb load and they were not at all sure that the aircraft would be able to get airborne within the airfield limits with so much extra weight. Defensive armament was limited to six .303in machine-guns, a pair in each of the mid-upper and ventral positions facing aft, and

two more in the nose, one freely mounted and the other fixed. Since the guns were not in turrets, they had limited traverse and there were significant blind spots all round the aircraft which they could not cover. These limitations of speed and firepower made the Hampden easy prey for enemy fighters.

Whenever Hampdens met Luftwaffe fighters they suffered badly, and the last straw for the Hampden as a day bomber came on 12 April 1940, when twelve aircraft of Nos. 44 and 50 Squadrons sent to attack warships off Norway were intercepted, and six were shot down. From that day on, the Hampden was strictly regarded as being available for night operations only, and the RAF finally had to accept the fact that its prewar plans for the conduct of the bombing offensive had been overtaken by events.

If the Hampden's armament and performance were less than impressive, the crew compartment was no better. The curious slab-sided design of the fuselage resulted in a maximum internal width for the cockpit of just three feet, and that left the four-man crew with little room for manoeuvre once they were airborne. It was necessarily the case that, unlike its twin-engined bomber cousins, the Hampden flew with a single pilot, and in this at least it pointed the way to the future. The experiences of the Hampden squadrons were used to illustrate the feasibility of single-pilot operation when it came to establishing the crew size needed for the four-engine bomber force.

The navigator spent most of his time in the Perspex nose cone ahead of and below the pilot's high-mounted seat. In many ways his lack of navigation aids was the most serious shortcoming in the bomber force of the time. No real effort had been made to find out how bombers might be made to fly long distances, by day or night and in all weathers, and arrive over their targets. Navigation methods were basic in the extreme, and were usually referred to by the crews as 'by guess and by God'. Map reading was regarded as almost essential, and that meant operating in reasonable weather, preferably in daylight. When it was necessary to fly above cloud, dead reckoning was used, and that required that the pilot should fly precise headings and speeds, and that wind velocities should be known with some accuracy.

Even in peacetime, on the rare occasions when crews flew long-range exercises (invariably by day over friendly territory and in good weather), it was found that dead reckoning could not guarantee a position within 50 miles after flying 400 miles. At night, map-reading by moonlight was preferred, backed up by star fixes worked out using a sextant. When night bombing became standard practice, crews had little hesitation in bombing on estimated time of arrival (ETA) if the ground could not be seen. In spite of the inevitable inaccuracies associated with these methods, the air staff had a touching faith in the capacity of crews to find their targets and hit them with precision. Disillusionment, when it came, would be complete. (On one celebrated occasion in 1940 a Whitley crew managed to identify the Thames as the Rhine and attack a Fighter Command airfield in Cambridgeshire rather than a Luftwaffe airfield in Holland.)

In the Hampden, both the navigator and the pilot were effectively cut off from the other two crew members by a metal door across the centre of the fuselage. Behind the door was an upper compartment with a hinged Perspex cupola for the wireless operator/gunner, and almost directly below him sat the ventral gunner. The space provided for the crew was not generous, particularly since it was cluttered with radios, gun mountings, ammunition boxes and the like. Communications being what they were, the wireless operator even had to look after two carrier pigeons in a wicker basket. As might be expected, the aircraft was not heated. Crew members were bundled up in layers of silk, wool, and leather to protect them from the often biting cold. In the Hampden, this bulky clothing meant that the crew's movement was even more restricted.

Taking all these problems into account, the Hampden operation undertaken on the night of 12 August 1940 was a remarkable feat of arms. A build-up of barges was under way along the Channel coast in preparation for the proposed German invasion of Britain, and one of the waterways though which a great many of the barges were travelling was the Dortmund-Ems Canal. Previous RAF attempts to close the canal had been unsuccessful, and a further raid using Hampdens was planned. Five Hampdens of Nos. 49 and 83 Squadrons were detailed for the attack, which was to be at low-level against an aqueduct carrying the canal over the River Ems. Earlier attacks had alerted the Germans to the threat, and the aqueduct was now heavily defended by searchlights and anti-aircraft guns.

Briefed to be the fifth and last to attack was a crew from No. 49 Squadron, Flight Lieutenant Roderick Learoyd (captain), Pilot Officer John Lewis (navigator/bomb aimer), Sergeant J. Ellis (wireless operator/gunner), and Leading Aircraftman Rich (gunner). Their aircraft was Hampden P4403, coded EA-M and known to them as *Pinocchio*. (Walt Disney's puppet was painted beside the cockpit on the left-hand side.) They took off from RAF Scampton at 2000 and set off south-easterly into a clear sky lit by a half-moon. Ten minutes before their time on target, they were in position just north of the aqueduct, waiting their turn to attack. They watched as the four aircraft ahead of them ran the gauntlet of fire guarding the canal. All four were heavily hit and two were shot down. The aqueduct remained intact.

At 2323, just six minutes after the initial attack, Learoyd began a shallow diving run along the canal, aiming to level out at 150ft for bomb release. By now the German gunners were more than ready, and the Hampden flew into a storm of anti-aircraft fire. Blinded by searchlights, Learoyd kept his head down and flew on

instruments at the direction of Lewis. Shells tore large holes in the starboard wing, and the aircraft was hit continually by smaller-calibre bullets. Learoyd held the Hampden steady until Lewis yelled that the bombs were away and then broke hard into a steep climbing turn. Once clear of the flak, the crew took stock of the damage.

Although the aircraft had been hit repeatedly and was full of holes, none of the crew was hurt. (Ellis even took the trouble to note that one of his carrier pigeons had laid an egg during the attack!) The hydraulic system had been ruptured and there was also the possibility of other unknown damage, so after nursing the Hampden across the English coast at 0200, Learoyd elected not to attempt a night landing. He stayed airborne until first light and landed safely just before 0500.

Post-raid reconnaissance showed that *Pinocchio*'s efforts had been rewarded. The aqueduct was severely damaged and barge traffic on the canal was disrupted for weeks afterwards. For his determination in pressing home an attack on such a heavily defended target, Flight Lieutenant Learoyd was awarded Bomber Command's first Victoria Cross.

*The artist writes:* I was privileged to meet Rod Learoyd, VC at an air event in 1991. He was the inspiration for my painting, and he helped me to portray the Hampden in its correct position over the aqueduct, as well as providing essential information on the raid. I always construct a kit of the aircraft I am going to portray, because it enables me to create a totally original image. A great deal of time is spent sketching for accuracy, but on completion of the painting I was satisfied that I had been very fortunate in meeting the actual pilot, and a Victoria Cross winner to boot, and that he approved of my work.

# Dorniers over Kenley

*Painting by Mark Postlethwaite*
*Text by John Ray*

THE DORNIER DO 17Z-2 DEPICTED IN THE FOREground of this painting has just taken part in one of the most daring Luftwaffe attacks of the Battle of Britain, and is trying desperately to escape from the pursuing eight-gun Hurricanes. The date is 18 August 1940, and the scene is occurring at about 1325. In the background lies the target of the raid, Kenley Aerodrome in Surrey, only sixteen miles from central London. The Dornier has dropped its bombs and is now racing back to the English coast, aiming to cross the Channel and reach the safety of France.

Throughout August 1940 the main Luftwaffe thrusts were against RAF airfields in the south of England. During a conference at the Hague on 1 August, Reichsmarschall Goering, C-in-C of the German Air Force, planned attacks moving progressively from the south and west towards London. In this way he hoped to grind down the RAF. By the 17th the Germans believed that Fighter Command was near the end of its tether. Luftwaffe Intelligence estimated that the RAF had only 300 serviceable fighters left. Heavy attacks on 8, 12, 13, and 15 August had stretched British defences, especially in the south-east, where Air Vice-Marshal Park's No.11 Group were attempting to hold off the might of Luftflotten II and III.

Luftwaffe commanders believed that by striking at airfields, British fighters would be destroyed either on the ground or in the air if they rose to defend their bases, and it was thought that a final combined onslaught on the 18th could break their opponents. As part of this offensive, plans were laid at the Brussels headquarters of Feldmarschall Kesselring, C-in-C of Luftflotte II, to bomb Biggin Hill (target 1017) and Kenley (1018), Park's two key aerodromes on the direct approach to London from the south-east.

Biggin Hill was to be raided by 60 Heinkel He 111s of KG 1, flying high with escort fighters, the type of assault generally made by German bombers during the battle. However, the strike against Kenley, allocated to KG 76, was to be a far more complicated operation. First, twelve Junkers Ju 88s would cross the coast near Dover and then fly north-west to the target, preceded by a fighter sweep by Bf 109s. At Kenley, the Ju 88s would dive-bomb hangars and other buildings. Five minutes later, 27 Dornier Do 17s would arrive and bomb from high altitude, trying to crater the ground and destroy defences. Then, nine more Dorniers would approach five minutes after that and strike from low level at any remaining targets. The well planned operation depended crucially on attacks being made in accurate sequence. A perfectly timed and co-ordinated operation could bring brilliant success; otherwise there could be a costly failure.

The most difficult part of the operation fell to the nine Dorniers of the 9th Staffel of the 3rd Gruppe of KG 76. Their aircrew were experienced in low-level flying from the recent French campaign, during which they had made many successful attacks on supply routes and aerodromes. The raid on Kenley would be more challenging. The aircraft would cross the Channel, skimming to the sea, underneath the relentless gaze of British Radio Direction Finding (RDF, or radar) stations, making their landfall near Beachy Head. Next they would approach Lewes, then follow the railway line running from Brighton to London, which passed within a couple of miles of Kenley.

The 9th Staffel were stationed on an airfield at Corneilles-en-Vexin, some twenty miles north-west of Paris. There, after breakfast on 18 August, their CO, Hauptmann Joachim Roth, briefed his men on the day's operation. He would fly in the leading aircraft to guide his formation to the target, and all would maintain careful formation until they were close to it. Their particular task was to hit buildings, including hangars, at the southern end of Kenley; photos of these were passed

round for inspection. Joining the mission were a visiting reporter, a photographer and two officers who were gaining battle experience.

The Dornier Do 17Z-2, nicknamed the 'flying pencil' because of its slim fuselage, had a wingspan of 59ft. Each aircraft carried a crew of four and was protected by three machine-guns. Unusually for Dorniers, those of Roth's Staffel mounted a 20mm cannon in the nose. For this attack each aircraft carried twenty 50kg bombs fitted with special low-level fuses so that the aircraft themselves would not be damaged by the explosions.

Soon after 0900 the operation was postponed for two and a half hours to allow an improvement in the weather. When the new order for take-off was given, they became airborne just before noon, leaving the French coast near Dieppe and skimming the waves until the chalk heights of Beachy Head and the Seven Sisters came into view just to their east. Several crew members then put on their steel helmets. As they passed over some RN ships in the Channel, desultory machine-gun fire was aimed at them, but all aircraft crossed the English coast unharmed a few minutes after 1300.

At this point, however, civilians of the Observer Corps, in a post high on Beachy Head, spotted them and took steps that were to have a drastic effect on the fortunes of the 9th Staffel's mission. Telephone messages raced inland and soon the staff at Kenley were aware that a low-level attack was moving in their general direction.

During the Battle of Britain, German Intelligence suffered from several weaknesses. They did not recognise the crucial importance of RDF to the RAF, and they failed to appreciate the value of certain aerodromes to Fighter Command. They believed Kenley to be merely another airfield, but it was a Sector Station. The Controller there had a total of four squadrons available, at his own base and at Croydon.

As the Dorniers flew north, following the line of the railway, people gaped then scattered. The bombers roared just overhead, using woods and hills as cover and

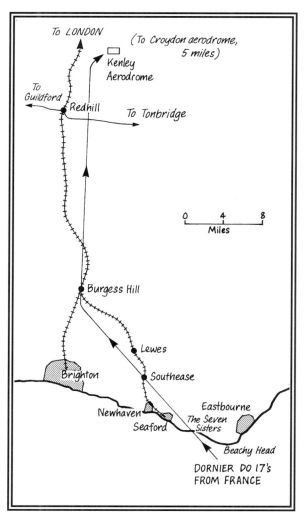

swerving to avoid pylons. On board Feldwebel Reichel's aircraft the visiting photographer, Rolf von Pebal, took some amazing low-level shots. Some show the Staffel approaching Beachy Head and crossing fields and

farms. Others were of the railway station at Southease and of civilians running for shelter at Burgess Hill, where houses and streets were machine-gunned. But the Observer Corps tracked them all the way, giving regular reports so that by 1315 officers at Kenley realised that enemy aircraft were closing fast on the airfield. Their own squadrons, Nos. 615 (Hurricanes) and 64 (Spitfires) had already been scrambled to meet KG 76's main formations, which had been detected by RDF as they came across Kent. As the picture became clear, the Controller rapidly called off the Hurricanes of No. 111 Squadron at Croydon and directed them to intercept the unexpected low-level assault.

At 1322 Roth's Dorniers climbed at tree-top level over the chalk ridge of the North Downs and swept towards the aerodrome. There they met two surprises. Firstly, the bombers which should already have devastated Kenley had not even arrived; secondly, the ground defences, having been given good warning, were ready and waiting. And already the Hurricanes of No. 111 Squadron were racing in to intercept.

Suddenly the airfield was alive with flames and explosions. A hail of fire rose from the ground as anti-aircraft and Lewis guns opened up, with the bombers replying as they crossed the airfield. The curtain of defensive shells and bullets caught several of the pursuing Hurricanes, one of which crashed at Wallington, killing the pilot. Feldwebel Petersen's Dornier, carrying the high-ranking Oberst Sommer as a visiting officer, was hit repeatedly and burst into flames. The pilot of another bomber was struck by a bullet and mortally wounded, the aircraft being saved by the navigator taking over control. At the further side of the aerodrome, parachute and cable rockets were fired into the air, catching two bombers, one of them Petersen's, which crashed into a bungalow, killing the crew.

Roth's aircraft was hit and caught fire, but staggered on to make a forced landing near Biggin Hill.

At the airfield there was chaos. Bombs exploded on hangars and buildings, which collapsed or burned, while columns of smoke and flame rose into the summer sky. Unexploded bombs cut furrows through the grass among dead and injured airmen, WAAFs and soldiers who were caught in the violent onslaught. On the ground a dozen stationary aircraft were destroyed or damaged, half of them Hurricanes of No. 615 Squadron. The airfield was out of action for about two hours as rescuers raced to help the wounded, put out fires and repair defences. By the evening Kenley, although shaken, was ready to resume its place in Fighter Command's defensive system.

The other bombers of KG 76, which should have launched the first strike, arrived late. They were intercepted by fighters and, although a few dropped more bombs on Kenley, many unloaded their cargoes elsewhere. Some of the Ju 88s turned back and attacked West Malling, an alternative target.

Seven Dorniers of Roth's Staffel remained to fight a desperate running battle with the pursuing Hurricanes as they raced back, hedge-hopping, to the coast. Every bomber was hit, two so badly that they crashed into the Channel before gaining safety. Nevertheless, they struck back. Their gunners shot down two Hurricanes, and another fighter was destroyed in error by gunfire from the ground as it returned to Croydon. The five remaining Dorniers, some carrying dead or wounded crew, finally reached France. Altogether the Staffel lost heavily, with five aircrew dead, five taken prisoner and several others wounded.

On 18 August the RAF and the Luftwaffe lost, as a combined total, more aircraft than on any other day of the Battle of Britain. On the German side, 100 bombers and fighters were destroyed or damaged. The RAF also suffered heavily, with 75 fighters destroyed or damaged and 62 other aircraft hit on the ground. What were the results for both sides of that momentous day?

The tenacity and skill of the defences, in which the civilian Observer Corps had participated prominently, showed the Germans that there would be no easy victory. They had failed to crush Fighter Command. Worried by heavy losses, Goering next day held a conference and ordered his fighters to give more protection by staying close to bombers during raids. He also ordered all-out strikes on airfields around London, still hoping to demolish Fighter Command.

For the RAF, nearly all the fighter casualties of 18 August were suffered by No. 11 Group. No aircraft from Nos. 12 or 13 Groups were damaged, and only two from No.10 Group were hit. As Park's outnumbered squadrons were bearing the brunt of battle, there was a deepening disagreement over air fighting tactics – the Big Wing controversy – between Nos. 11 and 12 Groups during the next three weeks of the battle.

Overall, in spite of heavy losses, especially of pilots, the RAF's resolute resistance continued. When the flames were extinguished and defence systems repaired, Kenley still had an important role to play in Fighter Command's response to the Luftwaffe. Two days later, Churchill's memorable speech referred to the young pilots as 'The Few', eloquently expressing the nation's debt.

*The artist writes:* This painting was commissioned directly by Arms & Armour Press for a book they were publishing which dealt with this famous raid. However, it was a painting that I had been considering for some time, ever since I had visited Kenley in 1992 and walked around this famous Battle of Britain airfield. Being a very well documented raid, it was easy to imagine the Dorniers swooping low over the treetops as I stood where, 52 years ago, the Spitfires and Hurricanes were dispersed.

I had always been interested in the Battle of Britain, ever since I was taken to see the film when I was six years old. This lifelong fascination, I suppose, culminated in me appearing on the TV quiz show The $64,000 Question, answering questions on this very subject. The fact that I walked away with the top prize was mainly due to misspent youth and a lot of luck!

# Hurricane Head-On Attack

*Painting by Jim Mitchell*
*Text by John Ray*

A STRICKEN DORNIER DO 17Z-2 OF 1/KG 76 is shown here in its final moments above London on 15 September 1940. The aircraft had already been under severe attack from half-a-dozen British fighters in turn; the wireless operator and the mechanic had baled out over the south of the city and were taken into captivity. Remaining on board were the captain, Oberleutnant R. Zehbe, and the bodies of two crew members killed by earlier bursts of fire.

Just before noon, Hurricane P2725 of No. 504 (County of Nottingham) Squadron, based at Northolt and flown by Sergeant R. T. Holmes, curved down into a head-on attack against the crippled bomber. The fighter closed with the Dornier, Holmes opened fire and, as the bomber started to break up, Zehbe baled out. The British pilot had flown so close that his machine struck the bomber, badly damaging its port wing and leaving him no option but to take to his own parachute. The Dornier started to spin, both wings outboard of the engines fell away, and the fuselage broke in two. The rear portion, containing the body of a gunner, came down over Fulham, and the tail landed on a rooftop at Vauxhall. The remainder of the aircraft plummetted down into the forecourt of Victoria Station, partly wrecking a shop. This most spectacular crash over the heart of the capital was witnessed by thousands of people.

The pilots experienced very different fates. Sergeant Holmes parachuted over Chelsea and descended in Ebury Park Road, where he slid down the sloping roof of a house and bumped into a dustbin. Naturally, his reception was friendly. The 27-year-old Oberleutnant Zehbe, already badly wounded, landed at Kennington and was soon surrounded by a hostile crowd of Londoners who had suffered heavily from German night bombing over the previous week. They attacked him before the police arrived, adding to his injuries. He died next day.

In one sense, Zehbe was doomed even before reaching London. Stationed at Nivelles, near Beauvais in northern France, he had taken off just after 1000 and reached the rendezvous point with other aircraft of the 1st Staffel and of KG 3 from the region of Antwerp over Cap Gris Nez. Climbing to 15,000ft, they all headed across the Channel towards Dungeness, escorted by Bf 109s. The route then passed directly over Kent, moving towards London. It soon became clear, however, that one of the Dornier's two Bramo-Fafnir air-cooled engines was not developing full power, and the aircraft slowly and inexorably fell behind. By the time the formation reached the capital, Zehbe's machine was well to the rear.

Suddenly British fighters, like a pack of hunting predators finding a weakened victim, pounced for the kill. Over south London a Flight of Hurricanes from No. 310 (Czech) Squadron attacked in turn, hitting the port engine, before two Spitfires joined in. It was at that stage that two of the crew jumped out, leaving Zehbe to his fate. Soon afterwards, Sergeant Holmes arrived to administer the *coup de grâce*.

Zehbe and his crew were experienced airmen who had taken part in a number of raids against Britain. On 18 August theirs had been one of the Dornier Do 17s which had launched a high-level strike against Kenley, where Roth's low-flying Staffel had been so savagely mauled by the defences. More recently, only eight days earlier, they had been in the massive force of almost a thousand aircraft which launched the first great

daylight raid on London, followed by bombing through the night. They helped to start the largest fires seen in Britain since 1666. By the next morning 306 civilians were dead and 1,337 badly injured, London's Dockland in the East End having been badly hit by the concentrated assault.

At that stage the airfields of No.11 Group, under Air Vice-Marshal Park, had been under intense strain for about three weeks, so the change of target had brought a measure of relief to the day-fighter force. That evening, Park flew over the capital in his own Hurricane to see the effects of the raid. Steps were taken to ease the burden of the hard-pressed pilots by bringing in experienced pilots from Groups outside the main fighting zone.

German leaders knew that Operation 'Sealion', the proposed seaborne invasion of Britain, could not take place until the RAF had been overwhelmed, but by the end of August Fighter Command was still unbroken. With the possible dates for landings running out, Goering was forced to review his policy, and the decision was taken to launch raids on the capital. In spite of the widely held belief that this was to avenge RAF raids on Berlin, the main reasons were strategic. The Germans wanted to smash economic targets, together with civilian morale, and force Britain into surrender. In addition, several Luftwaffe commanders, notably Kesselring, believed that the small residue of Fighter Command reckoned to be operational would be drawn to the city's defence and overwhelmed by German fighters.

Fortified by the erroneous belief that Fighter Command was almost beaten (some German pilots were told that the RAF was down to its last 50 fighters), Goering planned for a final assault on

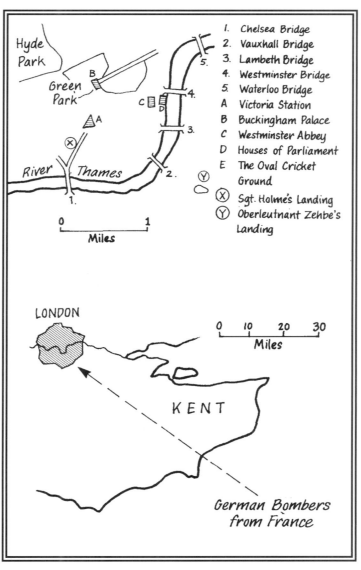

| | |
|---|---|
| 1. | Chelsea Bridge |
| 2. | Vauxhall Bridge |
| 3. | Lambeth Bridge |
| 4. | Westminster Bridge |
| 5. | Waterloo Bridge |
| A | Victoria Station |
| B | Buckingham Palace |
| C | Westminster Abbey |
| D | Houses of Parliament |
| E | The Oval Cricket Ground |
| ⊗ | Sgt. Holmes Landing |
| Y | Oberleutnant Zehbe's Landing |

German Bombers from France

London. However, his tactical application was at fault. He prepared two giant sledgehammer blows, one for the morning and the other for the afternoon of 15 September. These 'Valhallas' gathered slowly and laboriously over the Pas de Calais and were easily detected by British RDF stations on the Kent coast.

Thus Park was given ample time to prepare his response and have aircraft positioned to meet the intruders. As there had been no great daylight raid on London for eight days, morale had risen in No.11 Group. Replacement pilots were posted in, and some even trained, while plans were improved for meeting Luftwaffe attacks. After the argument over RAF tactics, Park made use of paired squadrons. Altogether that day he had 21 squadrons of Hurricanes and Spitfires available in his own Group and could readily call on ten other squadrons from Nos, 10 and 12 Groups, a figure that would have astounded Luftwaffe Intelligence.

The first massive German formation consisted mainly of Dornier Do 17s, including Zehbe's aircraft. It was heavily protected by Bf 109s, many of whose pilots chafed at having to fly slowly and close to their charges. They crossed the Kent coast and advanced inland on a bright morning, heading for the capital. With time on his side at last, Park soon had more squadrons flying than at any previous time in the Battle of Britain. He had planned for Spitfires to tackle the fighter escort while Hurricanes went for the bombers, and on that day the scheme worked. The Spitfires of Nos. 72 and 92 Squadrons from Biggin Hill were the first to engage at the coast, and soon German fighters were using up precious fuel in a series of dogfights which started at 23,000ft. Other Fighter Command squadrons from Kenley, Northolt, Hendon and Hornchurch joined in, while aircraft from Middle Wallop in No. 10 Group were called to help. Then, as the bombers approached London, they were met by the might of 60 fighters of No. 12 Group's Duxford Wing, led by Douglas Bader.

The sky was filled with fighters twisting in combat, while bombers tried frantically to maintain formation and avoid the hail of fire. The Dorniers could not break through, and scattered their bombs haphazardly over south London and Kent as they turned back in disorder. Hurricanes and Spitfires, for once outnumbering the enemy, hunted them across the sky. At this stage Zehbe's aircraft was hit repeatedly before plummeting dramatically over the centre of the capital.

A lull now ensued for two hours before the Germans returned. This gave Fighter Command an opportunity to refuel, rearm and prepare to meet the next attack. Three large formations, mainly of Heinkel He 111s and Dornier Do 17s heavily escorted by fighters, again aimed for London, crossing the coast at about 1400. The RAF's

response was firm as squadron after squadron moved towards the Germans. The Luftwaffe's targets lay in London, but few of their aircraft penetrated the defences. Many dropped their bombs in the suburbs, only to be confronted by two squadrons from No. 10, six from No. 11 and five from No. 12 Groups. In the mêlée, bombers were pursued over Kent and the Thames Estuary as they tried to escape. The sky was filled with vapour trails, aircraft diving and wheeling, bombers and fighters burning and men parachuting to safety. Once again Goering's battering tactics had failed at heavy cost.

Two smaller raids were launched later, one against Portland and the other against an aircraft factory at Southampton, but little damage was done. By the end of the day the Reichsmarschall's hopes had been dashed.

At first, claims by both sides were exaggerated, owing to the normal confusion of battle. Later counts showed that 58 Luftwaffe aircraft were destroyed during the day, while the RAF lost 29. These casualties were sufficiently heavy for German leaders to recognise that Fighter Command was still alive and well, and many German aircrew were amazed that so many Hurricanes and Spitfires

had opposed them. Two days later Hitler postponed Operation 'Sealion', and although further smaller daylight raids were made, the Luftwaffe turned to the night Blitz. In that campaign they would suffer fewer losses.

On the British side, Churchill spent some time on the 15th at No.11 Group's headquarters, watching the progress of battle with Park. By the evening Fighter Command could feel satisfied with the way in which the defences had reacted. However, the disagreement between the two AOCs, Park at No.11 Group and Leigh-Mallory at No.12 Group, concerning tactics and the size of formations required, continued.

As 15 September marked a watershed in the battle, it has become recognised as 'Battle of Britain Day'. The RAF's resolute defence was epitomised by actions such as that of Sergeant Holmes in his Hurricane. For Zehbe, who lies buried in Brookwood Military Cemetery, however, the day brought disaster, for which much blame must be apportioned to Luftwaffe Intelligence. Their fault was to underestimate the strength and powers of resistance of Fighter Command.

# The Northolt Raid

*Painting by Geoff Lea*
*Text by John Maynard*

IN THE YEARS IMMEDIATELY BEFORE THE FIRST WORLD War, Royal Engineer Surveyors three times visited the flat land west of Northolt Junction railway station and pondered its suitability as a military aerodrome. However, it was not until January 1915 that authority was given for work to begin on the site, and it opened two months later with the arrival of No. 4 Reserve Aeroplane Squadron from Farnborough.

Lying close to the main Oxford Road and bounded to the east by the railway, the new site was within easy reach of London. Its development continued throughout the First World War with the construction of hangars and the usual profusion of ugly military buildings. Northolt was first conceived as a base for the night defence of London, and to this end it was provided with the rudimentary landing aids then available. The first patrols were mounted in June 1915, when Zeppelin attacks were anticipated. Gradually, however, training became the principal activity, and after the USA's entry into the war in 1917 many Americans arrived there for flying training. That same year Northolt recorded its first and, as it turned out, only contact with the enemy in the war. On 13 June Captains Cole-Hamilton and Keevil took off to intercept raid being carried out by Gotha bombers over Essex. Sadly their aircraft was hit in the ensuing engagement and both men were killed.

In the inter-war years the airfield became the base for a wide range of diverse activites as the RAF struggled to survive on limited budgets while fulfilling its multifarious defence obligations. Thus bomber, fighter, coastal patrol and communications squadrons were all variously based at Northolt during the twenties. A mean-minded Treasury provided modest funds to drain the often waterlogged flying field and to erect permanent brick barracks, messes and administration blocks, and on the far side more modern hangarage was built.

Certainly by the time the Prince of Wales and the Duke of Kent arrived there to undertake their flying training the airfield was beginning to assume a more dignified, businesslike appearance, and No. 111 Squadron with its Bristol Bulldogs took up residence in July 1934. In 1936 Northolt passed to No. 11 Group, Fighter Command, and No. 23 Squadron moved in with its Hawker Demons from Biggin Hill and a welcome spell on detachment in Malta. Air Marshal Hugh Dowding had moved into the new Command Headquarters at Bentley Priory, in nearby Stanmore, on 14 July 1936, and began to establish in that strangely ugly building the defence system that would change the course of history a bare four years later.

In 1939 Northolt acquired two 800-yard concrete runways running north-south and north-east–south-west. Surprisingly it was among the very first RAF aerodromes to be so equipped. Early in the war the experts began to prepare a vast and complex camouflage scheme. Hedges were painted across grass and runways, and the hangars had plan views of back-to-back housing painted on their roofs. There was a great deal of argument about the efficacy of this elaborate ruse, which was only partly settled when the Luftwaffe took a perfect aerial photograph of Northolt with great accuracy on 31 August 1940. This perhaps proved that much time, ingenuity and, indeed, paint had been wasted on a site so clearly delineated by the railway and the recently constructed Western Avenue.

In June 1936 No. 111 Squadron had exchanged its Bulldogs for higher-performance Gloster Gauntlets, but some eighteen months later that squadron secured a place in history by taking delivery of the first of its Hawker Hurricanes. By Christmas Day 1937 'Treble One' had formed a flight of three.

The Hurricane started life in 1933 in Hawker's design office at Kingston, when chief designer Sydney

Camm began to scheme a single-seat, open-cockpit monoplane fighter based on the Hawker Fury biplane and powered by a Rolls-Royce Goshawk engine. It began as a simple concept with four guns and a fixed, spatted undercarriage. The specification writers of the Air Ministry had turned their backs for years on proposals for monoplane interceptors. However, over the next twelve months a positive torrent of innovation emerged from the Ministry and was welcomed by Hawker. Thus, when the prototype aeroplane emerged it was powered by the Rolls-Royce PV.12 engine, later named Merlin. It had a fully enclosed cockpit, a retractable undercarriage and provision for eight wing-mounted machine-guns.

The high speeds of combat by then envisaged made this daunting armament a necessity, since guns could only be brought to bear for seconds at a time. The Hurricane's eight .303in Brownings could punch ten pounds of metal travelling at some 2,000mph into the structure of an enemy aeroplane in just three seconds. Impressive though this was, it would very shortly prove to be barely adequate. In 1938, however, with 1,600 Hurricanes on order, the first squadrons to receive the type wrestled with a truly high-performance aeroplane. Treble One pilots had to accustom themselves to a maximum speed increased from 230mph to 318mph, a landing speed some 15mph higher than that of the Gauntlet, and a significantly greater ceiling and rate of climb.

Of course there were accidents. The first involved Hurricane L1556, the ninth production aeroplane, which dived into the ground alongside Western Avenue between Ickenham and Hillingdon, killing the pilot. In the following months there were forced landings at

Colnbrook and at Ickenham, as well as a landing accident on the airfield in July. However, the Squadron Commander, Squadron Leader John Gillan, achieved considerable Press acclaim by flying from Edinburgh to Northolt, a distance of about 400 miles, at an average speed of 408mph. The assistance of a tailwind component was of course acknowledged, but robust Service humour accorded Gillan the nickname 'Downwind',

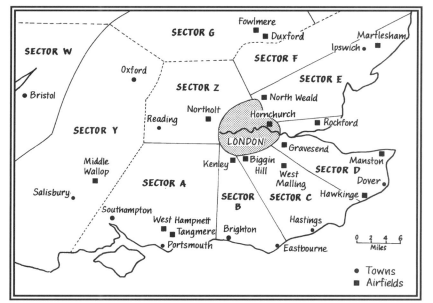

which he relished for the remainder of his short life. Men like Gillan, who were the heartbeat of the prewar Service, trained their regular squadron pilots to an exceptional level of competence and professionalism. Just enough of them survived the Battle of France and the early stages of the Battle of Britain to inspire and encourage the youthful volunteers who comprised the bulk of Fighter Command by August 1940.

War came on a bright sunny Sunday morning, and Northolt then had three fighter squadrons in residence, Nos. 25 and 600 with Bristol Blenheim Is and,

of course No. 111 with its Hurricanes. The Blenheim Is were designated night fighters, although they were ill-equipped for the role at that early stage of the war. About two weeks later No. 65 Squadron moved in with Spitfire Is. It was a time of watching and waiting while the apparent stalemate in France froze into immobility like everything else in the terrible winter of 1939. At Northolt, squadrons came and went, some over to France, others to bolster home-defence deficiencies. Early in January a new Station Commander arrived who would see the station through the great battle of the summer, and Heston was acquired as a satellite aerodrome. The camouflage pundits came to the fore again at about this time, and a dummy aerodrome was built on a golf course near Barnet, complete with a scattering of dummy Hurricanes to lure the Germans away from Northolt a few miles to the West.

The shattering German offensive through Holland, Belgium and France started on 10 May 1940. On 2 June the rear-guard of the British evacuation from Dunkirk waded out to the last ships, and Hitler's domination of continental Europe was almost complete. On 30 May, No. 609 Squadron flew its Spitfires from Northolt to help cover the evacuation, having arrived at the base only a fortnight earlier. Their first operation was not a success, since the returning aircraft became lost, several carrying out forced landings and one crashing near Harwich and killing the pilot. From then on things could only get better, and by 2 June the squadron scoreboard stood at a commendable seven, including two Bf 109s among the more vulnerable bombers. Ultimately, 609 would move south to Middle Wallop, in the centre of the battle by then raging over the South Coast. Before this, however, its Spitfires provided the escort for the de Havilland Flamingo flying from Hendon to France in mid-June with Winston Churchill on board. Churchill tried in vain to persuade France to fight on, but when he returned on 13 June it was clear that Britain would be standing alone.

Northolt was designated a Sector Station for Sector Z in Fighter Command's order of battle, and close by was Air Vice-Marshal Keith Park's No.11 Group operations room in the grounds of historic RAF Uxbridge. The remnants of No. 1 Squadron flew into the airfield on 20 June. They had been driven out of their French base at Berry au Bac by intense bombing in the third week in May, and thereafter had retreated from field to field across France until they withdrew to southern England from Nantes. By the end of the month No. 1 Squadron was up to strength and operational once again.

After suffering severe losses in combat with the increasing weight of Luftwaffe attacks, No. 43 Squadron rested at Northolt but returned to Tangmere in August. Increasingly the aerodrome was being used as a reserve base, combining recuperation and training with a rotation of operational squadrons. Amazingly it did not suffer under Goering's tactical switch to attacks on Fighter Command's airfields, which began on 12 August. Once the early summer haze had cleared on this beautiful fine morning across southern England, vital radar stations were seriously damaged or put out of action, whilst Manston, Lympne and Hawkinge were heavily bombed. As August progressed, Middle Wallop, Kenley, Biggin Hill, Martlesham Heath, West Malling, Tangmere, Croydon, Ford and many other stations suffered terrible damage, but surprisingly Northolt was ignored. Perhaps after all the elaborate camouflage scheme, which now included rivers and pools painted up the runways, was working.

When No. 1 Squadron moved to Middle Wallop it was replaced by No. 257 Squadron, but by the middle of August that unit had lost four pilots killed and eight of its Hurricanes. Park withdrew the Squadron to Debden, and the newly arrived No. 1 Squadron RCAF joined its RAF twin at Northolt. Meanwhile, an historic event had taken place at the airfield on 2 August, when No. 303 Squadron was formed, comprising Polish pilots under the command of Squadron Leader R. G. Kellett. This date marked the beginning of a close association between Northolt and the Polish people which has lasted to this day and is marked by the moving memorial which stands at one corner of the aerodrome. The Poles were fanatically dedicated to the defeat of the enemy, perhaps more so than the citizens of any other occupied nation. They knew only too well the likely fate of their fellow countrymen at the hands of the Germans, and most of them had close family still in Poland. The squadron became operational on 24 August, and in September it was No. 11 Group's top-scoring Squadron.

On 9 September the Hurricanes of No. 229 Squadron moved in to replace No. 1 Squadron, which went to Wittering for a spell away from combat. The history of No. 229 could be traced back to the First World War, when it briefly flew coastal patrols off Northern France and Belgium. Disbanded in 1919 after a bare year's existence, it re-formed at Digby in early October 1939 with Blenheim Is. At that time the intention was obviously to retain the unit's coastal patrol role, and its Blenheims were involved in the cold and infinitely tedious job of patrolling over North Sea convoys and fishing fleets. This was interspersed for a lucky few with various airborne development trails of RDF, before the squadron began its move into night defence. However, in March 1940 all of this came to an abrupt end with a switch to the day fighter role and re-equipment with Hurricanes. After action in France, No. 229 moved

back to Wittering and No. 12 Group to rebuild its strength. On 9 September it flew south to Northolt and participated throughout the closing stages of the great air battle, and especially in its climax on 15 September.

It was on 6 October, a Sunday morning, that the enemy finally arrived at Northolt. A bomber emerged from the clouds to cross the airfield at only a few hundred feet, machine-gunning and releasing two bombs. It returned moments later for a further attack, shooting up No. 229 Squadron's dispersal. The bombs fell between hangars and other buildings, but destroyed a taxiing Hurricane and killed its Polish pilot, Sergeant Siudak, in his cockpit. Also killed was air-raid lookout A.C.2 Stennett, who was on the roof of one of the buildings. A Hurricane of No. 229 flown by Pilot Officer V. B. S. Verity, a New Zealander, intercepted the raider and damaged it, but it sought refuge again in the low cloud, finally crashing at Leatherhead in Surrey and killing its crew.

Geoff Lea's painting, superbly depicting both the raid and the interception, was commissioned by the wife of Mr F. W. Edge, who had served with No. 229 almost since its formation at Digby in 1939. That Sunday morning in October 1940 he was in the squadron orderly room, a building alongside one of the hangars, when he heard machine-gun fire; not an unusual experience at the time. The arrival of bombs with shattering explosions brought a great chunk of concrete down through the ceiling and on to a desk just in front of Mr Edge. At that point he decided the time had come to take cover, and he ran outside to see a wrecked Hurricane, the craters, and, rather to his surprise, the hangars still standing. The Luftwaffe never returned to Northolt, but the memory of its Polish squadrons will remain forever with the proud inscription on their memorial: 'I have fought a good fight, I have finished my course, I have kept the faith'.

# Mackenzie's Wing Strike

*Painting by Brian Withams*
*Text by Michael Burns*

IN THIS IMPRESSIVE PAINTING BY BRIAN WITHAMS, just one of the very many remarkable incidents of air combat during the Second World War is depicted. Numerous unusual, eccentric or bizarre events took place over six years of air fighting. Some are now lost, but this example at least is a documented footnote in Battle of Britain history. In October 1940 Pilot officer Mackenzie's Hurricane ran out of ammunition in the middle of a combat after a series of actions in a rambling dogfight, so he determined to destroy the enemy fighter he was chasing by using his own Hurricane as a weapon against the Bf 109. The moment after impact is depicted in this painting.

Throughout most first-hand accounts of air combats told by pilots of any era there is one recurring comment. Squadrons and flights often became separated during the heat of battle, and on many occasions the individual pilot would suddenly find himself very much alone in the sky, where mere seconds before there was a mass of twisting and turning aircraft. This is illustrated very clearly in the painting by Brian Withams, depicting the one-on-one duel of the individual dogfight, which would often continue from 20,000ft down to wave-top level, ending only with a final burst of fire or a sudden break-off of the fight and a flee for home with minimal fuel reserves.

When Pilot Officer Kenneth W. Mackenzie joined a front-line squadron in late September 1940, the Battle of Britain was entering its final stage. He expected to be attacking large bomber formations, but found No. 501 Squadron smarting from maulings by raids by the large formations of aggressive Bf 109s that were escorting single Gruppen of Ju 88s. His main opponents would be fighters. So it was fortunate that, unlike many young pilots thrown into the battle, he was an experienced airman with an engineer's knowledge of aeroplanes, and had benefited from several weeks' rigorous combat training. Within a week he had five victories to his credit and had proven himself the very model of an aggressive fighter pilot, and one with unusual style.

His ambition to fly had been sparked in 1934, when Alan Cobham's flying circus came to his native Belfast. A flight in an Avro 504 convinced Mackenzie that his career had to combine engineering and aviation. At seventeen he became a founder member of the North of Ireland Aero Club, which was run by ex-RAF instructors. Flying Avro Cadets, he soloed after only six and a half hours and rapidly gained his 'A' licence. Between reading engineering at Queen's University, Mackenzie was absorbed by competition and aerobatic flying and learning about aircraft from club mechanics, but the signs of war stirred his patriotism. He was disinclined to join the élite Auxiliary Air Force, but the RAF Volunteer Reserve welcomed his flying experience. The VRs came from all walks of life, drawn together by a common love of flying. Mackenzie had the life he wanted, but his engineering studies suffered through his devotion to flying. He swiftly completed the Elementary Service syllabus at Sydenham, flying Hawker Hart trainers.

The VR was mobilised on 4 August 1939, but flying was halted and it was four months before Mackenzie was called up, and three more before he started flying training again. In May 1940, after two months further elementary training, he began ' real' flying on Harts at No. 3 Service Flying Training School, South Cerney. Assessed as 'above average', he was posted to No. 6 Operational Training Unit (OTU), Sutton Bridge, for training on fighters.

Mackenzie described his first solo in a Hurricane as a 'glorious experience', and instructors who had fought in France gave intensity to the combat training that soon followed. As to his own style, Mackenzie the engineer was emphatic that the only way to master the Hurricane was to fly it to its limits.

On 20 September 1940, Pilot Officer K. W. Mackenzie was posted to No. 43 Squadron, which at the time had been withdrawn from No. 11 Group, where the battle was mainly being fought, to No. 13 Group in the north of England. He was with them barely nine days, but intensive training under Frank Carey now gave him confidence in himself and in the Hurricane. On the 28th, only four days after flying his first operational patrol, he found himself in action when, at dusk and in poor visibility, his Section was vectored on to an intruder over Newcastle. The enemy turned out to be a Heinkel He 111, and Mackenzie opened fire from 400 yards. Although the Heinkel escaped, Mackenzie had fired in anger for the first time.

Next day Mackenzie was posted to No. 501 (County of Gloucester) Squadron at Kenley, in No. 11 Group, Fighter Command, where his direct manner, humour and aggressive spirit soon took him to the heart of the squadron. Together with No. 605 Squadron, this unit formed the Croydon Hurricane Wing, which in turn formed part of the Biggin Hill Sector.

No. 501 Squadron had operated in France with the AASF, and was already an experienced, highly motivated unit with a terrific team spirit. Its pilots, who included respected veterans of France such as 'Ginger' Lacey, 'Gus' Holden and 'Hawkeye' Lee, were a mixture of Regulars and members of the Auxiliary Air Force, leavened by a number of Polish fliers.

On 30 September the Luftwaffe mounted its last massive daylight bomber attack, but this served only to confirm the failure of these attacks, and henceforth it would put most of its effort into night bombing. By the end of September it was clear that the Germans had failed to achieve the air superiority essential to an invasion. Fighter Command was still unbowed, while Luftwaffe bomber losses had been severe. Nor had Luftwaffe fighters achieved the success that had been expected of them. Tied to the close escort of bombers, the Bf 109s had been unable to counter the Hurricanes and Spitfires aggressively, but now the Luftwaffe freed them to use their superior speed and climb in fighter combat above 20,000ft. Formations of Ju 88 fast bombers were now despatched, escorted by dozens of Bf 109 and Bf 110 fighter-bombers above them, and scores of Bf 109 fighters operating as high top cover.

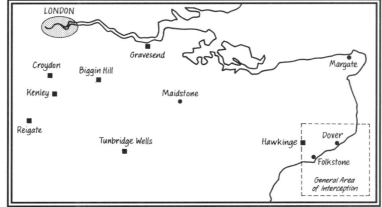

On 1 October Mackenzie was ordered to fly a sector familiarisation followed by an airfield 'beat-up'. His evident aerobatic skill and good reports from OTU and No. 43 Squadron had brought quick acceptance as part of the team. Allocated Hurricane Mk I V6799/SD-X fresh from servicing, he went over it with his ground crew to get to know it, driven by his engineering interest. Next day he took his mount to the limits. He liked SD-X.

On 4 October, Mackenzie made his first operational flight with No. 501 Squadron, a dull reconnaissance. But on only his second sortie he shared in damaging a bomber. Streams of fighters and bombers were using fog, rain and cloud cover to reach London. At 1100 the squadron scrambled to intercept Ju 88s near Folkestone at 8,000ft. Mackenzie and Holden spotted a Ju 88 1,000ft below, and Holden attacked from the rear quarter, firing from 300 yards with no results. Mackenzie pulled a tight turn for a rear attack and fired at 80 yards into the port engine, damaging it. The rear gunner hit Mackenzie's port wing. Both pilots attacked again, but lost the Ju 88 in cloud.

Next morning Hogan accosted him: 'Congratulations Mac, you're a mad bugger ... glad to have you with us!' Such acceptance delighted him, but he was preoccupied by something more practical. Since first firing the Hurricane's eight .303in machine-guns at OTU, Mackenzie had questioned the lethality of rifle-calibre bullets against metal aeroplanes at the recommended range of 300 yards and standard pattern. Now he pestered the chief armourer to harmonise his guns to a spot at 200 yards. With that he knew he would have destroyed the Ju 88. In common with other fine marksmen, spot harmonisation and getting in really close to produce a lethal cone of fire became an obsession.

On 5 October Fighter Command braced itself for the fighter-bomber high-altitude raids about to be unleashed. From 0900 raids of from a dozen to 40 Messerschmitts began coming in high and fast. Although No. 501 Squadron was fully serviceable and flew three times, they fought only once.

At 1245, barely fifteen minutes after landing from a 90min patrol at 28,000 frozen feet, the squadron was scrambled and ordered to climb to 20,000ft. At 18,000ft they surprised 30 plus Messerschmitts 2,000ft below, down-sun. Mackenzie attacked a Bf 110 but broke off to avoid another one. As he pulled up to attack a Bf 109 above him, another Bf 109 crossed his sights. He peppered it with a full-deflection burst from 100 yards which slowed the enemy, but Mackenzie took time to regain position. Unseen behind him as he trailed his prey at 1,200 yards, Holden shot a Bf 109 off his tail. Off Margate his Bf 109 dropped to 20ft above the sea. Mackenzie closed fast to his favourite range and a long burst from 100 yards sent it into the sea.

On 7 October, after a day's rest, No. 501 Squadron was scrambled at 1100 to intercept a large raid, but reached altitude too late. They landed at 1230 tired, but within half an hour were scrambled with all available squadrons against a raid of over 150 Bf 109s, Bf 110s and Ju 88s flying in waves at various altitudes from Calais to Dover. This so stretched No.11 Group that No.12 Group reinforcements were called in.

Croydon Wing was to patrol the Sevenoaks approaches at 20,000ft in standard wing formation; No. 501 Squadron flew west along the north bank of the Thames, with No. 605 two miles behind and above. Control vectored No. 501 Squadron on to raiders escaping south-east, and Hogan saw them, a pair of Bf 109s and then five more a mile to the east. They had seen the Wing, and made for the gap between the squadrons; No. 501 Squadron attacked and the dogfight began.

Evading a Bf 109, Mackenzie followed Hogan down as he attacked another. A long burst by Hogan inflicted several hits, then he broke right as the Bf 109 went into cloud. MacKenzie broke over the cloud at 6,000ft. He calculated that the German would not go straight through; he came out at right angles and turned for the Channel. Mackenzie had altitude, and half-rolled at full power on to the Bf 109's tail. Holding fire, he raked its radiator and engine from 150 yards. The Bf 109 lost speed and altitude until it ditched off Hythe.

Mackenzie had lost his colleagues but still had ammunition. He could see combats above him and hear Control reporting enemy positions. He climbed hard and patrolled the Dover-Folkestone line at 23,000ft, keenly watching his tail. At 1330 he saw eight Bf 109s

cross the coast, inbound from the east. They were 1,000ft above him, but with speed in hand and aerobatic skill, Mackenzie looped up and half-rolled off on to the last three undetected.

Suddenly, a Bf 109 appeared 200 yards ahead, just over him. Mackenzie's quick burst struck its radiator and cockpit and the pilot reacted violently, breaking hard and half-rolling into a dive, almost colliding with his attacker. By the time Mackenzie had recovered, the Bf 109 had pulled well ahead but was streaming glycol. At maximum boost, Mackenzie overhauled the German, who was in a shallow dive towards Folkestone. Past the harbour, he closed up and opened fire at less than 100 yards. Three seconds later his guns clacked and hissed. He was out of ammunition, but not of ideas.

Cruising at 180kt, slowly descending to 80ft, but taking no evasive action, the German made for France. Mackenzie was determined not to let him get within reach of his air-sea rescue service. He flew round him, came alongside, and signalled to him to ditch. Slumped across his controls, staring ahead, the German made no response. Taking getting in close to extremes, Mackenzie decided to knock off the Bf 109's tail with his Hurricane's undercarriage, but when he lowered it he lost too much speed, and hastily raised it.

He drew alongside the German's port three-quarter and brought his Hurricane's wingtip down on to the Bf 109's port tailplane, which broke off. He then pulled up to port as 3ft of his wingtip came off cleanly just beyond the aileron's outer hinge. The Bf 109 crashed and sank, but its pilot had drawn Mackenzie into a trap: two Bf 109s attacked him from above and behind. Standing patrols guarded the German rescue service. Skimming waves, twitching port and starboard, up and down, and out of ammunition, Mackenzie became the prey. The Germans were determined but poor shots, yet hit his radiator and back armour plate.

Near Folkestone the Germans turned back. Mackenzie's Hurricane would not make Kenley, so he decided upon a belly landing on the hill to the north of Folkestone. Fearing fire, he unstrapped for a swift escape. As SD-X decelerated, Mackenzie pitched forward on to the sight and split his jaw and broke teeth. But he got out quickly and was taken in hand by AA gunners.

While on sick leave he was awarded the Distinguished Flying Cross for five victories in less than a week. He returned to his squadron on 17 October raring to go, but there was no action until the 25th, when he claimed one Bf 109 and shared another. That afternoon he had another collision, with his wingman, Pilot Officer Goth, who died. Mackenzie was lucky to bale out and escape unhurt. The Bf 109s were now staying to fight it out; trying to eliminate Fighter Command. Mackenzie claimed three more to bring his score to ten, but it was a last desperate effort by the Luftwaffe. Fighter activity diminished sharply as the night-bombing campaign intensified. It was the end of the day battle and the beginning of the night Blitz.

*The artist writes:* When researching and creating Mackenzie's Wing Strike it was clearly important for Brian Withams to get as much background details and accuracy as possible, particularly given the split-second moment of the unique event he was depicting. 'I worked in collaboration with the pilot himself – "Mac" Mackenzie – who described chasing the German aircraft but having exhausted his ammo, he chose to fly alongside the enemy aircraft. Noting the pilot was looking neither left nor right but going flat out for the French coast, Mac positioned himself to place his starboard wingtip under the tailplane of the Messerschmitt and rolled, taking the tailplane off plus his own wingtip. As I remember he scraped home doing a "wheels-up" above the cliffs at Eastbourne..'

# Defiant Victory

*Painting by Jim Mitchell*
*Text by Mike Spick*

DURING THE SUMMER OF 1940, WITH THE BATTLE of Britain raging by day, Luftwaffe night bombing was of low intensity. At first this consisted mainly of nuisance raids and minelaying, because the day battle was confidently expected to create suitable conditions for the invasion of England which was to end the war. But when the daylight battle began to go badly for the Luftwaffe, night operations took on ever-increasing importance. Liverpool was heavily raided on four nights at the end of August, and the main weight of the attacks then fell on London, which was bombed on 64 out of 65 successive nights from 7/8 September .

The British night defences of the time were rudimentary to say the least. The anti-aircraft guns were dependent on sound locators, which were virtually useless. By October 1940 the first gunlaying radars were entering service, but these lacked accuracy and, in any case, were unreliable. Searchlights were adequate up to about 12,000ft in clear conditions, but it was easy for German bombers to stay above this altitude. The only real answer was the night fighter.

Night fighting had long been neglected by the RAF. Finding a German bomber in the night sky was akin to searching for the proverbial needle in a haystack, and although a sufficiently accurate ground controlled interception system and a reliable airborne radar set were under development, in late 1940 they did not yet exist.

Of the two radar-equipped night fighters available, the extremely capable Bristol Beaufighter was only just entering service, and was still suffering teething troubles. The Bristol Blenheim was numerically the most important night fighter, but it suffered from several shortcomings. Its performance was inadequate to allow it to catch a cruising German bomber unless it was exceptionally well placed when contact was made, it was demonstrably lacking in hitting power, the multi-paned glazing of the cockpit gave all sorts of unwanted reflections, adding to the difficulties of night operations, and its Airborne Interception (AI) Mk III radar was extremely unreliable.

Given these shortcomings in the radar-equipped night fighter force, single-seater day fighters, Spitfires and Hurricanes, were often put up at night to operate in the 'catseye' role. While it was a matter of sheer chance if these managed to make contact with a German bomber, occasional victories were scored. Finally, two squadrons of Boulton Paul Defiant Is were available.

The Defiant had its origins in Air Ministry Specification F.9/35, which called for a two-seater bomber destroyer armed with a powered gun turret. In theory, Defiants could formate on enemy bombers in a position where they were safe from return fire, allowing their gunners to take an unhurried aim. The theory came unglued in the presence of enemy fighters; after a couple of early successes, the two Defiant squadrons, Nos. 141 and 264, were shot to pieces in a handful of daylight actions. It could hardly have been otherwise. A single-engined fighter with the added drag and weight of a powered turret and a second crewman could not be expected to match the performance and agility of a single-seat fighter. The lack of conventional fixed forward-firing armament was a disaster, while the weight of fire of the four rifle-calibre Browning machine-guns in the turret was arguably on the light side.

Far too vulnerable for daylight operations, the two Defiant squadrons were transferred to the night fighter force. The aircraft was in many ways suitable for this. Its handling was docile and it had a sturdy, wide-track undercarriage, well able to cope with the exigencies of night landings. Its performance was good enough to allow it to catch the German bombers, and it had a two-man crew, which allowed the pilot to concentrate on instrument flying when necessary, while the gunner

maintained a visual search. Just one problem remained; finding the bomber in the first place.

There was at this time a rudimentary system of ground control, but it was far too inaccurate to allow the fighter to be vectored to within visual distance, which was normally no more than a few hundred feet. Placing it within several miles was the best that could be hoped for. Generally, the procedure was for the night fighter to fly station on a preset patrol line, and to stay there until ordered to go chasing after a bomber. The night sky is a big place, and all too often these excursions proved fruitless.

Even on occasions when searchlights succeeded in illuminating a bomber, it was often difficult to see it from the air. Only if the fighter was at a lower altitude could the fighter crew see the lit-up underside of a bomber; from above the enemy machine remained invisible. But even if a target could be seen, getting into a firing position before the bomber evaded the searchlight, or passed beyond its range, was another matter.

Chance visual sightings, though rare, posed no such problems. The bomber simply had to be close! The problem then became one of identification. Incoming and homebound German bombers were mixed in with British bombers on operations, training aircraft on night sorties and, of course, other night fighters. The greatest care had to be taken to confine tragedy to the enemy.

The night of October 15/16, 1940, saw the Blitz on London in full swing. The Luftwaffe launched some 400 bomber sorties, many of their crews flying twice during the hours of darkness. In reply, Fighter Command put up 41 sorties, but even with the advantage of a clear night and a bright noon, only two made

contact. In one instance a Blenheim gained a radar contact, but, as so often happened, the pilot was unable to close the range to reach a firing position. The other interception was made by a Defiant of No. 264 Squadron flown by Pilot Officer Desmond Hughes, with Sergeant Fred Gash as his gunner. Hughes later recalled:

'It was a bright moonlight night. Suddenly, out of the corner of my eye, I saw something move across the stars out to my left. If you are scanning the night sky it is normally completely still, so anything that moves attracts the eye. This just had to be another aircraft. I got Fred to swing his turret round and we both kept an eye on the black shape. We moved towards it and soon caught sight of a row of exhausts. It was a twin-engined aircraft. I slid alongside, below and to the right of him, and slowly edged in "under his armpit" while Fred kept his guns trained on the aircraft. Then we saw the distinctive wing and tail shape of a Heinkel – there was no mistaking it. I moved into a firing position, within about 50 yards of his wingtip and slightly below, so that Fred could align his guns for an upward shot at about 20 degrees. Obviously the German crew had not seen us – they continued straight ahead.

'Fred fired straight into the starboard engine. One round in six was a tracer, but what told us we were hitting him was the glitter of the de Wilde rounds as they ignited on impact. Fred fired, realigned, fired again. He got off two or three bursts. There was no return fire from the bomber – indeed, I doubt if any guns could have been brought to bear on our position on its beam. The engine burst into flames, then the Heinkel rolled on its back, went down steeply and crashed into a field near Brentwood.'

Ironically, the German raider was not one of those attacking London. It was Heinkel He 111 of Kampfgruppe 126, a specialist minelaying unit which that night was targeted against the Thames Estuary.

The night sky is a big place; a combination of over 400 German bomber sorties and 41 British night fighter sorties, on that clear moonlit night, produced only two contacts and one combat, and the latter was gained

Wittering

Duxford

Debden

Hunsdon

Castle Camps

Brentwood

Northolt

LONDON

Gravesend

Biggin Hill

Redhill

Tangmere

Durrington

Ford

Martlesham

Waldringfield +

Rochford

Manston

West Malling

Willesborough +

Key:
● Nightfighter Airfields
+ GCI Stations

by a catseye fighter rather than a radar-equipped aircraft. At the time of the encounter Hughes and Gash were patrolling a line to the east of London, astride the approach route of many of the bombers.

There are several points of interest in this combat. Pilot Officer Hughes's comment that he first gained visual contact out of the corner of his eye is significant. Peripheral vision is always more acute, especially for movement. Night fighter pilots were to learn to keep a contact in their peripheral vision while they closed the range, as the target was often lost when they looked directly at it.

At first the target would be merely a black shape, and only when the fighter crew got in very close could they make a positive identification, even in bright moonlight. Certainly the German crew were not keeping a very good lookout, but encounters with night fighters were extremely rare occurrences at this stage of the war, and were hardly regarded as a real threat. It should be remembered, however, that the Defiant, approaching rather lower, would have been lost to the German crew against the darkness of the ground, whereas the Heinkel was limned against the lighter background of the sky.

The use of tracer at night seems slightly surprising, since its usual effect was to dazzle the gunner and ruin his night vision. Nor was it an aid to aiming; tracer could in fact be very misleading. What told Gash that his shots were on target was the de Wilde ammunition, each hit with which caused a flash on impact, confirming that his aim was true.

At the time of this engagement, night fighting was in its infancy, with heavy reliance on catseye fighters. Just six months later the radar-equipped Beaufighter, operating under close ground control, was in the ascendant, and the tide of the night battle over Britain had turned.

*The artist writes:* One of several prints specially commissioned for *The Battle of Britain*,1990, by Alfred Price, this was not an easy painting to compose. The main difficulty was due to the fact that the event took place at night, which limited the colour available to portray the scene. Like most paintings I create, this portrayal is based on actual events and required a great deal of research to obtain complete accuracy when putting brush to canvas.

# Operation 'Colossus'

*Painting by David Shepherd*
*Text by Ray Sturtivant*

SHORTLY AFTER ITALY ENTERED THE WAR, ON 10 June 1940, the Air Ministry received letters from two civilians familiar with the country, suggesting that an attack be directed against the Acquedetto Pugliese system in Southern Italy. This was proposed as an important target because the aqueduct system carried drinking water across the Apennine Mountains to the arid province of Apulia, which included the strategic ports of Bari, Brindisi and Taranto.

In the ensuing months it became apparent that these three ports were being used for the shipment of troops to both North Africa and Albania, and consequently planning began with the aim of cutting the vital water supply by launching an attack on one of the aqueducts. Studies showed that an attack using the types of bomber then available was impracticable, and a seaborne raid was equally out of the question because the only vital and vulnerable points were too far from the coast. By this time, however, other options existed, and Admiral Sir Roger Keyes, the Director of Combined Operations, suggested the use of paratroops of No.11 Special Air Service Battalion. This proposal met with the approval of the Chiefs of Staff and, importantly, Winston Churchill, who was by then Prime Minister. The codename Operation 'Colossus' was adopted.

The Acquedetto Pugliese received its water from the River Sele, which flows into the Tyrrhenian Sea south of Salerno. The source of the river, from which the water was drawn, was near Calatri, in very mountainous country. The water was carried over the natural bed of the river by the Traquino Aqueduct, at the very fountainhead of the system. This was the obvious target, and detailed planning for an attack was begun.

It was clear that the only possible base for the intended raid was Malta, some 400 miles away. A force of elderly Bristol Bombay troop transports was at first considered, but these would have been inadequate for the task, and only four were available. Initial planning therefore centred on the use of five Armstrong Whitworth Whitley bombers, supplemented by the Bombays. The Whitley was later to be used extensively by airborne forces, but at that time it was serving only as a bomber; consequently the aircraft and crews would have to be drawn from Bomber Command. The Air Officer Commanding-in-Chief of that Command was reluctant to detach some of his best crews for this specialised task, especially as the preparation and execution of the operation was likely to take as long as a month, but he was prevailed upon to help.

As a result, on 15 December five selected Whitleys and experienced crews of No. 78 Squadron were flown from Dishforth to Ringway, Manchester, where they were attached temporarily to the Central Landing Establishment (CLE), later to become the Airborne Forces Experimental Establishment. Here ground crews started to fit special long-range tanks and modify the aircraft for paratroop dropping, while the unit's Development Section was kept busy improving the somewhat primitive supply containers for arms and stores.

Group Captain Harvey of the CLE, and Wing Commander J. B. Tait, DFC, who had been appointed commander of the Whitley detachment, soon drew attention to the immense maintenance difficulties which would be involved in the use of two quite different types of aircraft. The necessary modifications, and the training of pilots and paratroops, could not be achieved in the timescale envisaged. The Bombays were therefore taken out of the plan, and, at the prompting of the Deputy Chief of Air Staff, Bomber Command eventually agreed, somewhat reluctantly, to provide a further three Whitleys from No. 78 Squadron. These flew to Ringway on 30 December.

Here, all the Whitley aircrews received training in paratroop dropping, including the first night descents

by the 37 men of 'X' Troop, selected from No.11 SAS Battalion. The SAS troops also spent some time studying a scale model of the target, made using such information and photographs as were available, an urgent signal being sent to Malta for further aerial photographs to be obtained by the Martin Marylands of No. 69 (GR) Squadron. In case word of the operation should leak out, the cover story was to be of a proposed attack on a bridge in Abyssinia.

Final approval for the plan was given at a meeting at the Air Ministry on 11 January 1941, and next day preparations began in earnest at Ringway under Wing Commander Sir Nigel Norman, who was designated Operation Controller. Assisting him were Wing Commander Tait, now designated Attack Commander-Air, and the Attack Commander-Ground, Major T. A. G. Pritchard.

On 2 February the whole force of eight Whitleys flew to Mildenhall, which was to be their departure point from the UK, but bad weather then delayed their final departure for Malta. On 5 February, in advance of the main party, a Coastal Command Short Sunderland flying boat left for Malta with spares and ground crews, there being no Whitley spares on the island. An 'X' Troop officer, Lieutenant A. J. Deane Drummond, also flew in this aircraft, taking copies of the Operation Instructions for the AOC Malta and for the AOC-in-C Middle East. The Whitleys followed two days later, each carrying its own troops and parachutes, and reached Malta at 0900 on 8 February. Here they found enthusiastic help.

The attack was to take place on the first suitable night during the full moon period of 9-16 February. Meanwhile, the Malta-based Marylands had made many reconnaissance flights, but owing to cloud it was not until

the 9th that new photographs of the target were obtained. These revealed a second aqueduct across a tributary of the Sele, about 300 yards from the original structure. This raised doubts as to which was the intended target, but it

was eventually decided to attack the more easterly of the two. There was no time for further reconnaissance as the weather on the night of 10-11 February was favourable,

and there was considerable risk of the Whitleys being damaged on the ground by enemy air attack. This left no time for test drops of containers, the testing of fittings, or last-minute combined drilling of the teams, but it was decided to go ahead rather than risk aborting the operation later through bad weather.

At 1740 on 10 February Wing Commander Tait took off in 'K', in company with 'N' piloted by Sergeant Lashbrook, and 'W' flown by Flight Lieutenant W. R. Williams, to transport the covering party. They were to have been followed ten minutes later by 'D' (Sergeant G. W. Holden), 'E' (Pilot Officer P. B. Robinson) and 'J' (Squadron Leader P. S. Hoad) with the demolition party, and finally at 1800 by 'R' (Sergeant A. S. Ennis) and 'S' (Pilot Officer J. Wotherspoon), loaded with bombs for a diversionary attack on Foggia. Each aircraft in the main party carried a single bomb in addition to the troops and containers. In the event, 'J' was delayed by engine trouble, did not leave until 1817, and was unable to catch up with the others.

Course was set for Agrigento, on the south coast of Sicily, and from there over the mainland to the mouth of the River Sele, the intended rendezvous being over Mount Vulture, near the target, at 2130. Some cloud was met over the sea and fog over parts of Sicily, but the only opposition encountered by the five was some flak seen over Palermo. The cloud had dispersed by the time they reached the Italian coast, though some banks of fog lay in valleys; a thick bank been seen between the Sele and Ofanto valleys. Otherwise the weather was perfect, with visibility comparable to early dusk on a fine day. Detail on the ground stood out well, and snow-covered peaks, rocky valleys and clusters of picturesque mountain towns and villages contrasted sharply with their warlike intent. There was no difficulty identifying the objective and surrounding landmarks, and all of the aircraft arrived in the target area at about the intended time. The first drop was made at 2125.

Meanwhile 'J' had made a bad landfall on the Italian coast and followed a river partly obscured by mist until reaching the Adriatic. It then returned to the west coast at Scalea, flew up the Sele River and finally reached the objective at 2315, not dropping its paratroops until 2330. Unfortunately two of the aircraft, including 'J', were unable to release their containers. The packing and loading of these was a delicate task if the centre of gravity was to be so adjusted that the container would leave the bomb rack easily, but this had not been fully realised. The stick of troops from 'J', all Royal Engineers, was eventually dropped in a neighbouring valley, about two miles from the correct dropping zone. Consequently, when 'X' Troop assembled, Major Pritchard was without his senior Royal Engineers officer, Captain G. F. K. Daly, five of his sappers and much of his explosives.

In the meantime, things elsewhere had not gone according to plan. The paratroops were all dropped, but in four instances the containers did not go with them, a five-pin plug having been incorrectly fitted. Several aircraft had to make three or four runs up and down the valley to get the containers off. One full load, comprising ladders and five charges, and two other single containers each with seven Tommy guns, two Bren guns and ammunition, could not be dropped and had to be carried back to Malta.

Despite these setbacks, the troops made their way to the aqueduct with such explosives as they had. They could be seen moving around on the ground, and several times flashed torches as the aircraft passed over-head, to show that they had landed successfully. When they reached the aqueduct, however, they found that the centre pier was of reinforced concrete, not masonry as had been anticipated, and it was therefore much too strong to be destroyed. On the other hand, the end pier and the second smaller aqueduct were constructed of masonry, and sufficient explosives were available for the Engineers to attack both of these. Charges were placed in these structures, and at 0030 on 11 February they were fired. The two aqueducts promptly collapsed and water poured down into the ravine, making the operation a partial success.

The troop was then organised into three sections, and Major Pritchard gave orders for each to make its way independently to the mouth of the Sele, where the submarine HMS *Triumph* would wait to pick them up on the night of the 15th/16th. As it transpired, all had been taken prisoner by the 12th except for the section led by Captain Daly, which was captured only 12 miles from its destination on 15 February.

In the meantime, the Whitleys went on to bomb various nearby minor objectives before returning to Malta. On the return journey 'R for Roger', one of the diversionary aircraft, in which Wing Commander Norman was a passenger, successfully bombed the railway station and yard at Foggia, setting fire to a fuel train, the trucks of which exploded and caused large fires, and also badly damaged two other trains. The pilot then headed back towards Malta, and was able to see the paratroops assembling on the ground as he flew across the dropping zone. The other diversionary aircraft, 'S for Sugar', developed engine trouble and forced landed in Italy. The surviving seven aircraft flew back to Mildenhall on the night of 16/17 February.

As it transpired, the disruption of the Italian war effort was not as great as had been hoped. The end pier was easier to repair than the substantial centre pier would have been, and there were sufficient water reserves in local reservoirs to last for most of the repair time. Nevertheless, the attack undermined Italian self-confidence and resulted in effort being wasted on unnecessary defence measures. More importantly, however, the raid provided practical experience of the organisation and equipment which would be needed if future airborne operations were to be successful. On their return, Wing Commander Norman and Group Captain Harvey prepared a paper setting out the lessons learned, with invaluable suggestions for the future.

In David Shepherd's painting the aircraft of the first wave of attacking Whitleys, 'K', 'N' and 'W', carrying the covering party, are seen over the aqueduct that was the raiders' target. White parachutes bearing the SAS troops are seen descending behind the three aircraft, together with the blue parachutes to which were attached the stores containers that caused so much difficulty in two of the Whitleys. With a fine eye for detail, David has included in his painting the static lines for the parachutes that have been released. Once the whole 'stick' of parachutes had gone, the lines were hauled back into the aircraft by the dispatcher.

*The artist writes:* This painting by David Shepherd was found in the mess of one of the battalions of the Parachute Regiment. It initially caused the artist some difficulty in its identification, and in recalling the reason for its creation. While the Whitleys depicted are certainly an uncommon subject in aviation art, David Shepherd particularly enjoyed doing this painting because he has a great affinity with the aircraft of this period, through his memories of the war in the air as seen by a nine-year-old schoolboy.

# Beaufort Torpedo Strike

*Painting by Michael Turner*
*Text by Ray Sturtivant*

ALTHOUGH THE WAR AT SEA WAS FOUGHT MAINLY in the broad stretches of the Atlantic, the North Sea and coastal waters of Europe were also the scene of many engagements throughout the Second World War. It was particularly important to interfere with German coastal traffic to and from Norway, the source of important iron ore and the base from which enemy air and sea forces were operating in efforts to close off the British convoy routes to North Russia. A number of RAF squadrons were assigned the role of interdicting sea traffic off the coast of Western Europe, one of these being No. 42 Squadron.

This painting by Michael Turner shows a typical Beaufort attack by No. 42 Squadron on an enemy coastal convoy. The nearest aircraft has just released its torpedo, while AW-K is making the same run-in towards ships of the convoy just out of picture. The leading Beaufort is sweeping the ships with its machine-guns, to which individual ships' armament are replying.

The squadron had a history extending back to the First World War. During that conflict it had carried out artillery spotting and tactical reconnaissance missions in France and Italy, initially using the obsolescent B.E.2e and later its replacement, the R.E.8. Disbanded at Netheravon in June 1919, it became one of many squadrons to re-form in the expansion of the thirties, becoming a torpedo-bomber unit at Donibristle on 14 December 1936. Its initial equipment was again an obsolescent type, the Vickers Vildebeest biplane. It was not until April 1940 that the squadron received a modern replacement, in the shape of the Bristol Beaufort. As an alternative to a semi-enclosed 1,605lb 18in torpedo, up to 1,500lb of bombs could be carried.

The Beaufort had been slow to enter service, a major difficulty being the unreliability of its Bristol Taurus II engines. This problem was not finally overcome until the more powerful and reliable Pratt &

Whitney Twin Wasp was installed on the Beaufort Mk II. Designed to a 1935 Air Ministry Specification, 78 Beauforts were ordered the following year, but it was not until December 1939 that No. 22 Squadron at Thorney Island became the first operational unit to receive them. The first aircraft for No. 42 Squadron, L4489, arrived on 8 April, a further six arriving in the next few days. The unit code AW was applied to them, L4489 becoming AW-A.

By this time the squadron was at Bircham Newton in Norfolk, from where it had been carrying out North Sea operations under Wing Commander J. Waring. Later that month it moved south to operate across the English Channel from Thorney Island, but the aircraft were still plagued by engine problems. The squadron became operational on 5 June at Thorney Island, then later that month moved north to Wick, which was to be its home for the next nine months, Wing Commander R. Faville taking over in September. With the greater range of its new aircraft, anti-shipping and minelaying operations, as well as harbour attacks, could now be carried out along much of the coast of northern Europe.

On 21 June, a few days after arriving at Wick, No. 42 Squadron despatched nine aircraft, on temporary detachment at Sumburgh, for a dive-bombing attack with 500lb armour piercing bombs on the German battlecruiser *Scharnhorst*, which had been sighted off Trondheim. Under the impression that a torpedo attack was in the offing, attendant destroyers manoeuvred to try to intercept the raiders. Meanwhile, a swarm of about 50 Messerschmitt Bf 109s came up from Norwegian aerodromes to claim three of the Beauforts. The attack was unsuccessful, but no engine troubles were experienced for once and the other six aircraft returned safely.

Soon after this attack, all Beauforts were grounded because of the continuing engine problems, and

there was a genuine concern that the type might even be declared unsafe for operational service. Instead, 254 machines were returned to the manufacturer at Filton to be fitted with uprated Taurus Mk VI engines, the opportunity also being taken to make all the fuel tanks self-sealing. Not until 28 September was the Beaufort again declared operational.

The torpedoes themselves were far from perfect for their task, and the average hit rate for Beaufort-launched torpedoes was estimated in 1940 to be less than one in five. Another complication was that even practice torpedo attacks could be hazardous, as the pilot of L9942/AW-Q discovered on 30 September 1940, when his propellers bent on hitting the water as he misjudged his height over Sinclair's Bay, Caithness. The engines lost power and his aircraft sank into the water before he could gain height, the crew fortunately escaping injury.

Although designed primarily as a torpedo-bomber, the Beaufort was only rarely able to carry out an attack in this role. No. 42 Squadron's first torpedo operation of 1941 took place on 12 January. At 1330 that day, L9965/AW-M, piloted by Flying Officer Tregance and with sergeants Butt, Goldsmith and Godfrey as crew, attacked the 4,563-ton Norge-Transport *Toledo* in the entrance to Sognefjord, but the ship took avoiding action and the torpedo missed ahead. Meanwhile, the air gunner, Sergeant Goldsmith, silenced the deck guns and N1015/AW-F, piloted by Sergeant How and with Sergeants Powell, Spencer and Bower as crew, came in with four general-purpose bombs, one of which scored a direct hit on the stern of the transport. The amount of damage caused could not be seen owing to smoke forward. In fact the bomb failed to explode. As the aircraft departed, AW-M was

met by light anti-aircraft fire from an island in the entrance to the fjord, but both aircraft landed safely back at Wick.

The squadron continued to engage in various tasks, including convoy escort, and then on 9 February

came the opportunity for another torpedo attack. Following a report of the sighting of several German destroyers in Norwegian waters, a special strike of three aircraft was mounted, led by Flight Lieutenant Kerby in L9875/AW-C. He was accompanied by L9834/AW-V (Pilot Officer Harvey) and N1163/AW-N (Flying Officer Tregance). Flying in

clear weather, the three aircraft emerged from some cloud cover at 1225 to sight six enemy destroyers 3,500 yards ahead, steaming at about 20kt in close formation line abreast. The three aircraft made an immediate attack, dropping their torpedoes form a height of 80ft at ranges of 800 to 1,000 yards, and saw the missiles running towards the targets. The first two destroyers evidently realised what was happening and turned to comb the torpedoes successfully. The next two appeared bewildered, while the last two took no action. The aircraft then took avoiding action, but the crew of AW-C saw some black smoke, and the air gunner in AW-V reported seeing an explosion amidships, followed by black smoke, from the fifth destroyer. The aircraft all returned to base without damage.

On 1 March 1941 the squadron moved to Leuchars. The next day three aircraft, Flight Lieutenant Rooney in N4514/AW-R leading Sergeant Wilson in N1015/AW-F and Sergeant How in N1112/AW-J, carried out an attack at 1600 on a convoy of six merchant ships accompanied by an armed trawler, sailing at about 8kt. Owing to an electrical fault, Rooney's torpedo came adrift fifteen minutes before the attack, but he continued to lead the other two aircraft, raking the bridge of a 2,000-ton cargo vessel with his front gun. Wilson chose a 2,000-ton tanker as his target and dropped his missile from a height of 50ft at 800 yards range, only to see it just miss astern. How selected the same vessel as Rooney, dropping broadside from 80ft at 700 yards. As he turned away his rear gunner fired into the ship, then saw a brilliant flash amidships, from which flames then appeared to be spreading. These aircraft, too, returned safely.

As a whole, however, the Beaufort squadrons suffered continual losses both on operations and in train-

Approximate range of Coastal Command Beaufort Operations

Narvik

Trondheim

SHETLAND ISLES

ORKNEY ISLES

Bergen   Oslo

Wick

Stavanger

Inverness

Goteburg

Aberdeen
Dundee

Alborg

Edinburgh

Malmo

Newcastle

Lubeck

Hamburg

LONDON

Rotterdam

Dunkirk

Calais

Dieppe

ing. On 29 April the pilot of W6527/AW-P found himself unable to maintain height after one of his engines failed during a practice attack on the Tentsmuir range, Fife, and had to ditch. In his report on this incident, Wing Commander Faville expressed the view that it was extremely improbable that any Beaufort would keep height on one engine, and that pilots were beginning to lose confidence in the machine. He strongly recommended that the aircraft be re-engined with Twin Wasps. Instead, however, later production Mk Is were fitted with the Taurus XII.

Sightings of enemy convoys were uncommon, but on 3 August, still operating from Leuchars, Sergeant Morison in AW200/AW-R spotted one at 0745. A single merchant ship of around 3,500 tons was accompanied by two flakships and also a submarine on the surface. Five minutes later Morison attacked from the port quarter, dropping four bombs from 50ft. He claimed that the whole salvo had dropped on the submarine, which disappeared in convulsions of water. He then machine-gunned the spot where the submarine had been. However, postwar analysis of German records show no corresponding loss of a U-boat in Norwegian waters, though surface vessels sank *U-401* in the North Atlantic on that date.

Torpedo attacks by No. 42 Squadron in Norwegian waters were by now infrequent, but on 23 December 1941 three torpedo-armed aircraft took off from Leuchars and at 1542 sighted a 3,500-ton merchant ship steering 125° at about 10kt. The vessel appeared to be passenger-carrying, but had a cargo of barrels on deck. An attack was made by Pilot Officer Burchley in L9965/AW-M, who had left the formation. He machine-gunned the deck and bridge after dropping his torpedo. The vessel gave three warning blasts on her whistle, then put up heavy fire. As the aircraft turned away it also met flak from the shore, but all three aircraft made it home.

The squadron continued to operate from Leuchars until June 1942, when it was withdrawn from its task and sent out to the Far East, now re-equipped with the more suitable Beaufort Mk II.

*The artist writes:* This painting was done for my RAF pictorial history series and subsequently used on the jacket of Roy Nesbit's book abut Beaufort operations, a reverse of the situation concerning the painting of Gladiators over Malta.

# *Defiant Night Attack*

*Painting by Mark Postlethwaite*
*Text by John Ray*

THE BOMBER SHOWN HERE IS HEINKEL He 111P-4, Werk nr 2962, of 1/KG 55, coded GI+DL. With a crew of four it had taken off from an airfield near Paris just before midnight on 8 April 1941 to join a stream of bombers heading for the night's target, the city of Coventry in the Midlands of the UK. On board was a bombload consisting of one 500kg high-explosive bomb and many canisters of incendiaries.

After crossing the Channel, the bomber passed over the English coast near Portsmouth, flying northwards. At the controls was the pilot, Oberfeldwebel Soellner, but the most important crew member was the navigator, Hauptmann Otto Bodemeyer, who was Gruppen Kommandeur of 1/KG 55 and had flown in the Luftwaffe from the time of the Spanish Civil War. The other two crew were the flight engineer, Feldwebel Link, and wireless-operator Unteroffizier Kaufhold.

That night there was bright moonlight, which was a help to navigation but made the task of the defences easier. Below the Heinkel in the painting is a night fighter, the pilot of which has made a careful approach so that the bomber is silhouetted against the moon. He has then moved in for the kill.

The fighter, Boulton Paul Defiant N1790 of No. 151 Squadron, had taken off on patrol from RAF Wittering at 0048. It carried a two-man crew. Sergeant A. Wagner was the pilot, and behind him, in a power-operated turret with four .303in machine-guns, was Sergeant S. Siedengart. Just under an hour later they had seen the bomber about four miles south of Coventry, and had stalked it. Then, as Wagner closed in, Siedengart fired powerful bursts at the Heinkel, and its engines started to burn.

On board the bomber, Link was wounded and flames licked through the cockpit. Soellner tried to control the aircraft, but soon realised that it was too badly damaged to save. At that stage he ordered the crew to bale out, and both he and Bodemeyer left from the forward escape hatch. However, bullets from the Defiant had smashed the intercom, so Kaufhold and Link, in the rear fuselage, did not hear the message and were trapped inside the burning bomber. Fortunately for them the aircraft remained wings level and in a shallow glide until it reached the ground, where it bounced along, eventually breaking off its tail. Kaufhold and Link were miraculously thrown clear, both hurt but still alive.

All of the Germans were soon taken prisoner, and the capture of Bodemeyer gave the RAF particular satisfaction. For Kaufhold this marked a second period of captivity. The first had been in May 1940, after he had been shot down over Belgium, but he had been released when that country surrendered a few days later.

The broken Heinkel came to a halt just outside Roe's Rest farmhouse in Desford, Leicestershire, about 30 miles from Coventry. It was one of four brought down in Britain that night, three of which fell to the Defiants and Hurricanes of No. 151 Squadron.

The story of night air defence had been very different when the German Blitz on Britain started in September 1940. Then, the Luftwaffe, having suffered heavy bomber losses in daylight raids and having been unable to break Fighter Command, turned to attacks in darkness. They particularly targeted London, ports and industrial cities, changing their aim from destroying the RAF to demolishing economic targets and breaking civilian morale.

The Luftwaffe had three particular advantages in this new warfare. First, the RAF had no adequate fighter to counter night raids. Spitfires and Hurricanes were generally unsuitable, Blenheims were too slow and the Beaufighter was barely entering service. For RAF pilots, night fighting was very different from intercepting day raiders. They had to play a difficult cat-and-mouse game to catch bombers in darkness. Therefore the bur-

den of defence at night fell on Anti-Aircraft Command, which fired thousands of shells but hit few aircraft.

Second, two suitable radars were particularly lacking. One was needed on land for tracking intruders; that was Ground Controlled Interception (GCI). The other, Airborne Interception (AI), was required in a night fighter to bring the aircraft close to an intruder. The necessary developments in these radars were not made until early 1941, and until then the Luftwaffe bombers had little trouble from defences at night.

The third advantage for the Germans was their use of radio beams for guiding bombers to their targets in darkness. During this period three types of beam were employed: Knickebein, X-Gerät and Y-Gerät. They were comparatively simple to use and difficult to counter. Various devices were employed by British scientists to jam or distort them, but they could not prevent Luftwaffe bombers regularly getting through to their targets. On a number of raids the Germans first used a skilful pathfinder squadron, KGr 100, to drop incendiaries so that succeeding bombers could plant their loads on the fires below.

Consequently, from September 1940 until May 1941 the night Blitz caused thousands of civilian deaths and injuries, together with a massive destruction of buildings across the United Kingdom. Most heavily hit was London, which at the start of the campaign was raided on 54 consecutive nights from 7 September 1940. From bases in northern France, Heinkel He 111s, Dornier Do 17s and Junkers Ju 88s, mainly of Luftflotte III, flew either singly or in small groups in a steady stream to scatter high explosives, parachute mines, incendiaries and unexploded bombs on the capital.

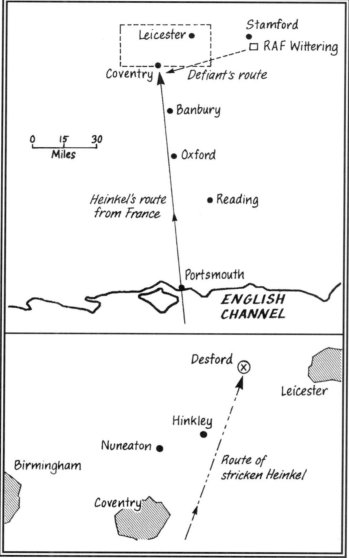

Between 7 September and 31 December 1940, 13,339 civilians were killed and about 18,000 seriously injured in London alone. Material damage was considerable, with the destruction or damaging of homes and factories, shops and schools, railway stations and docks. Many historic buildings were hit. In Britain overall throughout September some 250 people were killed and 350 injured every day. This brought great pressure on civilian morale.

During September only four German bombers were destroyed by night fighters, so the need for the RAF to take action was urgent. The concern felt by politicians and the Air Staff led, at least partly, to the replacement of Sir Hugh Dowding, the C-in-C of Fighter Command, in November 1940. He had led his men during the daylight battle, but the post was now taken by Air Vice-Marshal Sholto Douglas.

On the night of 14/15 November the Luftwaffe turned its attention to Coventry, an industrial centre. Guided by beams, 450 German bombers pounded the city until dawn, causing 1,500 civilian casualties as well as damaging factories. About 500 tons of bombs were dropped, destroying 100 acres of the city centre. A new word entered the language; the city had been 'Coventrated'. The 119 sorties flown that night by Fighter Command did not lead to the destruction of one single raider.

Attacks on other industrial cities followed. Major night raids were made on such places as Birmingham, Manchester, Sheffield and Nottingham. Although great damage was caused and thousands of civilians were killed or injured, industrial production was not greatly affected. In fact, it increased as factories continued to pour out the munitions of war.

Heavier raids were made on seaports and naval bases. Liverpool, Glasgow, Plymouth and Bristol were showered with thousands of bombs. Portsmouth, Southampton, Hull, Belfast, Newcastle, Swansea and Cardiff all suffered major attacks, in each of which they were blasted by at least 100 tons of high explosive. In a number of these cities, postwar buildings now cover the Lufwaffe's main aiming points during the night Blitz. In spite of considerable damage, however, Britain's sea trade and shipbuilding were not stopped, and the Royal Navy continued to operate effectively.

For the defences, the tide started to turn in the early months of 1941. An advanced ground-based radar was better at tracking German bombers over land in darkness, and an improved AI apparatus, carried by night fighters, enabled aircrew to intercept the raiders. This, combined with bad winter weather across Britain, led to a steady rise in German losses. The Luftwaffe continued to launch raids over London and other cities, but at greater cost. Between June and December 1940 Fighter Command shot down only 35 bombers at night, but during March 1941 they destroyed 22. This figure rose to 48 in April and peaked at 96 in May.

Much credit for this improvement was also taken by Bristol Beaufighters, which were employed in increasing numbers. Their armament of four 20mm cannon and six machine-guns enabled them to destroy bombers with devastating bursts of fire. Defiants, which

had not done well in day battles, also proved useful against night raiders. They were flown by various squadrons, including Nos. 151, 256 and 264. Some squadrons, such as No. 151, in which Sergeants Wagner and Siedengart served, also used Hurricanes.

Throughout the night Blitz London remained the prime target for the Germans. Altogether in that period the capital suffered 71 major attacks, during which a total of 18,000 tons of high-explosive bombs were rained down. Two of the worst nights resulted from fire raids. On 29/30 December 1940 thousands of incendiaries burnt in the City of London, destroying, among other buildings, the Guildhall and eight Wren churches. Then, at the end of their campaign, on the night of 10/11 May 1941, 550 bombers hit London for five hours. They killed 1,436 civilians and seriously injured a further 1,800, the greatest casualty toll of any single raid.

The intensive campaign came to an end in May, as the Germans eased up. The main reason was that Hitler turned his attention eastward to the Balkans and to his arch-enemy, Russia. Luftwaffe units were therefore moved in that direction from France.

This was an encouragement for the millions of

civilians in Britain's ports and industrial centres. The Germans had failed to achieve one of their main aims in launching the night Blitz. They could not break the morale of the people and thereby force the British government to seek peace. Some 45,000 men, women and children had been killed and almost 50,000 seriously injured; a million homes were destroyed or damaged. The stress was very great when bombs fell night after night, disrupting life, yet the civilian spirit, although severely tested, remained unbroken. In fact, morale improved, with a greater determination to fight on. Civilian defence services did sterling work and showed how ordinary people could play an active part in total war.

Thus ended the longest period of aerial assault ever suffered by any nation up to that time. The crew of the Heinkel shot down at Desford had taken a full role in this relentless campaign. For example, Unteroffizier Kaufhold had flown on raids against London, Glasgow, Hull, Plymouth, Greenock and Bristol. The Defiant's victory was a great boost not only for its two-man crew, but also for the British people.

Bomber Command learned a great deal from the Luftwaffe's night Blitz: the struggle was far from over.

# The Augsburg Raid

*Painting by Chris Stothard*
*Text by Peter Jacobs*

For Bomber Command, 1942 was destined to mark the turning point of the war. In February of that year the Command acquired at its head the man who was to inspire and lead it for the rest of the war, Air Marshal Arthur Harris. With the entry into service of the new four-engined Avro Lancaster bomber, Harris immediately realised the potential of the aircraft to enable his Command to strike at targets almost anywhere in Germany.

The first unit to be equipped with the Lancaster was No. 44 Squadron at Waddington, Lincolnshire, and the task of seeing the new bomber into squadron operational service fell to one of its Flight Commanders, Squadron Leader John Nettleton, a 24-year-old South African. No. 97 Squadron at Coningsby also took delivery of its first Lancasters and, during the early weeks of 1942, both squadrons worked long and hard to bring the type firmly into the front line of the bomber force. By the middle of April No. 97 Squadron had moved to nearby Woodhall Spa, and crews from both squadrons were often flying together at low level. Rumours of a special operation started to circulate.

A special training flight took place on 14 April, with the No. 44 Squadron crews led by John Nettleton and the No. 97 Squadron crews led by Squadron Leader John Sherwood. The training flight involved both squadrons flying independently to the south coast, then joining up for a long transit north to carry out a low-level simulated attack on Inverness before returning to base. By now, the strongest belief among some of the crews was that they were to take part in a raid against one of the German warships. The fact that the training flight had involved coastal features added strength to the rumour.

On the morning of 17 April the crews were briefed at their bases on the special operation. There was a certain amount of surprise when the target was finally revealed. It was not to be a German warship, as expected, but a factory at Augsburg in Southern Germany. Sergeant Bert Dowty was a 19-year-old air gunner of No. 44 Squadron at Waddington at the time. He had taken part in the very first Lancaster operations on the night of the 3/4 March, and Augsburg was to be his second 'op'. He recalls:

'When the target map was revealed there was a general feeling of almost disbelief. My immediate thought was one of total surprise as the usual target maps only covered one wall! But this was different, it was such a long way that even if we could get to the target, I could not see us making it back again.'

The choice of the Maschinenfabrik Augsburg-Nurnberg Aktiengesellschaft factory at Augsburg was interesting. Although the factory was one of the anti-U-boat targets, the company being a manufacturer of diesel engines, it was 1,000 miles away, deep in Southern Germany, and had not been considered one of Bomber Command's primary targets up to that point.

The plan was a particularly daring one. Six aircraft from each squadron, flying in two sections of three, would cross the Channel west of Le Havre. With the squadrons just two miles apart, the formations would then transit south at low level before turning east to pass south of Paris. They would then head towards Munich, as if to carry out an attack in that area, and then turn north towards Augsburg. The factory area was quite small, so pinpoint accuracy was needed for the attack to be successful. It was decided that the attack would be carried out at low level in the last minutes of daylight, so that the bombers could then return under the cover of darkness. Each Lancaster was to carry just four 1,000lb general-purpose bombs, all of them fitted with a delayed fuze. In support of the raid, diversionary attacks and fighter sorties over Northern France were planned in an attempt to keep the Luftwaffe fighters occupied.

At 1500 on 17 April 1942 the twelve Lancasters took off and set course. As they crossed the enemy coast the diversionary raids certainly brought up the enemy fighters, but they also nearly led to disaster. One group of enemy fighters returning to base spotted the rear section of the No. 44 Squadron Lancasters and gave chase. Almost immediately the first Lancaster, flown by Warrant Officer 'Joe' Beckett DFM, was shot down, and then the fighters turned on the second, flown by Warrant Officer 'Bert' Crum DFM. Bert Dowty was in the front turret as the Lancaster was attacked by Messerschmitt Bf 109s. He recalls:

'I could see up to six fighters around us. Both of our port engines were soon hit and set on fire, and the next thing I can remember is crashing into a field full of wheat. Fortunately our second pilot, Alan Dedman, had managed to jettison the bombs "safe" before we crash-landed into the field. The fact that Bert managed to get us down at all seems remarkable to me, and we certainly owe him our lives.'

The third Lancaster of the rear section, flown by Flight Lieutenant 'Nick' Sandford DFC, was also shot down, and then the fighters turned on Nettleton's lead section. The action had taken only a matter of minutes, and all three Lancasters of the rear section of the No. 44 Squadron formation crashed within two miles of each other, with Beckett's and Crum's Lancasters just 500 yards apart.

In Nettleton's section his number three, flown by Sergeant 'Dusty' Rhodes, was soon shot down before the fighters turned on Nettleton himself and his number two, Flying Officer 'Ginger' Garwell DFM. Both of the surviving No. 44 Squadron aircraft were hit time and time again, but, just when the end of both bombers seemed certain, the fighters turned for base, short of fuel. Remarkably, the No. 97 Squadron formation, just two miles way, had not been seen by the enemy pilots and had carried on.

The two remaining Lancasters of No. 44 Squadron, together with the No. 97 Squadron formation, continued to Augsburg without further incident.

The No. 44 Squadron aircraft, with Nettleton leading, pressed home a most determined attack on the factory. Sadly, Garwell's aircraft was hit during the run-in to the target and crashed just after releasing its bombs. Nettleton's Lancaster, now the sole survivor of the six No. 44 Squadron machines, turned for home.

The two sections of No. 97 Squadron Lancasters were over the target minutes later. By the time these aircraft were making their attack, every anti-aircraft gun in the target area was in full action and the crews were met by an almost unavoidable barrage of fire. The number two of the rear section was flown by Flying Officer Ernest Deverill DFM. His first wireless operator was 22-year-old Sergeant Ron Irons, on his fifth 'op'. 'By the time that we arrived over the target area the element of surprise had completely gone,' Ron explains. 'The German defences were very alert and were firing everything imaginable at us, including heavy gunfire.'

Nevertheless, Sherwood led the attack, making a straight-in and very low approach. The other two aircraft in his section, flown by Flying Officers 'Darky' Hallows and 'Rod' Rodley, followed Sherwood into the attack. Having released their bombs, both pilots saw their leader's aircraft fall and explode on impact with the ground. The rear section was led by Flight Lieutenant 'Jock' Penman DFC. By now the German gunners had established the exact line and height of the run-in to the attack, and all three aircraft of this section were hit. Ron Irons recalls:

'We were hit during the run-in to the target. Flak had hit the hydraulic pipes, which had put the gun turrets out of action, and hydraulic oil had caught fire under the mid-upper turret. I left my position to help the gunner, Ken Mackay, extinguish the fire. At the same time, our starboard inner engine had been hit and was on fire.'

The third aircraft of the section, flown by Warrant Officer Tommy Mycock DFC, had also caught fire during the run-in. He managed to hold the Lancaster steady just long enough to release its bombs on target before the aircraft blew up. The two remaining Lancasters in the section turned for home. Deverill's Lancaster, now flying on just three engines, faced a long and hazardous return journey.

The five surviving Lancasters from the twelve that had originally set out returned without further incident, although Nettleton's problems were far from over. Having suffered navigational problems during the return leg, and being desperately short of fuel, Nettleton eventually landed at Squire's Gate airfield, near Blackpool, at 0100 on the 18th; ten hours after leaving Waddington. The four surviving aircraft of No. 97 Squadron landed back at Woodhall Spa by midnight, Deverill's aircraft immediately being declared a total write-off.

Of the 85 men who had taken part in the Augsburg raid, 49 were missing, though it was later discovered that twelve had survived to become prisoners of war. The eight Lancasters that reached the target had caused sufficient damage to hold up production for several weeks. In the aftermath of the raid there were many discussions about its value, but the determination of the crews in carrying out such an attack must rank among the highest achievements in the history of Bomber Command.

For his outstanding leadership on the raid, John Nettleton was awarded the Victoria Cross. His citation concludes: 'Squadron Leader Nettleton displayed unflinching determination as well as leadership and valour of the highest order'. Sadly, Nettleton did not survive the war. He was killed during a raid on Turin on the night of 12/13 July 1943. Amazingly, John Sherwood survived the crash at Augsburg and, although he was initially recommended for a Victoria Cross, he was later awarded the Distinguished Service Order. Many of the other aircrew were decorated for their part in the raid, including Ron Irons, who was awarded the Distinguished Flying Medal. He went on to complete 36 operations.

Bert Dowty's adventures after being shot down en route to Augsburg are fascinating and, perhaps, typical of many others. He heard about the result of the raid on BBC radio while evading capture in France. Having crashed at Folleville, he was eventually caught on a train fourteen days later near Limoges, and was repatriated to the UK at the end of the war. For Bert Dowty the Augsburg raid later became a way of life. Ever since the end of the war he has spent much time researching the raid from the RAF and German points of view, and he has traced most of the French civilians who helped him during his attempted return to the UK.

The painting 'Daylight to Augsburg' by Chris Stothard shows the two Lancasters of No. 44 Squadron carrying out their attacks against the factory at Augsburg. The lead aircraft is KM-B, flown by Squadron Leader John Nettleton, who was later awarded the Victoria Cross. In the background is KM-A, flown by Flying Officer 'Ginger' Garwell DFM, which has already been hit and shortly after was engulfed by fire and crashed with the loss of three of its crew. The painting has been reproduced with the kind permission of the No. 44 Squadron Association, and special thanks go to Bert Dowty and Ron Irons for their assistance.

# The High Fighter

*Painting by Jim Mitchell*
*Text by Michael Burns*

IN THIS SUPERBLY DETAILED AND ATMOSPHERIC painting, artist Jim Mitchell has depicted an unusual and little-recorded aspect of the air war during World War Two. One of the highest and longest combats ever flown is the subject of this striking painting, which depicts a special high-altitude Spitfire IX intercepting a Luftwaffe Ju 86R-1 in an extended and difficult mission in September 1942.

By 1939 both the Germans and British had realised that technological advances made it inevitable that military flying operations would be conducted at very great heights, and had issued specifications for high-altitude aircraft. The principal design problems were those of controlling weight, increasing the aspect ratio of the mainplanes to decrease drag, raising supercharger operating height and improving airscrew efficiency to increase power, rate of climb and ceiling.

From late 1940, Junkers Ju 86P reconnaissance aircraft regularly flew over Britain well beyond the reach of RAF interceptors. Although these intrusions were mainly nuisances, the British took the threat of high-altitude bombers very seriously. The threat became real when a new phase in the bombing campaign against Britain opened in late August 1942, and Ju 86R-1s began high-altitude bombing operations over Southern England. Although it was unknown to the British, only a pair of these aircraft were operational, but the stakes for the future were considerable.

On 24 August a Ju 86R-1 dropped one SC 50 bomb on Camberley, Surrey, from 38,000ft; another raid followed later that day. The next day one flew in at 34,000ft and dropped bombs in Hertfordshire. By now the defences were alert, but they were unable to prevent a raid on Coventry on the 28th which killed 48 people. On the 29th two Debden Spitfire VIs, dedicated high-altitude fighters, chased a Ju 86R-1 which bombed Histon, but the fighters failed to reach its 39,000ft altitude. Raids on Bristol, Cheltenham and Newport followed. Then, on 5 September, when a Ju 86R-1 bombed Luton in Bedfordshire, a Manston Spitfire VI opened fire on it at a height of 36,500ft, but stalled and could not press home the attack. On 9 September two pilots from Debden struggled to 38,000ft by dint of firing their Brownings to jettison weight in order to chase a raider over Clacton, but failed to intercept. No British fighter in service seemed able to reach the Ju 86P-1.

Extensive and barely recognisable developments of the prewar Ju 86G bomber, the Ju 86P and improved Ju 86R were able to fly at very high altitude because of their reduced weight, supercharged diesel engines, glider-like long-span tapered wings and pressurised two-man cabins. The only true stratospheric bombers of the war, they were also the first bombers with fully pressurised cabins to see action. Oxygen masks could be used up to around 30,000ft, but to fight higher a pressurised, heated cockpit was needed to protect aircrew from the hypothermia and compression sickness resulting from low atmospheric pressure that reduced blood oxygen content. The Junkers cabin had a pressure differential of 8lb/sq in above that of the surrounding atmosphere at 45,000ft. Although this allowed the crew to breathe without masks, the cabin would explode if punctured by gunfire. If the Ju 86 were attacked, the cabin had to be depressurised and repressurised afterwards.

The P-1 and R-1 bomber sub-types could carry four SC 250 or sixteen SC 50 high-explosive general purpose bombs, but they carried only one 250lb bomb for sorties at their performance extremes. The P-2 and R-2 reconnaissance subtypes carried an area-cover camera and two more split vertical models. The Ju 86P was powered by two supercharged Jumo 207A diesels, 16.6-litre, six-cylinder, in-line two-stroke compression-ignition engines with two-piston cylinders. The Ju 86R-1's

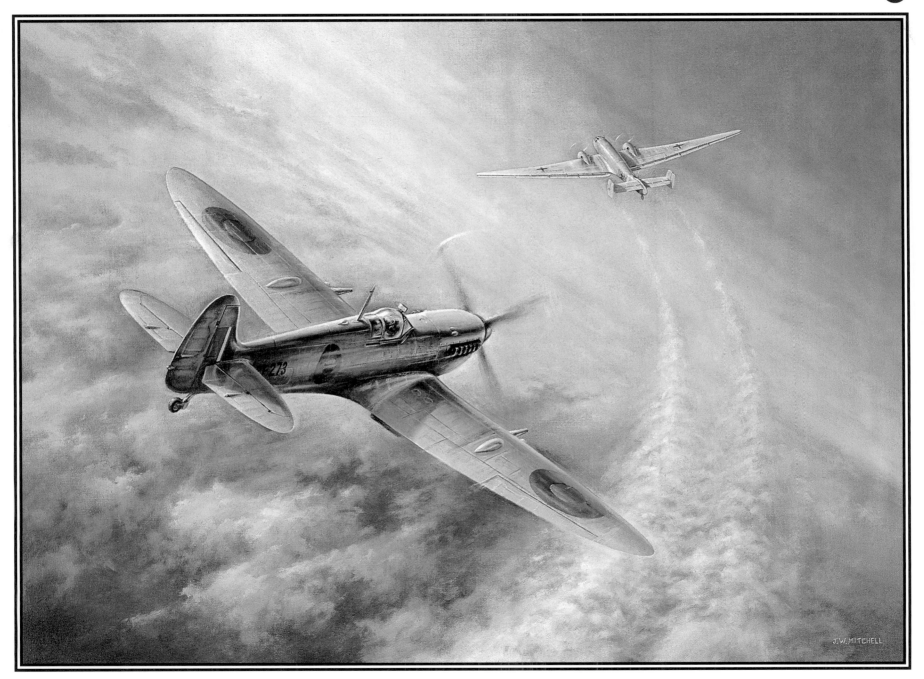

twin Jumo 207B two-stage diesels were rated at 1,000hp for take-off and 750hp at 40,000ft, and even greater wingspan gave it a service ceiling 4,000ft higher than that of the Ju 86P, a remarkable 49,000ft.

They were the only diesel-powered bombers in service during the Second World War. The Germans had rejected diesel-powered bombers before the war, so this reversion needs explanation. The original Ju 86 of 1934 had been designed to use the Jumo because it appeared to offer advantages in fuel efficiency, thus allowing greater range or payload, but in service from 1936 the 600hp Jumo 205 proved a disappointment. Strength and efficiency were the factors leading to the reversion to diesels in the Ju 86P and R. A diesel achieves more fuel efficiency than a petrol engine through higher compression, but it must be much stronger to withstand the higher pressures, an advantage for the additional pressures involved in supercharging. The penalty was weight, which is critical in high-altitude aircraft.

However, the primary attraction for the limited German supercharger technology of 1939 was that high compression extracts so much energy that exhaust gases emerge at lower temperatures than those of a petrol engine. This made the supercharge cooler and more dense, which reduced the problems of producing both the exhaust-driven turbo first stage and the mechanically-driven second stage of the 207B. Nitrous oxide injected into the second stage cooled the charge and released oxygen for combustion for further high-altitude boost.

In May 1942 one of the Ju 86P-2s which daily flew down the Suez Canal at 40,000ft, recording vital

Allied shipping movements, was knocked down by a Spitfire VC stripped by Aboukir Depot and fitted with the high-compression Merlin 46 engine and a four-bladed airscrew. But RAF Fighter Command had no fighter capable of reaching the Ju 86R-1 bombers attacking Britain in August 1942. Neither the pressurised Spitfire VI with its single-stage Merlin, nor the unpressurised Spitfire IX with the two-stage Merlin was

up to the task. A 'special à la Aboukir' was needed.

The Spitfire HF Mk VI had a pressurised, heated cockpit in a Mk VB airframe with extended wings and a two-speed geared single-stage supercharged high-compression Merlin 47 driving a four-bladed airscrew. It entered limited service in the spring of 1942, but the RAF did not yet understand the tactical or operational use of high-altitude fighters. The airfields of Gravesend and Kenley were too far forward, allowing insufficient

distance to climb over 30,000ft to intercept a Ju 86. Even when they were moved back to Debden, several pilots struggled but failed to intercept the first raids.

Rolls-Royce, meanwhile, had decided that any further increase in the Merlin's high-altitude power must come from a mechanically-driven second-stage supercharger. This required a liquid intercooler to lower the excessive temperature, and thereby increase the density, of the induction charge passed from first to second stage. This produced the Merlin 60 series for the new breed of Spitfire, the Mks VII, VIII and IX, and these engines were capable of being 'tuned' to develop extra power at great altitudes.

Produced specially to meet the high-altitude challenge, the Spitfire HF Mk VII had a pressurised, heated cockpit, a revised airframe and a Merlin 61 engine, but as it was not yet operational the RAF turned to the new Mk IX with the same powerplant. Intended as a stop-gap Mk V conversion while the Mks VII and VIII were perfected, the standard Mk IX had a better performance at altitude than the Mk VI, but still could not reach the Ju 86's operating altitude.

In the first week of September 1942 the High Altitude Flight was formed at RAF Northolt to find a method of beating the Ju 86R-1. Under the codename 'Windgap' it was initially equipped with a pair of Spitfire IXs modified to fight in the stratosphere. The RAF had learnt from the Mk VI; Northolt was far enough from the Sussex and Kent coasts for the Spitfires to climb to high interception altitudes and follow a raider west.

The Mk IXs allocated to the Flight, BF271 and BF273, had been converted from Mk VCs in August

1942 at Rolls-Royce Hucknall by installing the Merlin 61. Directed from the first Mk IX squadron, No. 64. They were modified to an 'HF' specification. Increased boost for higher compression and slightly lower propeller reduction gearing optimised their rate of climb and altitude performance. They were stripped of anything superfluous to their task, including camouflage, armour and machine-guns, leaving only the two inboard 20mm Hispano cannon. Lightweight wooden Jablo propellers saved 70lb. Resprayed in a lightweight blue-grey photographic-reconnaissance (PR) finish, when fully modified they weighed 450lb less than a 1942 Mk IX. The cost was pilot comfort – there was no heating or pressurisation.

The two aircraft were taken on charge by the High Altitude Flight on 6 and 5 September respectively. The first scramble occurred on 11 September, but although the pilot reached 45,000ft he failed to intercept the raider.

Next day, Pilot Officer Prince Emanuel Galitzine was scrambled in BF273 against a Ju 86R-1. He intercepted it at 41,000ft near Southampton, but the German climbed above 45,000ft. Aching, intensely cold and struggling with cockpit misting, Galitzine pursued it. The Spitfire had to be held rock steady and flown very accurately, with smooth control movements and gradual attitude changes, or it would stall and lose altitude.

Galitzine gained sufficient altitude to attack from above the Ju 86R-1 and from dead astern. One shell from his first burst struck its port wing, but the cannon-fire and the Ju 86's vapour trail produced a mist in his cockpit, forcing him to fly on instruments for 30 seconds. What was worse, his port cannon had jammed, and each time he manoeuvred to attack and fire, the cannon's recoil slewed him to port and he tumbled from the sky. The raider escaped, but the Luftwaffe now knew that the Ju 86R-1 was no longer invulnerable over England.

On 16 September, the Flight took on charge a very formidable high-altitude interceptor. In only ten days de Havilland had converted the prototype two-stage Merlin 61-powered, pressure-cabin Mosquito bomber MP469 as a counter to the Ju 86R-1. Four 20mm cannon replaced the transparent bomber nose, armour was removed, and smaller fuel tanks without bullet-proofing, and smaller wheels, were fitted. It became a single-seater. Pointed wings increased span by 5ft. Even with heavier engines with four-blade propellers the modified aircraft was 2,300lb lighter than a Mosquito Mk II.

Twin two-stage Merlins in the stripped, wooden airframe gave it more horsepower per pound that the Spitfire Mk IX. With two hours' fuel reserve it could reach 42,000ft in 35min; with less it bettered the Spitfire Mk VII, attaining 45,000ft. Its moderately pressurised cockpit, 2lb/sq in, reduced the effect of altitude by 12,000ft. It meant breathing oxygen, but the cabin was lighter and less vulnerable than the Ju 86's fully pressurised 'egg'.

At last, on 23 September, Spitfire VIIs BS121 and BS142 arrived at Northolt. But the autumn weather broke and Ju 86R-1 operations ceased after just twelve sorties, although the RAF did not initially realise this. The last attempted interception was on 2 October, but the Ju 86R-1 retreated before it could be engaged. That winter the Flight gained valuable experience, tackling many high-altitude problems including pneumatic, armament, radio and electrical malfunctions. Medium Sea Grey upper surfaces and PR Blue undersurfaces were adopted as standard for high-altitude fighters.

On 25 January 1943 the retitled Special Service Flight joined Mk VI-equipped No. 124 Squadron at North Weald. By then it operated the original Mk IXs, Mk VI BR326 and Mark VIIs BS121, BS142, and EN285, which had arrived on 29 December. As it was feared that Ju 86R-1 night raids might start, Mosquito MP469 had become the first of five NF Mk XV night-fighters with airborne interception (AI) Mk VIII radar, and shortly began operational trials with No. 85 Squadron.

In late April the Flight deployed three Mk. VIIs to south-western airfields. Frequently scrambled, they intimidated the enemy, who often ran as the Spitfires closed. The final victory was gained over a Focke-Wulf Fw 190 near Plymouth on 15 May. In June, No. 124 Squadron received the Spitfire Mk. VII and absorbed the Special Service Flight.

The Ju 86P-2 and R-2 remained excellent reconnaissance aircraft for the Germans throughout the war if they evaded interception, but by 1943 high-altitude Spitfires were regularly destroying them. The Junkers' phenomenal ceiling, their only defence, could not be improved. In contrast, by 1943 the PR Mosquito had a better combination of speed, range, altitude and versatility than any other reconnaissance aircraft. Luftwaffe fighter pilots who struggled to 30,000ft to make an interception found the Mosquito pilot turning up boost and disappearing. Most PR aircraft managed occasional sorties over Europe, but PR Spitfires and Mosquitoes regularly made long penetrations with minimal losses. The RAF had gained stratospheric air superiority.

*The artist writes:* Like 'Defiant Victory', this was not an easy painting to compose because the feeling I was trying to get in the scene was the sense of isolation and cold felt by the pilots at high altitude during this particular episode of the war. During the research the pilot described the condensation trail as 'like following in the wake of an ocean liner', and this comes over in this final version.

# 127 Wing Fighter Sweep

*Painting by Michael Turner*
*Text by Ken Delve*

IN MICHAEL TURNER'S SUPERBLY DRAMATIC PAINTING, Spitfire IXs of No.127 Wing, led by the famous ace Johnnie Johnson, swoop low over a German fighter airfield in Northern France. The Luftwaffe Fw 190 fighters, ammunition dumps and flak emplacements are all targets as part of the general Allied air-superiority campaign. Shell bursts fill the air as all enemy defences open up on the low-flying attackers; groundcrew duck and run for cover. Within moments the Spitfires have swept through, and all that is left is billowing smoke from burning aircraft and vehicles.

Airfield attacks such as that depicted here, although increasingly dangerous as Luftwaffe defences become heavier, were an increasingly important task for Allied fighter forces. The strategic aim of achieving air superiority required destruction of all enemy air power, in the air and on the ground. Operation Pointblank began in 1943 with the aim of eliminating the Luftwaffe fighter force. It was the priority target at aviation factories, where Bomber Command and the US 8th Air Force would expend much effort to destroy potential fighters at source; and it was the number one target at airfields, where medium bombers of the 2nd Tactical Air Force and, later, the US 9th Air Force would create as much destruction as possible, and where sweeps by Allied fighters were the third line of attack.

In Michael Turner's stunning painting, Supermarine Spitfire IXs of No. 127 Wing swoop low over a German fighter airfield in northern France, strafing aircraft and other targets as part of the Allied air superiority campaign. Shell bursts fill the air as the defending light flak emplacements open up on the attackers; groundcrew duck and run for cover. Within moments the Spitfires have swept through, and all that remains is billowing smoke from burning aircraft and vehicles.

Losses among the American daylight bomber force had continued to rise into the early part of 1943, and it was obvious that the Luftwaffe was by no means a spent force. If the Strategic Bomber Offensive was to continue its day and night pounding of German industry, the Luftwaffe's fighter strength simply had to be curbed. The strategic aim of achieving air superiority required the destruction of all enemy air power – in the air or on the ground. This became even more essential as part of Operation 'Pointblank', when the Luftwaffe became the priority target. While Bomber Command and the 8th Air Force attacked the factories, expending much effort to destroy fighter production, the medium bombers of 2nd TAF and, later, the 9th Air Force, coupled with the sweeps by Allied fighters, brought as much havoc and destruction as possible to the fighter airfields.

No. 127 Wing formed at Kenley on 11 July, 1943. With an initial strength of two Canadian squadrons equipped with Spitfire IXs, the Wing was part of Fighter Command, and as such was soon involved in offensive operations over northern Europe.

'Fighter leadership consists not in scoring personal victories but in the achievement of success with the whole Wing. My job would be to lead and to fight.' So wrote that great air combat pilot and leader of No. 127 Wing, 'Johnnie' Johnson, whose personal Spitfire, coded 'JE-J' was at the forefront of the fighter offensive. While the Spitfire had proved to be a superb defensive fighter, its lack of range prevented it from performing the escort role that was now needed. This meant that the bombers could have an escort only as far as the middle of France; after that they were on their own, and the German fighters simply waited until the escort had left before pouncing. The survivors could rest assured that on the return journey they would be met by an aggressive bunch of Spitfires lurking at the extremes of their range and determined to protect any stragglers. Frustration was high both among fighter crews and the crews of the bombers. The fitting of a 90-gallon drop tank doubled the Spitfire's fuel capacity and certainly

improved the situation, but it was not until the advent of the North American Mustang III, with its superb range and combat performance, that a true escort fighter became available. In the meantime, therefore, the Luftwaffe had to be attacked wherever it could be found.

During 1942 the tactic had been that of the 'Circus', in which a bomber force would attack targets in France, aiming to 'raise and engage that portion of the Luftwaffe fighter strength based on the Western Front'. This was the logical follow-on to the previous concept of fighter sweeps, which had proved to be a waste of effort because the Luftwaffe refused to rise to the bait. The bombing of important targets left the defending fighters no choice but to take on the bombers, at which point the escorting RAF fighters were meant to intervene. However, a Bomber Command analysis showed that although bomber losses were low, at around 3 per cent, the associated Fighter Command statistics were not so good. In 9,486 sorties they claimed 118 enemy aircraft, but for a loss of 166. This should not really have come as any great surprise, as in essence the tactic was little different from that employed, without success, by the Luftwaffe over Britain in 1940. Nevertheless, something had to be done to cut the continuing heavy losses in Bomber Command and in the 8th Air Force, and fighter sweeps against Luftwaffe fighter bases became the order of the day.

Attacking airfields was not an easy task; they were amongst the most heavily-defended targets in occupied Europe, bristling with quadruple 20mm AAA guns that put up a fierce amount of fire. The gun positions were usually arranged to give murderous crossfire kill zones, and 'flak-traps' were set up on the most likely lines of attack. In the face of such opposition it was very difficult for pilots to target aircraft on the ground, a fleeting pass with a burst or two being all that could be managed. To stay in the area and make a second or third pass

was to court disaster. ' Johnnie' Johnson recalls one such hairy occasion:

'Two days later we tried the same tactic and almost came to grief. The tactical bombers were operating in the Paris area and I led a section of Spitfires down to the deck to sweep the numerous airfields scattered around the circumference of the French capital. After 20 minutes at low level I was lost, although I knew we were a few miles south of Paris. I put the map away and concentrated on flying the various courses I had worked out before leaving base. About another five minutes on this leg and then turn to the west to avoid getting too close to Paris. Our horizon was limited to about three miles over level country, but was considerably reduced when we dipped down into a valley.

'We crossed the complicated mass of railway lines which indicated that we were close to Paris. We sped across a wide river and ahead of us was a heavily wooded slope, perhaps rising 200ft above the river. We raced up this slope, only a few feet above the topmost branches, and found ourselves looking straight across a large grass airfield with several large hangars on the far side.

'The gunners were ready and waiting. The shot and shell came from all angles, for some of the gun positions were on the hangar roofs and they fired down on us. I had never seen the like of this barrage. Enemy aircraft were parked here and there, but our only thought was to get out of this inferno. There was no time for radio orders. It was every man for himself. It seemed that all our exits were blocked with a concentrated criss-cross pattern of fire from a hundred guns. My only hope of a getaway lay in a small gap between two hangars. I pointed the Spitfire at this gap, hurtled through it and caught sight of the multiple barrels of a light flak gun swinging on to me from one of the parapets. Beyond lay a long, straight road with tall poplars on either side and I belted the Spitfire down the road with the trees forming some sort of screen. Tracer was still bursting over the cockpit. Half a dozen cyclists were making their way up the road towards the airfield. They flung themselves and their bicycles in all directions. I pulled up above the light

Fighter Command approximate range of operations 1941–43

flak and called the other pilots. Miraculously, they had all come through the barrage.'

As an interceptor day fighter the Spitfire had much to commend it, including speed in level flight and in the climb, but none of its good features, except perhaps its manoeuvrability, suited it for the low-level environment. This type of mission was far better left to other aircraft types. Although Spitfires were given a bomb-carrying capability, this again was not ideal and had really come about in the face of an increased requirement for close air support and a dearth of true fighter activity. In the period immediately after the D-Day landings the ground forces were in danger of being bogged down, and in the absence of heavy weapons they had to rely on air power as 'flying artillery'. The Spitfire squadrons carried out a good deal of this type of work, and after a while became

quite proficient. The 20mm cannon proved to be a remarkably good air-to-ground weapon against all manner of 'soft-skinned' vehicles, although it was unable to cause any serious damage to the average German tank.

The aircraft which truly specialised in intruder operations against enemy airfields was the de Havilland Mosquito, which undertook this role both day and night with some success – and a fair degree of loss. The night intruder element conducted a vital campaign against German night fighter airfields such as Venlo, Deelen and Leeuwarden in Holland. Not only were day bomber losses on the increase, but the German night fighter force was in a period of resurgence. If a night fighter found the bomber stream it could wreak great destruction, multiple 'kills' becoming quite common. Therefore every enemy fighter that could be prevented

from taking off was one less flying against Bomber Command.

The anti-airfield operations of day sweeps and night intruders were an essential part of the overall Allied air effort, an integral part of the campaign to achieve and maintain air superiority. It is amazing how resilient the Luftwaffe proved to be during these final years of the war, there being no shortage of fighter aircraft at any stage, although this was at the expense of other types and required the continued production of dated designs. In the end it was other factors, particularly a shortage of trained pilots and the disruption of fuel supplies, that reduced the Luftwaffe's effectiveness. A classic air combat aircraft, the Spitfire also proved that it had the teeth and ability to take part in the ground war.

# Bridge-Busting Bostons

*Painting by Geoff Lea*
*Text by Peter Cooksley*

THE ALLIED INVASION OF EUROPE, WHICH WAS FINALLY to result in the continent's liberation from the yoke of Germany's National Socialists, was no hastily-assembled affair, but one for which extensive and detailed preparation had to be made during the years preceding 1944. As the summer of the fateful year approached, the pace quickened and, with it, the demands on the three Services, not least upon No. 2 (Bomber) Group of the RAF. The Group had been in existence from as early as March 1936, including among its units the Hawker Hind biplanes of No. 52 Squadron. Eight years later the Group was operating very different aircraft, two of its Wings flying Britain's deadly, wooden Mosquito, and four squadrons having North American B-25 Mitchell bombers.

Two of the three squadrons making up the Group's No. 137 Wing were unique in flying another United States type, the Douglas Boston. This type had begun to be shipped to England in the summer of 1941, the first examples going in November to No. 88 Squadron at Swanton Morley, Norfolk, to replace the Bristol Blenheims they had flown since July. With their new Bostons they participated in shipping strikes, and made their first sortie against a land target with them on 12 February 1942. On 8 March they made the memorable attack on the Matford works at Poissy, flying in at very low level to evade the enemy defences. Another target at much the same time was the Phillips Radio Company works at Eindhoven.

The following summer saw the Bostons of No. 88 Squadron engaged in another historic action, attacking the gun positions that had to be silenced in preparation for the Dieppe raid of 19 August. Experience gained in this way, as well as during sorties against vessels in Le Havre and the power station at Caen, made No. 88 Squadron ideal for service with the 2nd Tactical Air Force, which it joined in June the following year, and the unit continued to give yeoman service during such actions as that in November, when the suspected headquarters of the Nazi Todt organisation, in the village of Audinghen, was bombed.

While turning away from delivering its attack on this target, a Boston of No. 88 Squadron was hit by anti-aircraft fire. The pilot's collarbone was broken and his face badly gashed, but he was at first not fully aware of his injuries because he was stunned. As consciousness returned, the pilot officer found his aircraft in a dive which had already cost some 2,000ft of altitude, but he was unable to pull it from its death-plunge as his arms were paralysed by his injuries. Thinking quickly, he realised that it would be possible to pull back the control column with his knees, and in this way the machine was coaxed into level flight and the crew were ordered to bale out. However, they hesitated to do so because it meant abandoning the captain. By now some feeling had returned to his arms, so an agonising trip home was begun which ended with a successful emergency landing at Hawkinge.

Illustrated here is an No. 88 Squadron sortie at about the time when the destruction of V-weapon sites and ammunition dumps were the order of the day. It is possible to determine the period from the aircraft markings, which indicate a time after July 1942, when the fuselage roundels, previously encircled by a broad yellow border, had been replaced by alternative markings with the yellow border and the white inner circle reduced in area to avoid compromising the disruptive effect of the upper surface camouflage. The fin flash was also altered at this time, being reduced to a square with its sides measuring no more than two feet in length, and with the central area a mere twelfth of that total. Code letters, too, were changed, appearing in the dark red as seen on RH-X in this painting.

The nose of the aircraft bears a personal motif depicting a cartoon Scottie dog. Humorous personal

markings were not to be augmented by pin-up girls until later, and frequently a simple name sufficed. (A Boston named *Gloria* has only recently been discovered in dense tropical jungle. One of 35 raiders attacking enemy positions on Papua New Guinea on 16 April 1944, it fell to ground fire and lay undiscovered and virtually intact for 40 years.)

With the number of pre-invasion sorties rapidly increasing, No. 88 Squadron was to called upon to make a total of twenty attacks against railway centres and marshalling yards in France between the middle of April and the end of May 1944. By this time, after several changes of base, the squadron was stationed at Hartford Bridge (later known as Blackbushe) in Hampshire, although a detachment had been made to their earlier home station, together with another to Beaulieu while they still retained their Bostons.

The Boston of No. 88 Squadron seen here is one of a number attacking a bridge in France, a type of sortie that had its origins in the First World War. It did not really come into its own until the second conflict, although the technique was developed during the uneasy peace that divided the two. The original idea was simply to use level bombing, from various heights, to pinpoint targets and destroy them. This technique was used by the USA and the air forces of most European nations, though the Luftwaffe tended to favour dive-bombing, believing that it ensured even greater accuracy.

The Douglas Boston employed for such work had originally been known in the USA as the DB-7. Designed by Northrop but constructed by Douglas, it was produced in 1938 as a development of the DC-5 civil airliner, and was built for a US Army attack-bomber competition in which it competed with the Glenn Martin 167W and Stearman X-100. The Douglas entry had the misfortune to be destroyed on a

test flight which killed the pilot and his passenger that same year, but it was ordered in numbers by France.

In fact, the potential purchase of the tactical bomber by the Armée de l'Air was the reason for the presence of the second occupant at the time of the accident. This was Capitaine Chemedlin, who represented the French Purchasing Commission which was eventually to order 100 DB-7s, increasing this to 380 in February 1939. The first examples to be delivered before the French collapse were assembled at Casablanca in North Africa, but these were few in number and the residue was taken over by Britain the following summer. They were powered by Pratt & Whitney Twin Wasp radial engines, later replaced by Wright Cyclones that increased available power by 60 per cent. This required an increase in the fin and rudder area, resulting in the type being designated the Boston III by the RAF when it first joined the strength of No. 88 Squadron.

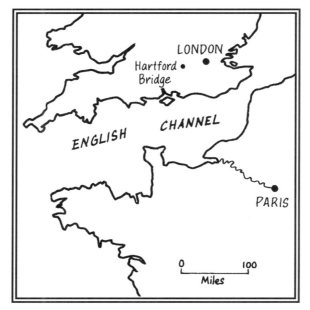

As operational British tactical bombers, these aircraft differed in a number of ways from their original French counterparts, including the introduction of an optically-flat transparent panel for the bomb-aimer, additional armour, and, of course, British instrumentation. The positioning of the engines and exhausts aft of the cockpit eliminated glare, especially distracting in poor light, and made the Boston popular with pilots.

Perhaps it was coincidence that some of the RAF squadrons equipped with the Boston had formerly been flying an earlier design associated with attack-bomber operations, the Fairey Battle. A single-engined aircraft, and based on a different concept of air warfare, its maximum speed was only 240mph, making it some 60mph slower than the Boston of only three years later. During that period the squadrons flying either type were still engaged in similar work, namely the destruction of tactical targets.

An early Second World War example of such operations had occurred on 11 May 1940, when, in an attempt to halt the advancing tide of Hitler's Wehrmacht, eight Fairey Battles of Nos. 88 and 218 Squadrons had been despatched to bomb the roads along which enemy columns were advancing on the border of Luxembourg. Whether this target was attacked, or even reached, is unknown, for such was the strength of the enemy that all but one Battle failed to return. Casualties of such magnitude prevented either squadron participating in a sortie made by RAF aircraft the following day, a Sunday, when the Battles of No. 12 Squadron were ordered to destroy the bridges, already in enemy hands, that spanned the Albert Canal. That action is remembered by the name of the pretty town that lay between the two crossings – Maastricht.

That such actions were essential, and would certainly be so again, was shown by the fact that, only two days before, Nazi Germany had unleashed its Blitzkrieg on unsuspecting Holland and Belgium, sending its armour racing across the countryside. The Albert Canal seemed to offer the only point where its progress might be stopped, and to this end all of the crossings had been destroyed; all, that is, except two, which were even then in the hands of enemy paratroops and heavily defended.

To deny even these to the Nazis, two tactical bombers were despatched to make an approach at 1,000ft and deliver a diving attack, but they were so severely damaged by ground fire while attempting to destroy the concrete bridge at Vroenhoven that both were lost, one falling in enemy-held territory. Simultaneously another action calling for the destruction of bridges was being carried out not far away at Veldwezelt, where the metal bridge was bombed in a low-level sortie only 50ft above the water, using eleven-second delay fuzes. This attack was made in the face of fire from an estimated 300 guns of all calibres positioned around the target, offering little chance of survival for the two attacking aircraft. Two crew members of one Battle were posthumously awarded the Victoria Cross, the RAF's first such awards of the Second World War. The deed emphasised the dangers of attacking communication bridges, whether the operation be performed by bridge-busting Battles or, as here, by Bostons.

# Gibson Over the Eder Dam

*Painting by Maurice Gardner*
*Text by Ron Dick*

MAURICE GARDNER'S PAINTING OF WING COMMANDER Guy Gibson's Lancaster over the Eder Dam captures a moment during the celebrated Dams Raid of 16 May 1943. It had long been recognised that an industrial nation deprived of the power to drive its factories would lose the capacity to fight. The trouble was that coal, oil and hydro-electricity did not offer themselves as easy targets for a bomber force. In Germany's industrial heartland, the Ruhr, much of the power came from the energy of the water stored behind a number of dams, but such huge structures seemed impregnable.

Had it not been for some original thinking by an unconventional British scientist, the RAF might have left the dams untouched. Dr Barnes Wallis was fascinated by the problem of the dams. He refused to accept that it was impossible to deliver a successful blow against them, believing that it was just a question of devising an effective weapon and the best means of delivering it. Early investigations were discouraging, suggesting that a bomb of conventional shape would have to weigh as much as 70,000lb to carry sufficient explosive to breach a dam. Even then, it would have to be dropped from a great height and within a few feet of the dam wall to do the job. Barnes Wallis persisted, and later research indicated that, if a bomb could be made to settle against the dam beneath the surface of the lake, the explosion would be concentrated by the water and the shock wave would crack the wall even when manageable amounts of explosive were used.

High- or medium-altitude bombing was clearly impracticable if the bomb was to be induced to settle at a chosen point, and, if dropped at low level, a conventional bomb would skip across the surface of the water before smashing into the concrete and exploding too high up the wall. Nevertheless, low-level bombing was the one method which was almost guaranteed to get the bomb against the dam.

Starting from there, Barnes Wallis' solution was to design a bomb shaped like a depth charge. It was to be mounted sideways in the aircraft, and given back-spin before being dropped. Released while flying very low, at exactly the right speed, and at a precise distance from the dam, it would bounce along until it struck the wall and then roll down the dam to a particular depth before exploding. When a successful design was eventually achieved, the bomb was 7ft in girth and weighed 9,250lb.

The only aircraft capable of carrying such a weapon was a heavily modified Avro Lancaster. Both the familiar upper turret and the bomb doors had to be removed. As can be glimpsed in Maurice Gardner's painting, uncompromisingly angular brackets were mounted in the open cavity of the aircraft's belly. When the cylindrical bomb was hung on these it projected well below the line of the fuselage, and this did not enhance the Lancaster's aerodynamics. Overall, the weight of the aircraft was up and the top speed was down, although handling did not seem to be seriously affected.

Barnes Wallis' unconventional ideas were not universally welcomed. Air Chief Marshal Sir Arthur Harris, C-in-C Bomber Command, was openly sceptical at first. He was tired of 'half-baked inventors', he said, and described the dams scheme as 'far-fetched'. However, he agreed that trials should be held and, when these proved promising, he gave his approval for the formation of a special squadron to carry out the raid. He had someone in mind to lead the new squadron. His choice, Wing Commander Guy Penrose Gibson, was then commanding No. 106 Squadron and about to complete his third tour of operations. He had amassed a total of 173 operational sorties, and had been awarded the DSO and the DFC. A bar to the DSO was on its way. He was only 25 years old.

Guy Gibson arrived at RAF Scampton, near Lincoln, in the middle of March 1943 to take up his new

command. He had been told only that his squadron would be involved in a vital operation, that it must be able to fly low at night, and that it would have to be ready in about two months. As the crews assembled at Scampton it became clear that their targets were to be dams, and that this was to be no ordinary squadron. The men had been drawn from all over Bomber Command, and collectively they represented the highest levels of operational experience and excellence in RAF bomber operations.

In the following weeks these select crews became No. 617 Squadron. Making practice flights against a dam in Wales, they mastered the difficult art of flying at very low level at night, and they also developed the devices and techniques required to deliver their special bomb with extraordinary accuracy. The problem of precise height was solved by fixing two spotlights on each Lancaster so that their beams intersected on the water when the aircraft was flown at a height of exactly 60ft. Range was determined by a simple wooden triangle with an eyehole mounted at one corner and a nail at each of the others. This basic device was designed so that the bomb-aimer looked through the eyepiece and released the bomb when the nails lined up with towers on top of the German dams. While the bomb-aimer concentrated on range, the navigator watched the spotlights and advised on height, the flight engineer handled the throttles and controlled airspeed, and the pilot maintained the line of attack and held the aircraft steady during the run. The crews grasped the techniques quickly and were soon delivering bombs with consistent and unprecedented accuracy.

On 15 May 1943, just two months after the squadron had been formed, Guy Gibson learned that his targets were to be the Ruhr dams, and was told that the attack would be carried out on the following night. The date had been chosen to take advantage of both a

full moon and the period when the lakes behind the dams would be at their highest levels.

Nineteen crews of No. 617 Squadron were available for the raid, and they were divided into three waves. The first wave of nine aircraft, led by Gibson, was briefed to attack the Mohne Dam as its primary target. If the Mohne was breached, those who still had bombs were to move on to the Eder and then, finally, to the Sorpe. The second wave of five aircraft was to tackle the Sorpe first, and a third wave of five was to be an airborne reserve, backing up the others as necessary. The operation was to be flown at low level throughout.

Just before 2130 on 16 May, the first No. 617 Squadron Lancaster took off from Scampton. To take account of the longer route planned for those aiming for the Sorpe, it was an aircraft of the second wave. But it was not the Lancaster of Flight Lieutenant Joe McCarthy, No. 617's only American and the wave's intended leader. His own aircraft was unserviceable, and transferring to the spare made him half an hour late. Gibson led the first wave off soon after the second, and they set off on a more southerly course for the Mohne, in groups of three. When the reserves took to the air nearly three hours later, No. 617's whole available strength was committed to the squadron's first and most famous battle.

The second wave was the first to fly and the first to suffer. Munro's aircraft was severely damaged by flak just after crossing the Dutch coast and had to turn back. Rice struck the surface of the Zuider Zee, tearing the projecting bomb from its mountings and scooping tons of water into the fuselage. Miraculously the aircraft bounced, and was able to turn for home. The aircraft flown by Barlow and Byers just disappeared soon afterwards, leaving McCarthy's crew, some 60 miles behind, the sole survivors of those going to the Sorpe.

The first wave, far to the south, was less troubled. Soon after midnight Gibson lifted his Lancaster over the hills cradling Mohne Lake and marshalled his forces. He found that his nine had become eight. Astell had been shot down by flak north-west of Dorsten. As the force gathered and circled the lake, a number of guns opened up from both the shore and the dam's towers. Gibson took note and began the attack himself, swinging down over the lake to settle the aircraft just 60ft off the water and aiming at the centre of the dam. As the heightfinding spotlights came on, the defenders were able to concentrate their attention on the light source, and the flak became intense. Gibson's gunners took on the towers as the Lancaster raced for the dam.

For Gibson's crew, everything worked well. The bomb bounced across the water, hit the dam and slid beneath the surface of the lake. Seconds later it exploded, raising a huge column of white water; but the dam did not break. After waiting for the lake's surface to settle, Gibson ordered the other Lancasters to attack in turn. The second aircraft, flown by Hopgood, was hit by flak on the run-in. His bomb overshot the dam and the aircraft crashed soon afterwards. Martin followed, with Gibson trailing his coat over the dam to draw some fire, and delivered his bomb despite being heavily hit by the German gunners.

Gibson and Martin then joined forces to cover Young and Maltby during their attacks. Both bombs found their mark, and Maltby's proved decisive. As the water settled again after his run, the dam suddenly crumbled and the lake roared through a gap 100 yards across and 100ft deep. The torrent raced down the valley, destroying villages, roads, bridges and power lines in its path.

Gibson turned away from the devastation and ordered the Lancasters still carrying bombs to set off for the Eder. It was after 0100 on 17 May when they reached the area of the dam, and a heavy mist was gathering in the valleys. The Eder was not easy to find. Not only was the visibility worsening, but the dam was hidden in a much deeper fold of the hills. Gibson spent some time circling the area before he was sure that he was in the right place. The other crews still had not found the target, so, as Maurice Gardner's painting shows, Gibson attracted their attention by flying across the dam and marking it with a flare.

It was fortunate that the problems of attacking the Eder were not compounded by flak. The Germans may have believed that the surrounding hills would provide sufficient protection against low-flying aircraft. They were close to being right. Shannon was the first to try, and he pulled away for a rest after making six unsuccessful attempts to reach the correct position for releasing the bomb. Maudslay's bomb was dropped on his third run, but it struck the top of the dam and exploded, taking aircraft and crew with it. Shannon tried twice more before releasing his bomb with great accuracy. The last available bomb was in Knight's aircraft. It was dropped on his second run and, in a reprise of events at the Mohne, the towering white column over the dam was followed by the crumbling of the dam wall and the irresistible rush of water into the valley.

At the Sorpe, McCarthy found that his Lancaster was alone. As with the Eder, the approaches to the dam were difficult, and several runs were made before the bomb was dropped. It exploded against the dam, but the wall held firm. Three of the reserve force delivered bombs. Burpee had earlier been shot down near Tilburg, en route to the Rhur, and by the time Anderson reached the dam it was hidden by fog and no attack was possible. The Sorpe resisted 617's efforts and survived the onslaught.

The remaining two Lancasters were sent against the Schwelme and Lister dams. Townsend succeeded in bombing the Schwelme but failed to destroy it, but Ottley's aircraft had been shot down by flak near Heisen on its way to the targets. On the return trip the Lancaster of the deputy leader, Squadron Leader Young, was hit by flak and had to be ditched in the North Sea. The crew did not survive. Of the 133 men who had set out for the dams, 56 did not return. Two members of Hopgood's crew survived as POWs, but the rest were killed. It had been a very costly operation, as Sir Arthur Harris had known it would be.

Thirty-four decorations were awarded, including a Victoria Cross for Gibson and DSOs for Martin, McCarthy, Maltby, Shannon and Knight. Ten DFCs, four bars to DFCs, two CGMs and twelve DFMs made up the list. The unprecedented number of awards for a single operation reflected the magnitude of the achievement.

The performance of the No. 617 Squadron crews had been superlative, but the direct results of their efforts were disappointing. Much later, when it was possible to assess the effects of the raid on the German war effort, it was realised that the disruption to the Ruhr's industries had been minimal. It was true that the damage was catastrophic in those areas immediately downstream of the Mohne and Eder Dams. Villages, roads and railways were washed away, coalmines were flooded, and a number of small factories and power stations were engulfed. For a while it made things difficult for the Ruhr, but never impossible. The Sorpe Dam held enough water to keep the factories going while the Mohne was repaired, which took a few months. It might have been different if the Sorpe could have been breached, but that was probably beyond the capabilities of even No. 617 Squadron. Unlike its concrete neighbours, it was an earth dam with a concrete core, and the Barnes Wallis bomb was not the right tool for that particular job.

The longer-term results of the raid were much more rewarding. On the German side, valuable resources were diverted to the defence of dams and other strategic targets. For the RAF, it opened the door to a whole range of new possibilities for the use of the bomber force. No. 617 Squadron was retained as a special unit, and went on to use its modified Lancasters to drop the massive Barnes Wallis Tallboy and Grand Slam bombs against particularly difficult targets.* More importantly, the squadron led the way in developing many of the precision marking and bombing techniques which so transformed Bomber Command's capabilities and effectiveness in 1944 and 1945. The astonishing accuracy in weapon delivery achieved by No. 617 Squadron during the Dams Raid did much to change the way that RAF commanders thought about the bomber offensive, and was one of the first steps along the road to the precise application of air power so graphically demonstrated in the Gulf War of 1991.

*The artist writes:* This painting was created following a request by aviation author Alan Cooper to produce a scene to use as the main cover on his forthcoming book on 617 Squadron. We decided it would be appropriate, and perhaps a little more unusual, to illustrate the moment when Wing Commander Guy Gibson finally located the Eder Dam during that epic Dambusters raid. The Eder was beginning to be shrouded in mist, and it took several runs before Gibson was able to mark the dam accurately with a flare and signal the other crews with him to begin their attack.

---

* In fact, two RAF squadrons were equipped with Lancasters modified to carry the Barnes Wallis 'earthquake' bombs. Nos IX and 617 Squadrons both attacked special targets such as the battleship *Tirpitz*, U-boat pens and viaducts with great success.

# F-Freddie Fails to Return

*Painting by David Shepherd*
*Text by Tony Mason*

THIS PAINTING IS AN EMOTIVE AND SYMBOLIC TRIBUTE to the crews of Bomber Command, and specifically to the contribution of the Lancaster bomber in the Second World War. David Shepherd has therefore given his Lancaster (one of his favourite aircraft) a fictitious code; VM-F was never allocated to a squadron aircraft. Until September 1944 Lancasters usually operated by night, and this portrayal is either of an imminent loss during an early morning return from a night raid, or of a victim in the last months of the war, when Bomber Command increasingly launched daylight attacks on targets deep inside Germany. F for Freddie, with its port outer engine burning, will not return to its base in England.

Mere words do scant justice to Bomber Command's contribution to the defeat of Hitler's Germany. Its first operational sortie was flown on 3 September 1939, and its last took place in the early hours of 3 May 1945. In the course of the campaign 47,268 aircrew were killed or listed as missing on operations, and a further 8,305 were lost within the Command to non-operational causes. Most of the 55,573 were officers or NCOs. By comparison, in the whole of the slaughter of the First World War, the British Army lost 38,834 officers.

In the early years of the war Bomber Command was ill-prepared to carry out the tasks envisaged for it. In the words of the Official History, it was equipped neither to penetrate into enemy territory by day nor to find its target areas, let alone its targets, by night. The road to success was to be long and hazardous.

In January 1941 the first Lancaster prototype flew at Woodford. A development of the twin-engined Avro Manchester which had entered squadron service only two months previously, the Lancaster had increased wingspan, four Rolls-Royce Merlin engines, a modified tailplane and a new undercarriage. Following trials at Boscombe Down, the first production aircraft flew on 31 October 1941 and the first squadron aircraft joined No.

44 (Rhodesia) Squadron on 24 December 1941. Initially, the Lancaster could carry a 14,000lb bomb load over a combat radius of 1,660 miles, but its bomb bay could accommodate single bombs of more than 4,000lb, giving it a major operational advantage over its contemporary, the Handley Page Halifax. Later in the war it would carry the 12,000lb Tallboy and 22,000lb Grand Slam bombs. With the advent of the Lancaster, Bomber Command acquired the hitting power necessary for the effective strategic bombardment of Germany. Altogether, 7,373 Lancasters were built. Of 955,044 tons of bombs dropped by Bomber Command in its campaign, almost two-thirds, 608,612 tons, were dropped by Lancasters in the last three years of the war. Of almost 7,000 Lancasters delivered during the war, almost half, 3,345, were lost on operations, together with 21,751 crew members.

The improved hitting power of Bomber Command was accompanied by improved navigation and bomb aiming. Gee, introduced in early 1942, was a system which allowed a navigator to calculate his position by timing the reception of pulse signals from three different ground stations. Later in 1942 the Oboe system also used harmonised pulse signals to give a bomb aimer his position over the target. In early 1943 a ground mapping radar, $H_2S$, was added to the navigation/bomb-aiming equipment on the Lancaster. The effectiveness of the entire force was enhanced by the introduction of the specialist Pathfinders. From March 1943 Bomber Command began the heaviest phase of its attacks on Germany, progressively being joined by the bombers of the United States Army Air Force.

Until July 1943, attacks were concentrated on the industrial heart of Germany, in the Ruhr. Essen, Cologne and Duisberg were heavily bombed on several occasions. Against these and other industrial centres 18,506 sorties were flown, from which 872 aircraft failed to return. A further 2,126 were damaged.

In July and August 1943 Hamburg was devastated by combined attacks by Bomber Command and the US 8th Air Force. In ten days more than 3,700 sorties were flown. The air defences were surprised by jamming and overwhelmed. Albert Speer, responsible for German industry, was extremely concerned lest such weight of attack be extended to only six more industrial centres. Then, in November, Bomber Command began its hardest battle, over Berlin, which was to last until March 1944. During the winter of 1943–44 35 major operations were flown, including 9,111 sorties against the German capital. Of these, 7,256 were flown by Lancasters.

But as Bomber Command's threat to German industry grew, so the German High Command expanded the defences against it. In March 1943 Hitler demanded extensive strengthening of flak defences. As a result, by the end of 1943 over 20,000 heavy anti-aircraft guns had been deployed to protect the Reich, manned and supported by two million servicemen and civilians. In the words of Albert Speer, every square metre of German territory became a front line.

Fighter defences also were considerably strengthened. Over a six-month period in 1943 aircraft numbers were doubled. Fighter control units were increased, and high priority was given to the electronic battle being waged against Bomber Command. Increasingly, the German night fighters used the bomber's own radar emissions, identification friend or foe (IFF), H$_2$S, and even their radar warning systems, to home on to their airborne targets.

The core force of Messerschmitt Bf 110s was strengthened during 1943 by Junkers Ju 88s and Heinkel He 219s. Fighter tactics were refined, particularly by exploiting 'shräge Musik' upward-firing cannon to hit the Lancaster's vulnerable underbelly. Fighter controllers became adept at placing the interceptors ahead of or among the bomber streams. Frequently they were thwarted by Bomber Command's jamming and deception

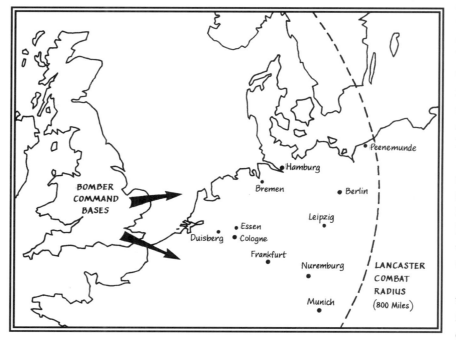

countermeasures, but there were too many German radar units and the bomber streams were too long for British electronic countermeasures to give complete protection from the fighters. There was no specialist flak suppression force.

Consequently, the heavy toll on bombers and their crews continued through the 'Battle of Berlin' on the 1,150-mile round trip from bases in eastern England to the German capital. That bleak winter, 1,047 aircraft were destroyed and another 1,682 damaged. In January alone over 2,000 aircrew were lost.

In the spring of 1944 the Command made a major contribution, with the Tactical Air Force and US allies, to the interdiction of North-Western France, making a well documented impact on German ability to reinforce the Normandy invasion areas. As the Allied forces moved towards the German frontier, the German air defences progressively lost the forward units of the early-warning network. The complementary daylight raids of the USAAF bombers, now escorted deep into Germany by P-51 Mustangs, imposed increasingly heavy losses on German day fighters. Their reinforcement by night squadrons further relieved pressure on Bomber Command.

In the last nine months of the war the offensive spearheaded by the Lancasters reached a crescendo. By 1945 1,300 bombers were available every day. In the last four months 181,000 tons of bombs were dropped; nearly one-fifth of the Command's aggregate for the entire war.

Despite fierce opposition from individual night fighters until the end, the German air defences collapsed under the weight of a combined bomber offensive which had overwhelmed the radar defences, cut the flow of fuel to the fighters, denied opportunities for replacement training and inflicted unsustainable losses on German aircrew. The war in the air, as on the ground, had been won.

It has been estimated that 7 per cent of the total British war effort was consumed by the bomber offensive. If so, the return on the investment was incalculable. The cumulative impact of the bombing campaign permeated all theatres of the war from 1942 onwards because of the German need to allocate resources to home air defence. The diversion of two million men has already been noted. Thirty per cent of Germany's total gun output and 20 per cent of heavy ammunition production were allocated to air defence. Sufficient aluminium was used in flak fuses alone to build 40,000 more fighters. By the end of 1943 70 per cent of all Luftwaffe flak personnel were deployed in the west to counter the bomber offensive, together with 75 per cent of heavy AA guns, which were mainly 88mm dual-purpose AA/anti-tank weapons. Meanwhile, on the Russian front, 'flak forces were too weak to accomplish even the most urgent necessities'.

At the outbreak of war Germany had 820 fighters of all types. In September 1944 production peaked at 3,000, or three-fifths of total aircraft production in that month. Nine thousand Ju 88 bombers were produced, but a further 4,200 were the night fighter variant.

Despite the desperate requirements of the Russian front, the Normandy invasion and the Mediterranean theatre, 25 per cent of all German fighters were defending the homeland. Although the Soviet Air Force enjoyed a 6 to 1 numerical superiority, German squadrons were withdrawn from the eastern front in 1943 to reinforce the air defences in the west.

Consequently, Allied ground forces and tactical air forces everywhere benefited considerably from the bomber offensive. Allied tactical fighters won air superiority against depleted and outnumbered opponents. Allied ground forces suffered fewer enemy air attacks because of the friendly air superiority established over their heads and the reduced number of German bombers available for counterattack. Allied armoured forces benefited from the diversion of 88mm guns to air defence. Allied close-air-support aircraft took advantage of the priority given by the Germans to flak installations protecting the homeland rather than ground forces.

The direct impact of the bombers on German industrial production spread across the entire war effort.

Whereas the interdiction of the Normandy invasion area had a primarily regional impact, the destruction of the German oil industry reduced all war-fighting activites to an increasingly impotent minimum. The expansion of the German wartime economy was constrained by destruction and the compulsion to disperse from industrial centres for survival. This dislocation may be compared with the ability of the USA, immune from air attack, to plan and implement a massive, unhindered wartime expansion of industrial production.

For the greater part of the war, only Bomber Command could take the fight back to Germany. In many senses Bomber Command's offensive was the 'Second Front' long before Allied troops set foot in Normandy. In the desperate years of 1940, 1941 and 1942 the daily bulletins announcing Bomber Command's attacks the previous night were welcomed by the grimly beleaguered British population. Across the Channel and North Sea, the nightly drone of Merlins gave heart to the occupied peoples, reassuring them that the war went on, that Germany was itself being attacked and that ultimately the invader would be expelled.

Most bulletins would be accompanied by the comment that a certain number of aircraft had failed to return. Usually the official figures were very small. The aircrew knew better. The odds against them completing the specified 'tour' of 30 sorties were heavy. They had an exacting, lonely and vulnerable duty, in which loyalty to one's crew colleagues, personal determination and individual integrity and bravery took them night after night to their targets. For the greater part of the war they had no escort fighters and no mutually supporting formation defensive fire. Once engaged in combat they were outmanoeuvred, outgunned and outpaced by German night fighters.

Today, all air forces know that air superiority must be won before any other activity can succeed without grievous loss. From 1939 Bomber Command

fought for almost six years without such superiority. Its inestimable contribution to the industrial collapse and ultimate defeat of Hitler's Germany may never be precisely quantified. The price paid by the aircrews, however, most definitely can. We see it in the fate of F for Freddie.

*The artist writes:* In the early 1960s I painted this picture of Avro Lancasters returning from a raid over Germany, when I perhaps had more freedom to paint what I really wanted; before the time arrived when, due to the success of my wildlife painting, I have happily been in the position of having a full order book of commissioned work for years ahead.

I remember the exciting and emotive days of the Second World War, when, as an eight-year-old schoolboy, I was living in North London in the middle of the Battle of Britain and the Blitz. Aeroplanes of that period have always been my favourite, and there is a very special place in my heart for the Lancaster, perhaps because I have been lucky enough to fly twice in PA474, *City of Lincoln*, belonging to the RAF Battle of Britain Memorial Flight.

In the painting I endeavoured to portray the all-too-familiar scene of a Lancaster hit by flak and struggling home on three engines, the crew wondering whether they will make it safely home to their base in Lincolnshire. One further point of possible interest is the fact that I included one Halifax, to make people look at the painting with more than just a cursory glance. It certainly worked, because a lot of people have commented on this, possibly questioning the fact that it could have occurred in reality. It obviously did during the war, on many occasions.

I sold the painting to the RAF for some £50.00, I believe, all those years ago, and as far as I am aware it hangs in the Sergeants' Mess at RAF Cottesmore.

# Halifax Attack

*Painting by Geoff Lea*
*Text by John Maynard*

AT 2150 ON THE NIGHT OF 30 MARCH 1944 CHRIS Nielson, captain of Handley Page Halifax III BM-N of No. 433 Squadron, Royal Canadian Air Force (RCAF), lifted his heavily-laden aircraft from the runway and began a gentle climb over the dark, rain-soaked Yorkshire countryside close by the village of Skipton-on-Swale.

Airfield construction had begun at the Swale-side site late in 1941 with the main runway running more or less parallel to the river and the complex of buildings adjoining the main road to Northallerton. There would be three runways, and a typically long, meandering perimeter track encompassing the site and giving easy access to the aircraft dispersal hardstandings which became for so many a last living touch of England.

By the high summer of 1942 the army of workmen began to move away from the disfigured land. Three maintenance hangars towered above the surrounding fields, ready to receive the bombers for servicing, or for the repair of battle damage. The largest spanned 120ft and was almost twice that length and 27ft high; amply proportioned to harbour the Halifaxes that would ultimately provide Skipton's striking power. Everywhere there were squat ugly huts. Wooden huts, corrugated Nissen huts, sweating pre-cast concrete huts. Where there were no huts there was mud, churned by boots and bicycles into an inescapable mire. Only in brief mid-summer did mud turn to hard rutted earth, and then, too, came eye-stinging dust and grit, blown everywhere by the wind across the flat land and the slipstreams' violent zephyrs.

From such natural inhospitability flew the aircraft of Bomber Command, rising into the wide skies of East Anglia and Yorkshire, which had become the great citadel from which were flown the nightly sorties against the enemy's centres of industry and population. Such was the vital importance attached to this citadel that its creation absorbed a huge proportion of Britain's resources. In 1942 a peak of airfield construction was reached, with a new base opening every three days after an average building time of only six months. Nearly a third of the nation's total civil engineering workforce, 127,000 men, were employed on this great endeavour, for the RAF's massive offensive was perceived as fundamental to victory for the Allied cause. Its direction and undisputed justification sprang from the leaders of the great world alliance; there were no hesitations, no misgivings. Free peoples revelled in the awful damage being inflicted on a cruel, barbaric enemy, and the oppressed of occupied Europe took strength and welcome optimism from the nightly sound of the heavy bombers.

Indeed, between the early summer of 1940 and the crossing of the Rhine almost five years later, this was the only possible offensive aimed at the black heart of Nazi Germany. There was one lingering sadness which has never gone away; the cost of this mighty onslaught in terms of aircrew lives. Almost by definition these were the very best of their generation. Fit, intelligent and brave, they share with the subalterns of the Somme a uniquely poignant place in the awful catalogue of war. Their chances of surviving more than a fraction of the sorties that comprised an operational tour were minimal. In total, the squadrons of Bomber Command lost nearly 9,000 aircraft in action over Europe, and in them some 38,000 RAF aircrew, 10,000 Canadians, 4,000 Australians, 1,700 New Zealanders and 1,500 men of other nationalities died. The airmen of Bomber Command represented 2 per cent of the total of Britain's armed forces, yet their dead accounted for more than 14.5 per cent of the nation's casualties on active service.

Skipton-on-Swale was, from the start, a Canadian base. In August 1942 No. 420 Squadron RCAF moved there from Waddington with the last of its Hampdens and its newly acquired Wellington IIIs. The station

transferred to No. 6 Group in May of the following year, when No. 432 Squadron RCAF formed there with Wellington Xs. In September No. 433 Squadron came into existence at Skipton, its badge including the spiny porcupine representing the Porcupine District of Northern Ontario, which had adopted the unit soon after it was formed. However, it was not until December 1945 that His Majesty King George VI finally approved the badge and its uncompromising motto, *Quis 'y frotte s'y pique* ('Who opposes it gets hurt').

At its formation, No. 433 Squadron was equipped with Halifax IIIs, and it embarked on intensive training for three months. It was to be the fourteenth and last RCAF bomber squadron to be formed overseas. They went to war early in January 1944, dropping mines in the waters around the Frisian Islands. Such 'easy' operations only counted as half a trip towards completion of a 'tour', and it was another fortnight before No. 433 carried out its first unqualified attack; on the ultimate target, Berlin. Six of the squadron's aircraft bombed, and a seventh, returning early with a mechanical problem, released its load on Kiel. That night, 18 January, the 'Big City' experienced a fairly light attack; the weather was appalling, as it had been for most of the month. Two nights later the bombers were back in business, with 769 aircraft taking off for Berlin and returning after a successful attack with a reasonably acceptable 4.8 per cent loss

rate. The Porcupines were blooded, and they had taken the squadron code 'BM' across Germany and into battle.

The Halifax was the second four-engined heavy bomber to enter service with Bomber Command, the first having been the Short Stirling. The Halifax IIIs, which No. 433 Squadron were the first to receive, were

much modified from the Mk. Is that had undertaken their maiden sortie with No. 35 Squadron to Le Havre on 10 March 1941. Gone was the ungainly and heavy powered forward turret, and an elegant long nose gave the aeroplane a far more pleasing and aerodynamic appearance. An incidental advantage of this was the generous area of uninterrupted black fuselage, which enabled the Canadians to indulge in colourful nose art to rival even the masterpieces of the US 8th Air Force.

More Halifax IIIs were built than any other variant. They incorporated Bristol Hercules radial engines in place of the earlier Merlins, a four-gun mid-upper turret

and larger, much-modified vertical tail surfaces, introduced to overcome an often fatal tendency to tail stall which could occur on final approach in battle-damaged aircraft with two engines feathered on one side. In addition, Handley Page had responded to Service criticism with a range of less-dramatic modifications designed to save weight, reduce drag and improve overall operational performance. Thus the new Halifax emerged as a popular, sturdy aeroplane with a commendable ability to absorb battle damage, proven versatility, and a reasonably forgiving nature. One thing that it was not, however, was another Lancaster.

By the end of 1943, Canadians constituted well over half of Bomber Command's Dominion-born pilots. All of the Canadian squadrons, fourteen in No. 6 Group, were Yorkshire based, with one exception – No. 428 at Middleton St George, County Durham. In addition there was a Canadian Pathfinder unit, No. 405 Squadron at Gransdon Lodge in Bedfordshire. The RCAF squadrons rapidly acquired traditions and standards of their own. They were the only Dominion force in sufficient numbers to warrant their own Group. This generated a mostly friendly independence, causing them to regard the relative formality of the RAF with a mixture of amusement, scorn and disbelief. Even so, they acknowledged that Service as positively libertarian when compared with other British institutions. However, their admiration for the British pub was unbounded, and the Busby Stoop just outside the airfield boundary was a fine example.

By 30 March, Nielson and his crew, some of whom were British, had 29 operations to their credit. The prospect of a rest was enticingly close, and was made all the more welcome by the reality that they had flown against the enemy on 32 occasions, though six of these were 'half-price' mining missions. That night, as they gained height through cloud and rain, heading for the assembly point, they all knew that the trip ahead was long, complex and significant. Their target was Nuremberg, a city which, apart from being an important centre of aircraft production and national government, was the very spawning ground of Nazism. Here Hitler staged his massive rallies, here he numbed and hypnotised minds to inspire racial hatred and the prospect of world domination by his so-called master race. There was therefore a fatal attraction about this city, one which perhaps caused the command structure from Churchill and Harris downward to contemplate its destruction with an enthusiasm which, that night, warped good judgement.

With its name *Nielson's Nuthouse*, coined from its identifying letter, colourfully emblazoned on its port nose panels, Halifax BM-N crossed the east coast of England. Around it flew no fewer than 700 other main force aircraft and an additional 135 Pathfinders and intruders. A creditable 120 bombers of this total were put up by the Canadian squadrons of No. 6 Group. Their course was set to take them over Bruges and Charleroi and on to Bonn before they eased south over Fluda on their heading for Nuremburg. There were some long straight sectors to be flown, no feints, no real diversionary tactics; tonight they were relying on the cloud-safe, dark March sky.

During their approach to the German border it became increasingly clear to Nielson that things were going disastrously wrong. The cloud was thinning, and in strengthening high-altitude winds a night of icy, gin-clear moonlight was in the making. The situation could hardly have been worse for the bombers. They faced an unusually long flight to the target, demanding maximum fuel conservation, across the heavily defended skies of northern Germany while exposed by a brilliant moon and buffeted by strong winds. The German night fighter pilots could scarcely believe their eyes. So clear and numerous were their targets that they abandoned the normally welcome restraint of ground radar control for free-ranging attacks on targets of opportunity. They were rapidly spoilt for choice, and the path of the bomber stream became pinpointed by the pyres of blazing aircraft falling to the frosty ground.

*Nielson's Nuthouse* turned south with just over 100 miles to go to the target. Before them lay the River Main, and to their right Schweinfurt, the scene of so much American heroism in daylight attacks. Nielson later recalled that at about this time visibility was so clear that, far ahead, he could see patterns of town and city streets seeming to sparkle with frost and moonlight like cobwebs. As they flew over Bamberg the Halifax was suddenly stricken by shattering impacts and explosions which immediately ignited the starboard inner engine. As the crew fought to regain a semblance of control they concluded that their aircraft had been hit by a night fighter firing from below, probably using the new 'schräge Musik' vertically firing 20mm twin-cannon installation. Many crews died in this way, never knowing what had hit them.

Anticipating that the enemy aircraft would return for the kill, Nielson dived the Halifax in an effort to extinguish the fire and take immediate evasive action. He called for the engineer to feather the propeller on the burning engine, but they were already leaving a wide fiery trail across the blackness all around them. Sudden-ly the fighter came in again, attacked, and almost immediately broke off to avoid a lethal cloud of debris as the Halifax exploded. Miraculously Nielson, his rear gunner and his wireless operator were blown clear and parachuted to safety close by the tragic remains of the *Nuthouse* and the five other members of her crew. They had been eight in number that night because they were carrying a supernumerary pilot in the jump seat. The extra man was often considered an unlucky passenger in the airmens' poignant catalogue of superstition.

That night, 11.8 per cent of the attacking force did not return. It was a loss that would remain unsurpassed, but even so it took no account of aircraft returning damaged beyond repair, or those that crashed attempting to land the next morning on fogbound airfields.

Geoff Lea's painting was commissioned by Fred Panton, the brother of the *Nielson's Nuthouse* engineer who was killed over Bamberg. The precise circumstances of his brother's death remain matters for dignified family grief which have no place in a painting. Instead, an earlier action has been recorded; perhaps it happened, perhaps it did not. When you look at the picture, remember Bomber Command's 55,000 dead. Remember that they and those that led them fought for you against a most monstrous tyranny. Be proud of them, for there can be nothing but pride in what they did for your freedom and for mine.

*The artist writes:* This painting was commissioned by Fred Panton, the brother of Pilot Officer Chris Panton, who was flight engineer in *Nielson's Nuthouse* and was killed in action that night over Bamberg. Having visited the crash site and the cemetery where his brother lies, Fred wanted a painting to symbolise the war in the skies, highlighting the elegant beauty of the aircraft while demonstrating its terrible vulnerability.

# Beware the Lion

*Painting by Geoff Lea*
*Text by Ken Delve*

THE BROAD BLACK-AND-WHITE INVASION STRIPES on wings and fuselages of these patrolling Spitfires immediately identify the subject of this painting by Geoff Lea as air support for the invasion of Normandy by the Allies in June 1944. For the largest combined forces operation ever mounted in the history of war, the Allies assembled unprecedented numbers of bomber, fighter and transport aircraft to achieve total air superiority over the beachhead. By and large, the invading armies were able to fight and advance without the worry of Luftwaffe intervention, but only because vital and hard lessons had been learnt from an abortive operation two years previously.

On 19 August 1942 an Allied force, primarily made up of Canadian units, stormed ashore at Dieppe in what some have termed 'a raid in force' and others a disaster. Its one certain purpose was to serve as proving ground for the inevitable large-scale Allied invasion of the Continent.

The Battle of Dieppe was supported by the largest array of RAF squadrons yet employed on a single operation, some 68 squadrons being airborne. For many squadrons it was their most hectic day since the Battle of Britain, with up to three sorties being flown during the day. The Allied commanders sought to use air power to redress the firepower imbalance being suffered by the ground forces, while the Luftwaffe were equally keen to prevent such intervention. The air battles over and around Dieppe were by far the largest yet experienced, and losses on both sides were roughly equal. However, for the Allied planners it reinforced the accepted doctrine that air superiority was an essential prerequisite to any major amphibious operation.

The brunt of the air combat was borne by the Spitfire squadrons of Fighter Command, some 48 of which were available for use, including four equipped with the new Spitfire IX. While the fighters had a cru-

cial part to play in providing an air umbrella, it was also an opportunity to employ tactical air power – fighter-bombers and medium bombers – in defence suppression and close air support. The RAF flew some 3,000 sorties in the space of sixteen hours on 19 August 1942. In response, the Luftwaffe flew just under 1,000 sorties. Whilst the fighter cover prevented any substantial Luftwaffe interference with the operation, and certainly kept the enemy clear of the vulnerable shipping, in the air combats it was the Luftwaffe that ended the day with the higher score, the RAF losing 106 aircraft to all causes and the Germans losing 48.

Dieppe has gone down in the military annals as a failure, but although it was very expensive in casualties for the Canadian troops, it nonetheless provided vital lessons that could only have been gained in the operational theatre, and it thus helped pave the way for improved tactics and operational concepts that would be invaluable in June 1944.

Throughout 1943, Allied air strength in the European Theatre of Operations (ETO) continued to grow as ever more American bomber and fighter units arrived to swell the 8th Air Force. The increasing pace of American daylight operations also proved that the Luftwaffe's day fighter strength in the west was by no means depleted. Bomber losses assumed horrendous proportions, and there was pressure for the Americans to abandon daylight bombing and join Bomber Command in the night offensive, although losses in Bomber Command were themselves quite significant.

The experience of the Dieppe air battles and the effectiveness of the German fighter force in 1943 led the 'Overlord' planners to believe that a comprehensive fighter plan to achieve and maintain air superiority over the bridgehead was essential to success. Consequently they created the largest and most complex fighter plan of the war. In the months leading up to D-Day much of

the offensive weight of air operations was aimed at the German fighter defence system; radars, airfields, production centres, etc., but the assumption remained that the Luftwaffe would field a strong force against the landings.

The Directive issued to the fighter forces stated:

'The intention of the British and American fighter forces is to attain and maintain an air situation which will assure freedom of action for our forces without effective intervention by the German Air Force, and to render maximum air protection to the land and naval forces in the common object of assaulting, securing and developing the bridgehead.'

A veritable air armada of P-51 Mustangs, P-47 Thunderbolts, P-38 Lightnings and various marks of Spitfire was ranged ready for battle as RAF units of Air Defence of Great Britain (ADGB) and the 2nd Tactical Air Force joined with the American VIIIth and 9th Fighter Commands. The overall plan was for the American units to provide the bulk of the escort and high-cover patrols, while the low cover, especially over the beaches, was provided by RAF Spitfires. The entire invasion area was to be given a layered screen of fighters, the first squadrons to be in position by 0425 on the morning of 6 June 1944. The screen was to be maintained for what was considered to be the 'peak operational period', from 0500 to 1000, and then for two further critical periods during the day.

The Allied fighter Order of Battle (ORBAT) seems very impressive, with the RAF providing 55 squadrons of Spitfires, plus a number of Mustang and Mosquito units, the most significant squadron of which

were the twelve night-fighter squadrons from Nos. 11 and 85 Groups; the American contribution comprised 27 squadrons of P-51s, 51 squadrons of P-47s and 21 squadrons of P-38s. Thus the overall fighter strength of some 2,000 aircraft looked very impressive on paper, but the scale of the task it was called upon to perform was equally large, both in terms of geographic area and timescale. Furthermore, it was considered that the overcrowded airfields in England would make ideal targets

FIGHTER PATROL LINES & AREAS FOR D-DAY

for German tip-and-run fighter-bombers, so each airfield was required to maintain a fighter flight on standby.

The P-51s and P-47s formed an outer fighter screen reaching down almost as far as Paris, the idea being to 'sanitise' a wide band of airspace on all sides of the assault area. Should enemy aircraft penetrate the outer screen, they would face additional fighters over the beach areas, with high cover provided by three

squadrons of P-47s and low cover by six squadrons of Spitfires. Meanwhile, the P-38s provided convoy cover over the myriad of ships filling the English Channel. The set patrol areas were to be occupied throughout the allotted periods, but once a squadron had been relieved on station it was free to go on a roving low-level mission to attack ground targets, these usually being elements of the enemy's communications network such as trains and motor transport.

Control of Allied fighter operations over the ships and beaches was exercised by various ground-controlled interception (GCI) units. The area nearest the English coast was covered by the Ventnor site, and the remainder of the operational area was split between three Fighter Director Tenders (FDTs), one of which, FDT 217, also acted as the co-ordinating vessel. In addition, each HQ ship had its own air operations centre, and all of these were tied into FDT 217 for co-ordination. The role played by the FDTs in the early hours of the operation was essential to ensure effective control of the large numbers of aircraft in the area, to prevent wasted effort, and to provide the most rapid response to any developing threat. It was intended that by nightfall on 6 June the control of air operations would pass to a number of land-based GCI units. In addition to the standing patrols, almost every other type of air mission was given a fighter escort, all of which helped drain the numbers of available fighters. However, by early afternoon it was obvious that no great Luftwaffe reaction would be forthcoming, and certain fighter units that had been held in reserve were released into the battle, albeit primarily in the fighter-bomber role.

Air attacks on German airfields had proved so effective that the Luftwaffe was unable to generate offensive sorties in northen France; but even so a pre-planned reinforcement of the northern bases was attempted with mixed success, some of the formations being jumped by roving American fighters. Although for most Allied fighter pilots it was to be a day of little action, some units were lucky. One was the 355th Fighter Group, whose P-51s, flying out of Steeple Morden on an evening sortie, came across a number of Ju 87 formations and promptly carved them to pieces, claiming fourteen of these unfortunate aircraft in the space of a few minutes.

A typical record of an RAF unit involved during the day was that of No. 602 Squadron. One of its pilots later recorded his impressions of the evening patrol:

'We flew along the Cotentin peninsula. There were fires all along the coast and a destroyer surrounded by small boats was sinking near a little island. Our patrol zone was the area between Montebourg and Carentan. We were covering the 101st and 82nd American Airborne Divisions while the 4th Division, which had just landed, marched on Ste Mere-Eglise. We couldn't see much. The sky was full of American fighters, in pairs. They were wandering about rather haphazard, and showed a tendency to come and sniff at us from very close to; when they seemed too aggressive we showed our teeth and faced them. One Mustang coming out of a cloud actually fired a burst at Graham, whose shooting was as good as his temper was bad, who opened fire in return, but luckily for the Mustang he missed.'

By the end of the day many of the Allied fighter pilots had become rather frustrated by the lack of aerial action. The Luftwaffe had not appeared in numbers, and for most of the airmen the day had consisted of two or three rather boring patrols. There is no doubt that the black-and-white recognition stripes painted on all tactical aircraft prevented a number of 'own goals', especially the all-too-common instances of ground, and particularly naval, forces firing at any aircraft in their area.

When the statisticians collated the sortie details for 6 June, they counted 5,350 fighter missions (3,648 by American units, over 2,000 of those being registered by 9th Air Force fighter Groups), ranging from close escort of the airborne force package to various types of defensive patrol. It was certainly a magnificent effort, and one that paid tribute to planners, groundcrew and pilots alike.

# Bombing Caen Steelworks

*Painting by Geoff Lea*
*Text by Peter Cooksley*

TODAY, IF ONE WALKS DOWN THE RUE ST JEAN IN Caen to the church that gives the road its name, at the junction with Rue Romain, there is little to suggest that much of the sacred building has been restored since the Second World War. Visitors are not reminded of that conflict until they turn into the parallel Avenue du 6 Juin, with its nearby Place de la Resistance. Like the church of St Pierre to the north, where the roof of the nave and the tower are modern copies of the originals, the restoration testifies to the fact that this ancient town, famed for lace and for its university and library, but also having an industrial complex of blast furnaces, a harbour and port installations, was virtually destroyed in the summer of 1944.

After many months of preparation, and a minor delay when the date was postponed from 5 June owing to adverse weather, the early morning of the following day saw the dawn of the Allies' D-Day (J-Jour). It began with the landing before dawn of the 6th Airborne Division, including glider troops, east of the River Orne, and the successful capture of the bridges spanning the river and the canal at Benouville, the latter destined to become known as 'Pegasus Bridge' in honour of this action. Thus started the Battle of Normandy, the province which had Caen at its centre. The local part of this engagement was to pass into history as the Battle of the Lower Orne.

The British had landed in three sectors near Ranville, Varaville and Touffreville, with the immediate objectives of securing the double bridge over the canal and destroying those over the River Dives and its tributaries between Troarn and Varaville. All of these objectives were gained before the day was ended, and after two more days a semicircular bridgehead was established at Le Mariquet and Herouville, but only after bitter fighting. The enemy counterattacked near Breville on 10 June in an attempt to split the east and west sec-tions of the Division, and only after harsh conflict was Breville captured on the following day. The position was finally consolidated, at the cost of heavy casualties, and the line was held pending the order to advance to the east in the direction of Le Harve. But the order was not given until 17 August, by which time many changes had taken place in the immediate vicinity of Caen. One of the first significant changes had occurred on 28 June, when the British 2nd Army had crossed the Odon, south-west of the town, which still lay in enemy hands. The contribution of No. 320 Squadron, RAF, to the capture of Caen is recounted here.

It seemed almost an act of official contrition by the USA that its new North American B-25 light bomber was named Mitchell, in memory of the cele-brated General unjustly disgraced fifteen years before. The aircraft was also being supplied to Britain under the Lend-Lease Act of March 1941, and the first examples were soon arriving in the UK, although only in small numbers. It was not until 1943 that the first B-25s were taken on charge by No. 320 Squadron, simultaneously with a move to Attlebridge, Norfolk, a matter of weeks after being transferred to No.2 Group, Bomber Com-mand. It was a significant change for this Dutch squadron, which had hitherto specialised in operations against shipping, originally flying Fokker T.8W float-planes. From these the unit had converted to its first landplanes, Avro Ansons, before being equipped with Lockheed Hudsons which it flew initially from Leuchars in North Scotland, quickly gaining a reputation for low-level attacks against targets ranging from single ships to the larger convoys.

Now, the role of No. 320 Squadron was to fly operations against railway marshalling yards, airfields, gun positions, flying-bomb sites and road and rail bridges. This allowed experience to be gained in work which culminated in one of its trickiest Second World

War operations. Additional emphasis had been given to the role by the Allied invasion of the European continent, when the targets were extended to include gun emplacements on the French coast, choke points, troop concentrations and V-weapon bases.

Before this, the squadron had undergone a number of changes. The previously mentioned transfer to No. 2 Group, Bomber Command, and the formation, with Nos. 98 and 180 Squadrons, of No. 140 Wing, equipped throughout with the Mitchell. This twin-engined light bomber with a crew of five was to prove popular despite a certain initial distrust of the nosewheel undercarriage, which was something of a novelty at the time. This feature had been anticipated in Britain by an experimental General Aircraft Monospar and the same company's Cygnet and Owlet light aircraft. The sole example of the Owlet, an open-cockpit two-seater introduced in 1940, had been pressed into service to familiarise pilots with the tricycle undercarriage, a characteristic of such US-designed aircraft as the Bell Airacobra fighter and the Douglas Boston light bomber, both of which were acquired by the RAF. It was not long before the Mitchell's unfamiliar undercarriage gained popularity, largely for the enhanced view it afforded on landing, and this, coupled with the aircraft's undemanding handling characteristics, made the Mitchell well-liked by aircrews.

Sorties were still being carried out from No. 320 Squadron's base at Swanton Morley in Norfolk, whence the unit had been detached from Dunsfold, Surrey, in May, and the squadron was part of the RAF's Tactical Air Force (TAF) when Operation 'Overlord', the Allied invasion of Europe, had been launched on 6 June 1944. Like other participating aircraft, the Mitchell IIs of 320 had been marked with the black and white identification stripes which were to be retained only on the lower surfaces after September. One of the Dutch squadron's

first Overlord sorties was that made on 10 June in company with Nos. 98, 180, and 226 Squadrons, all flying Mitchells. The 61 aircraft dropped their 500lb bombs from 12,000ft on the headquarters of Panzer Group West. This important HQ, which the Nazis had established at Chateau La Caine, could be identified by the very large number of road vehicles parked nearby, and great damage was done among these. Still more was suffered by the Chateau itself, where the casualties included General von Dawans, the Chief of Staff.

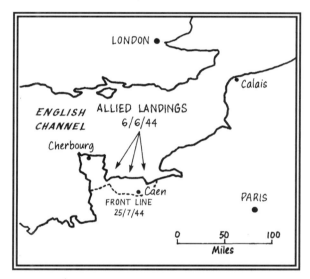

On the ground three days later, however, there was little progress to be reported by the Allied armies before Caen. An advance was held up in the vicinity of Colombelles, south of the main town, by enemy troops of the 21st Panzer Division, who had occupied the Mondeville steelworks and established a number of observation posts and gun positions within the site. A request was received from Division via the air liaison officers that the works be heavily bombed.

This was to be no ordinary tactical operation. A high degree of accuracy was called for, British land

forces being a mere 1,500 yards away. Taking part in the attack with No. 320 Squadron were Nos. 98 and 226 Squadrons, also flying Mitchells, although those of the Dutch squadron were probably newer. (The earlier aircraft purchased from Dutch funds had been replaced by others formerly belonging to Nos. 98 and 180 Squadrons, the deficit being made up by No.46 Repair and Servicing Unit, the Mitchell Pool at Hartford Bridge.)

The operation against the steelworks was planned for the early evening of Thursday 22 June, using 48 Mitchell bombers supported by 24 Bostons. The approach was to be made from directly over the sea, the formation dropping its mixed load of 284 500lb and 48 1,000lb bombs on the factory before turning east and heading for home, thus avoiding the heaviest of the Caen anti-aircraft defences, which at the steelworks alone consisted of some twenty or thirty 88mm guns.

As the run-in was made over St Aubin, it was clear that the reports of good visibility were correct. There was only a slight grey haze hanging over the sea, and at a range of ten miles the entire French coast from Le Harve to Cherbourg could be made out. Between those two points lay the five beaches, codenamed Utah, Omaha, Gold, Juno and Sword, where Allied ground forces had been landed only sixteen days before.

The Mitchells flew in five boxes of six machines each, twelve of them belonging to No. 320 Squadron. They included NO-K, seen in the painting, which was probably FV970. Despite the intensity of the defensive fire, only one of the high-explosive bombs dropped that summer evening by No. 332 Squadron failed to find its mark, falling outside the designated 'yellow' area. As the final aircraft delivered its load, the enemy sent up a crimson smoke-shell, signalling the guns to concentrate on the attackers as they re-formed, but the groundfire seemed to lose accuracy at this point and only a few bombers sustained minor damage. Among the crews only two air-gunners were wounded. However, the enemy suffered severely, the situation being summed up in the subsequent report, which claimed that the steelworks had been completely cleared of 'enemy grenadiers'.

Six days later the British 2nd Army crossed the River Odon, south-west of Caen. On 7 July the area was subjected to a night attack by 450 RAF heavy bombers, which saturated the defences and dropped 2,300 tons of high explosive. So deep were the bomb craters that they posed serious problems for the troops of the 2nd Army which were to take Caen on 9 July, having advanced some three miles under cover of darkness during the previous night, against fierce opposition. But now the enemy was attempting to repulse the attacking army without the advantage provided by the Mondeville steel factory, with its multitude of observation points. Small wonder that the 51st Highland Division was to send a signal of congratulation and thanks for a job well done. The professionalism of the accomplishment is illustrat-ed by the fact that an error of less than one per cent with British troops so close by could easily have resulted in a 'friendly fire' calamity of massive proportions.

As the invasion continued, carrying the victorious Allied armies into the heart of Europe, No. 320 Squadron changed bases frequently in support of the ground war. The initial move on to the continent was to Brussels/Melsbroek, but very soon the advance parties were penetrating into Germany itself. The squadron's first such move, on 29/30 April 1945, was followed by a second at the beginning of May to Achmer, where it remained until August.

Established on 1 June 1940 from a nucleus of Dutchmen who had elected to carry on the fight against Nazi Germany, No. 320 Squadron had not at first been a specialist tactical bombing squadron. Nonetheless, its first operational mission as a bomber unit, on 17 August 1943, had been an attack by five Mitchells on the railway marshalling yards at Calais; a precursor, perhaps, of what was to come. Assaults on special targets were originally performed by fighter aircraft engaged on 'Rhubarb' offen-sive sweeps, the first to be mounted by the RAF being undertaken by a pair of Spitfires which attacked targets of opportunity on the European coast on 20 December 1940. It was not until 10 January the following year that anything similar to No. 320 Squadron's historic mission was attempted and bombers were first used for 'Circus' operations. On that occasion six Bristol Blenheims, escorted by three squadrons of Spitfires and Hurricanes, made a daylight assault on the Pas de Calais area.

In the spirit of what had gone before, twelve of No. 320 Squadron's Mitchells were directed against railway marshalling yards once more, this time at Itzehoe, in Schleswig-Holstein, on 2 May 1945. One aircraft had to abort. Although no one knew it at the time, this was to be the Dutchmens' final offensive sortie, for on 2 August the squadron was disbanded and its personnel, so long fighting from foreign soils, were dispersed. Their motto had been *Animo libero dirigimus* (We are guided by the mind of liberty), and although No. 320 Squadron had existed for only five years and eight weeks, they had kept that motto well.

# Typhoons at Falaise

*Painting by Frank Wootton*
*Text by John Maynard*

DURING THE FIRST DAYS OF THE EARLY SUMMER OF 1944 the Hawker Typhoons stood parked alongside the landing grounds among the hedgerows of south-east England. Purposeful aircraft, deep chinned and wide tracked, they had the air of prize fighters waiting ready in the fields. Wild flowers and meadowgrass softened their belligerent lines and blurred the stacks of bombs and rockets, the scattering of tents, the vehicles and the bowsers that were all around. There was a stillness over the land, the weeks and months of preparation were clearly over, and the Typhoon pilots looked back on action-filled weeks attacking cross-channel targets such as port installations, railways, aerodromes, shipping and radar sites.

On the morning of 5 June, No. 164 Squadron had flown from Thorney Island to strike the coastal radars of St Valery with rockets and cannon fire, and now teams of groundcrew were painting wide black and white identification stripes around wings and fuselages. In the early evening two pilots flew across the Channel to the Cherbourg peninsula for a last reconnaissance, and returned full of excitement to tell of the sea congested with shipping on its way to France. That day eighteen squadrons of Typhoons were assembled within the RAF's Second Tactical Air Force, occupying the advanced airfields in the far south of England at Hurn, West Hampnett, Holmsley South, Thorney Island and Needs Oar Point. Total security had sealed off southern England, but local people moved fairly freely and the final preparations for D-day were watched by entranced schoolchildren and by elderly men who recalled their own experiences thirty years before in Picardy. At Tangmere, Air Vice Marshal Saunders, AOC 11 Group, gave his squadron commanders a last briefing and concluded: 'Gentlemen, you are all now on the brink of the greatest adventure of all, and I have no doubt as to the outcome of your part in it...' Early next morning twelve

squadrons of Typhoons began to attack the batteries and strongpoints behind Sword beach as the landing craft came in out of the grey dawn. The long hard battle for Normandy was beginning.

The Typhoon had been developed by Hawker Aircraft under the design leadership of Sydney Camm, creator of the Hurricane. However, while the Hurricane represented measured progress from the biplane era in terms of power and structure, the Typhoon was a radical new concept. Tough and heavy, it evidenced Camm's hallmark of great structural strength combined with heavy armament, and its new engine, the 2,100hp Napier Sabre, delivered almost twice the power of the Hurricane's Merlin. The Typhoon first flew, from Langley, just over a month after the outbreak of war in 1939. Its subsequent lengthy development programme was beset with difficulties, which more than once threatened the type's cancellation. In particular, the Sabre engine ran into serious early problems, but Napier persisted in its efforts to find solutions, encouraged by Lord Beaverbrook, Minister of Aircraft Production, who came close to staking his reputation on the outcome. Meanwhile, the aeroplane was also in trouble owing to a disappointing rate of climb, poor altitude performance, and finally tail flutter, which led to a number of fatal crashes when the whole tail unit detached in flight.

Despite these grave setbacks there was enough that was good about this rugged, fast and stable aeroplane to encourage the belief that it could be developed into a valuable and effective weapon. By early 1943 it had been operating as a low-level interceptor and fighter-bomber for some months, and had achieved significant if modest success during the Dieppe landings in August 1942. But it was in early 1943, when the Aeroplane and Armament Experimental Establishment at Boscombe Down perfected the 3in rocket projectile

with a 60lb warhead, that the Typhoon's enduring place in the history of warfare began to emerge. By the end of that year squadrons of Typhoons were flying low-level rocket strikes against the German defences on the coast of France and shipping in the Channel. Each aircraft could carry eight rockets, delivering firepower equivalent to a broadside from a cruiser in an apocalyptic nightmare of screaming, tearing noise and shattering explosions.

The small town of Falaise lies south of Caen, some 30 miles from the beaches where the Allied armies came ashore in Operation 'Overlord'. The selection of the Normandy coast as the assault threshold combined the element of surprise with the advantage of excellent beaches east and west of Arromanches. The Germans had assumed that the invasion would be mounted over the shortest possible sea crossing, and had accordingly concentrated their strongest defences and reserves in the Pas de Calais. Indeed, for a day or two after the Allied landings they continued to believe that these were a feint. Problems began for the Allies with the start of the advance inland. The country was criss-crossed by narrow lanes, thick hedgerows and dense copses in an undulating confined landscape reminiscent of Cornwall. It was unsuitable for the rapid movement of armour, and there was an urgent imperative to get clear of this so-called Bocage country if the momentum of the invasion was to be maintained. In fact, it was not until 25 July that the American Third Army, under the command of General Patton, broke out of the western side of the front and initiated a classic armoured advance which took him to the outskirts of Le Mans by 6 August.

Meanwhile, after the high ground of Mount Pincon had been secured by the 13th/18th Hussars, the British and Canadians started a slow and strongly opposed advance south from the eastern flank of the Normandy line. A few days earlier Hitler had decided to intervene in the development of the battle. He per-

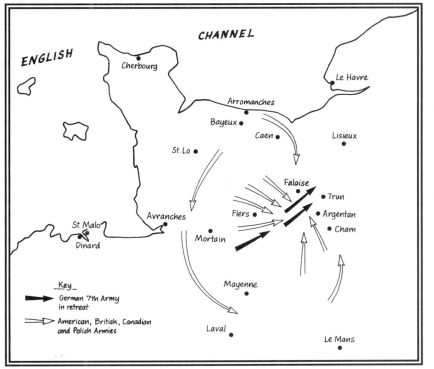

ceived that it might be possible to sever Patton's lines of communication by launching an attack in the direction of Montain, which he believed could force a way through to the sea at the base of the Cotentin peninsula. On 6 August the German Seventh Army began its advance.

The Typhoons had crossed the Channel to begin operations from landing grounds in Normandy from the end of June onwards. The airfield construction units

had performed near-miracles, carving out reasonable runways and dispersals across the coastal fields. At least air supremacy over the bridgehead was absolute, but the unhealthy accuracy of German artillery fire remained to be endured. Crossing from Hurn, No. 197 Squadron took up residence on airfield B.3 at St Croix, while No. 198 came over to B.10 at Plumetot and No. 174 Squadron left Holmsley South for B.6, near Camilly. This last unit had scarcely settled in before the Typhoons were pulled out to Bazenville, whence they put up 288 sorties before June ended. This was battlefield support with a vengeance, and the aircraft took off from the hastily levelled fields in great clouds of dust. Unsurprisingly, it was not long before the temperamental Sabre engines began to develop starting problems. Many aircraft had to return to England for engine changes, and there were hasty modifications to incorporate more effective filters in engine air intakes.

Landing grounds proliferated behind the front line. Coulombe and Martragny came into operation, and B.9 was levelled for the Canadians at Lantheuil. A Belgian, Squadron Leader Geerts, returned to the continent in command of No. 609 Squadron, which landed at Plumetot in early July and joined in the new 'Cab Rank' attack technique. This entailed the aircraft flying standing patrols which orbited the battle area, in touch with visual control points (VCPs) through VHF radio. The VCPs were RAF officers in tanks and reconnaissance vehicles who called down the rocket-firing aircraft to deal with enemy opposition such as dug-in tanks and gun emplacements. Very precise identification of targets and accurate map referencing by the exposed VCPs was conducive to a long life. The procedure came as near to perfection in close air support as was possible in July 1944, and the Typhoon squadrons' expertise and precision improved daily.

By nightfall on 7 August the enemy advance on Montain began to lose its momentum. The Americans mounted unceasingly ferocious counterattacks, and the intervention of aircraft striking at the German armoured columns was proving a crucial element in frustrating their plans. The Typhoons caught the long lines of tanks as they moved westward on the narrow roads, with few opportunities to disperse across open country. Within two days it was clear to Von Kluge that his attack had failed, but since permission to retreat was withheld by Berlin, the agonised General could only fight on and contemplate the gap behind his army closing as American, Canadian and British forces advanced towards each other from north and south, close by Falaise.

Throughout those hot, historic days of high summer the Typhoons excelled. For their pilots it was a new dimension in fighting experience. They even exchanged their Air Force Blue for khaki to avoid confusion with German field grey in the fluid proximity of battle. The dusty, makeshift airstrips were perhaps only ten minutes' flying time from the battlefield, leaving little time to adjust the gunsight, fine-tune rheostats, switch on the camera and select rocket salvo patterns before initiating an attack. At least there was little call for navigational finesse. The killing ground was marked by an acrid haze fed by more dense columns of billowing smoke. There was no opposition from the Luftwaffe, but the danger of collision in the crowded sky and the courageous flak gunners' accurate fire were ever-present perils.

The aircraft dived ever more steeply, jinking and skidding in early evasive action until the moment came for steady flight to draw the sight on to the target, hold it there and fire. Then there would be another second or

two to catch a glimpse of the missiles' smokey trails heading down until, stick hard back, the Typhoon was hauled skywards once again. Back at the landing ground there would be a queue of Typhoons in the circuit, another lining up at dispersal for rearming and, after every few trips, one for refuelling. The pilots remained strapped in the sweltering cockpits, debriefed by an intelligence officer on the wing root before leaving in a storm of noise and grit for another sortie through the hot, jolting low-level air to the Falaise battle.

The German withdrawal, finally agreed by Berlin, rapidly assumed the appearance of a rout as the Typhoon attacks were supplemented by a barrage of artillery firing from all round the shrinking perimeter into the chaos of the retreat. Nonetheless, elements of the German army fought with great courage as they struggled to break free of the trap and head north-east towards the Seine. Perhaps the saddest victims of the carnage were the horses on which the Wehrmacht continued to rely to haul its supply wagons. In the dreadful aftermath the bodies of men and animals were mingled with the shattered steel of the fighting vehicles and the burning wrecks of the transport. Through sheer fighting discipline, and urged on by the desperation of their position, some 30,000 Germans escaped to fight another day, but 50,000 dazed and terrified men surrendered and a further 10,000 lay dead in the fields and lanes of the gentle French countryside.

The German Chief of Staff later reported that, of the 2,300 tanks and self-propelled guns committed to battle in the aftermath of D-day, only just over 100 were pulled back from Falaise and across the Seine. The Normandy battle, perhaps the hardest and most vital of all in 1944, was over. Ahead of the Allies lay the fast, rolling plains of Northern France, and British tanks would enter Brussels on 3 September. Von Kluge, now under suspicion for complicity in the July plot to assas-

sinate Hitler, was summoned to Berlin by his mad and monstrous leader. Deeply ashamed of the fate that had befallen the Seventh Army, and anticipating the tragedy that would shortly befall his country, he killed himself during his journey home through France.

A year later, when peace had returned again to Europe, the Typhoons began to fly home. In ones and twos they landed at Lasham in Hampshire, and soon there were lines of them there. With their camouflage and insignia faded and Perspex discolouring, they stood like weary resting warriors awaiting fresh orders, new uniforms. But the breakers came, and soon there was scarcely one left in the length and breadth of England.

Frank Wootton completed his painting of the Falaise battlefield on 18 August 1944. In it, aircraft of No. 121 Wing, which comprised No. 174, 175 and 245 Squadrons, cross the smoke-stained sky. Below them lies evidence of the destruction of an army.

*The artist writes:* I was fortunate to be attached to a Typhoon Squadron during August 1944, one of the most exciting periods of the war. The German Army that had once driven all before it to occupy Holland, Denmark, Norway and France now turned away from the Allied forces that landed in Normandy on D-Day, 6 June. Rocket-firing Typhoons took a heavy toll of the retreating German forces, and the aircraft, flying in pairs, did not have far to fly to the target areas and so were busy throughout the daylight hours.

Alongside the airstrip where I worked, a school blackboard mounted on an easel gave the score of German tanks, armoured vehicles etc., in a deadly mounting tally, often several hundred a day. It brought to mind the well-known words of Nelson: 'It is warm work, and this day may be the last to any of us at a moment, but mark you, I would not be elsewhere for thousands.

# Tempest and the Flying Bomb

*Painting by Geoff Lea*
*Text by Ken Delve*

THIS UNUSUAL AND ATMOSPHERIC PAINTING BY Geoff Lea illustrates a period during the Second World War when Britain's home air forces were again thrown back on to the defensive, against a threat to which there was no ready answer or precedent to act upon. Barely one week after the momentous Allied invasion of Normandy, Germany opened a new age of warfare with one of the weapons with which it hoped to reverse the course of the war. In the typically poor light in which many interceptions were made, a Hawker Tempest fighter closes on the distinctive pulse-jet exhaust of the Doodlebug — the V1 Flying Bomb.

At 0418 in the morning on June 13 1944 the peace at Swanscombe, near Gravesend, Kent, was shattered by a fierce explosion. The first of Hitler's new 'terror' weapons had landed on English soil. Within an hour three more of these V1 flying bombs had come to earth, one crashing into a railway bridge at Grove Road, Bethnal Green, in London, and causing six deaths and a substantial amount of damage.

Almost a year earlier the Allies had established a reasonable intelligence assessment that such pilotless aircraft were at an advanced stage of development in Germany. Increased efforts were made to secure more detailed information, and by October it was reported that unexplained emplacements were being constructed in the Pas de Calais and Cherbourg areas. On 3 November good photographic reconnaissance imagery confirmed the presence of concrete platforms orientated on London. These were soon being referred to as 'ski sites' owing to their distinctive appearance. With the added intelligence that the test site at Peenemünde housed 'small aircraft', and that test firings had been observed, it became clear that the weapon would soon be ready for operational use. The defence planners realised that the programme had to be halted or, at the very least, delayed.

During the latter months of 1943 the destruction of elements of this new weapon assumed a high priority for all offensive aircraft. The heavy and medium bombers of Bomber Command and the American 8th Air Force were tasked against these 'Crossbow' targets, and also undertook missions against the development, production and storage centres. Meanwhile, the medium bombers and fighter-bombers of the American 9th Air Force and the 2nd Tactical Air Force (TAF) also attacked the ski sites. The ferocity of these combined offensive missions led to many delays in production, but it required a great bomber effort to achieve adequate results, and even then the hoped-for level of destruction was often not achieved.

It was evident that the weapon would eventually reach operational status, and that London would be on the receiving end. Thus, in December 1943 a series of studies were undertaken to determine the most effective air defence structure to protect the capital. It was very much a return to the early days of air defence, with a plan for three zones; fighter aircraft, anti-aircraft guns and balloons. However, the problem could not have arisen at a worse time, as the planning staffs were devoting time and resources to building the invasion force, and were reluctant to commit any additional aircraft and guns to the defensive scheme. Nevertheless, in the light of the increasing weight of intelligence that the attack would not be long delayed, and that an ever-increasing number of new launch sites were being discovered, it was clear that resources would have to be devoted to the scheme.

The revised 'Diver' plan of February 1944 called for eight day-fighter squadrons, plus a number of night fighter units, but for a lower total of anti-aircraft guns. Civil Defence plans were revised and evacuation plans dusted off ready for implementation if required. The bombing campaign continued, but it could not destroy

the ever-increasing number of launch ramps. It was now only a matter of time until the first bombs arrived, and only then would the validity of the defensive concepts be tested.

In the 24-hour period from 2230 on 15 June to 16 June 1944, British records show 151 reported launches, with 144 V-1s crossing the English coast. Of those, 73 reached the London area. The defences notched up only a modest score, seven falling to the fighters, fourteen to the guns and one shared. A further eleven were shot down by the guns of the Inner Artillery Zone. The Hawker Tempests of No. 150 Wing at Newchurch had been at readiness for defensive patrol since dawn on 15 June. Early the following day the Wing Leader, Wing Commander Roland Beamont, and his No.2 were airborne on such a patrol when they sighted a V1. Giving chase, the fighters were eventually able to carry out an attack and Beamont scored his first flying-bomb kill, the missile crashing near Faversham.

Overall, however, it was an inauspicious start. Too many bombs had reached the London area, but there was no simple solution to the problem. The V1, spanning a little over 17½ft, made a very small target, and it flew fast (300–400mph) and low. One first had to find this small target; then came the challenge of actually shooting it down. The official RAF account of the campaign summarised the speed problem: 'as for the fighters, the short time in which interception had to be made, demanded that they should be quickly and accurately directed on to the course of the bomb'.

Many of the coastal radar stations had been modified to improve their chances of tracking the V1s, and the ground controlled interception (GCI) principle remained the primary operational mode, all 'Diver' operations, as they were known, being controlled through the Biggin Hill sector operations room. A good radar set-up often meant the difference between success

and failure. However, the pilot still had to acquire the target visually to make the kill. In certain light conditions the bomb's pulse-jet motor was a real give-away, making the bomb visible from a long way off. At other times it was almost impossible to pick up.

Although No. 501 Squadron was the last of the Tempest units to enter the campaign, it became one of the most significant. By 29 July the squadron had received its full complement of Tempest Vs, and was taken off operations to carry out intensive training in 'Diver' techniques, but was tasked to specialise in the night role. The squadron moved to Manston on 2 August to cover the area from the Kent coast to the North Downs. Its new commanding officer was Squadron Leader Joe Berry, already a V1 ace from his service with No. 3 Squadron, the top-scoring squadron of No. 150 Wing.

The first kill went to Flying Officer Bill Polley in Tempest EJ585 on 5 August. He later recalled some of the problems of attacking these weapons:

'Very often we were too close to our targets before we got the opportunity to fire, and the big danger was getting an airburst. On one occasion I was chasing a V1 too quickly and I knew that I was overhauling the bomb too quickly and that I was very close to the armoured balloons. I fired a long burst and pulled up steeply to starboard, almost above the V1, just as it exploded. The blast caught my left wing and tumbled the aircraft in a series of snap rolls. After what seemed an eternity the aircraft regained its stability ... As my gyros had tumbled it was many ageing moments before I realised that I was upside down.'

This passage highlights a number of problems faced by the fighter pilots. Each Fieseler Fi 103 flying bomb carried a warhead containing 1,870lb of high explosive, and this produced a huge debris hemisphere when it exploded in mid-air. It was very likely to cause

fatal damage to any aircraft that was too close. There are numerous recorded incidents of aircraft receiving severe damage after flying through the debris, and others in which the pilot did not survive to tell his story. Two aspects caused pilots to open fire on their targets within this lethal range. Firstly, the small size of the flying bomb made judgement of distance tricky, especially in poor light, when the gunsight could not be used with the target wingspan setting; secondly, the bombs could take a surprising amount of damage without being destroyed, so pilots closed the range to ensure destruction. The other aspect highlighted by Bill Polley is that of confliction with other elements of the defensive scheme. In the very early days of the campaign the squadrons of No. 150 Wing complained of being fired at by the anti-aircraft guns, while the gunners complained that the fighters had strayed into the gun zones. No doubt both were correct. The balloons did not complain, but they were lethal to friend and foe alike.

Joe Berry made his stance very clear. 'The squadron must consider itself expendable, and thus will take off and try to effect interception in every weather condition ... even though all other squadrons are grounded.' It was very much an all-weather, day and night campaign for the V1s, so the defences had to make a suitable response. Although the single-seat squadrons, especially No. 501, flew many night missions, it must also be remembered that the Mosquito units were active during the night hours, using Airborne Interception (AI) radar to locate their targets. The Tempest pilots flew along set patrol lines, the ends of which were marked by searchlights, and each patrol lasted some two hours. The sector controller provided positions of target and fighter, with the aim of putting the latter in an advantageous position to achieve a kill.

The Tempest V, with its Napier Sabre engine giving it a top speed of around 440mph, did have a performance margin over the bomb. The squadron received a number of aircraft in polished, bare-metal finish, the reduction in weight and drag giving a few more precious miles per hour. Aircraft were also stripped of non-essential equipment; all very reminiscent of the efforts to give the Home Defence B.E.2c of 1916 a fair chance of getting at the Zeppelins.

The first phase of the flying-bomb campaign ended on 1 September 1944, with the Allied capture of those launching sites within range of London. Although the campaign never returned with the same intensity, from 4 September to 14 January 1945 the City was subjected to attack by V1s launched from Heinkel He 111 mother aircraft over the North Sea. Defensive patrols remained in force, but there was even less warning of attack, so the ideal solution was to destroy the parent aircraft before they launched their weapons. As part of this revised policy, No. 510 Squadron moved to Bradwell Bay on 22 September.

The final element of the V1 story lasted from 3 to 29 March 1945, with the weapons being used against the advancing ground forces in Holland.

In the overall campaign the Germans launched some 9,252 flying bombs, of which just under 5,900 crossed the English coast and 2,563 reached the London area. The defences claimed 4,262 destroyed, a very respectable 72.3 per cent of those that crossed into England. The threat posed by the V1 was enormous, and it was a weapon the like of which no-one had seen before. That the defences were able to react so quickly and so effectively is a tribute to all concerned.

# Dakotas at Arnhem

*Painting by Michael Turner*
*Text by Tony Mason*

IN 1980 A DISTINGUISHED PARATROOP OFFICER, Major General John Frost, who 36 years previously had commanded the 2nd Battalion The Parachute Regiment at Arnhem, compared airborne operations with ' normal' army land warfare. He said: 'It obviously takes time for anyone to adjust to different circumstances, and one of the greatest was the realisation of utter dependence on another service in the shape of the RAF'. Michael Turner's painting depicts RAF Dakotas flying over the glider landing ground at low level, dropping supplies to the beleaguered British airborne forces at Arnhem in September 1944. Wreckage and Horsa gliders are scattered beneath the Dakotas, which face the full fury of German flak. The picture evokes one of the most heroic and tragic operations mounted by the British armed forces in the Second World War.

Market Garden was the codename of the plan to drop three and a half divisions, approximately 35,000 men, of the First Allied Airborne Army behind German lines over two and a half days to seize nine bridges over the Maas, Waal and Ijssel (lower Rhine) rivers. Thereby, they would outflank the main German frontier defences, establish a bridgehead over the Rhine, accelerate access to the V1 flying-bomb launch sites in Holland and open the way for a thrust deep into the heart of Germany. The 82nd and 101st American airborne divisions were to attack the southern bridges, while the 1st British Airborne Division was to be dropped at the furthest point from Allied ground forces, at Arnhem. Meanwhile, XXX Corps of the British 21st Army Group was to advance the 64 miles northwards to Arnhem through a corridor including the bridges to be taken by the US troops. It was widely hoped that a successful operation would bring the war in Europe to an end before January 1945.

The plan depended for its success on the ability of the lightly armed airborne forces to seize their objectives and be relieved and reinforced by XXX Corps within two or three days. In the meantime the airborne troops would be dependent on Allied air forces for their delivery, their resupply and, to offset their own lack of heavy weapons, close air support.

The airlift was provided by Nos.38 and 46 Groups of the RAF and the US 9th Troop Carrier Command. While No.38 Group comprised 240 Short Stirlings, Armstrong Whitworth Albemarles and Handley Page Halifaxes, No.46 Group had 279 Douglas C-47 Dakotas. The great majority of these aircraft were allocated to Arnhem, with 1,053 US Dakotas largely supporting the southerly Eindhoven and Nijmegen sectors. In planning the operation, considerable attention was paid to the vulnerability of large formations of glider tugs and transports flying at 100-150mph and at heights between 500 and 2,500ft over enemy-occupied territory.

The strength of the Luftwaffe day fighters had dwindled during 1944. On the other hand, the night fighter force was still formidable. At such heights and speeds, however, the transports were particularly vulnerable to anti-aircraft artillery. Many of these guns were radar laid and therefore equally effective at night. Indeed, there was some concern that flak would be a greater threat to the operation than opposition on the ground. In the event, there would be no moon for the period planned for the operation, a factor which reinforced the decision to mount both delivery and resupply flights by daylight. Protection of the transport force would be shared between a number of commands and roles. Bomber Command would attack Luftwaffe fighter airfields and local flak positions before the first tows and drops on 'D' day, 17 September. Aircraft of the US 8th and 9th Air Forces and RAF Air Defence of Great Britain (ADGB) would provide escort and flak suppression along the routes to the drop zone areas. The Sec-

ond Tactical Air Force RAF (2nd TAF) was to attack ground targets in the dropping/landing zone areas immediately before the arrival of the transport aircraft.

The initial phase of the airborne assault was very successful. By the end of the first day not one RAF transport aircraft had been lost and the great majority of troops had been delivered accurately and safely to their correct zones. No fewer than 1,113 bomber and 1,240 fighter sorties were flown in support. Unfortunately, intelligence about the strength and disposition of the German forces on the ground proved to be very inaccurate, and the British paratroops came under heavy fire from the outset, which prevented them reaching their objectives in the town. On 18 September, the second day, the remainder of the 1st Airborne Division was delivered by 458 aircraft and 296 gliders, again with a high level of accuracy and safety. There was, however, a significant increase in flak density, and the first supply drop by Stirlings from between 500 and 1,000ft was also opposed by machine-gun and small-arms fire. Nonetheless, only four transport aircraft and 34 gliders were lost from the entire Allied force flying to all three river areas.

By Tuesday 19 September, however, the Arnhem operation was not going according to plan. Bad weather delayed the arrival of the Polish brigade, and a breakdown in communications between the 1st Airborne Division and Army headquarters obscured the serious situation developing on the ground. The Germans continued to reinforce their flak batteries along the transport aircraft approaches and ground dropping zones (DZs).

The first large-scale resupply run took place during the Tuesday afternoon, when 145 Dakotas and Stirlings dropped their loads accurately on Dropping Zone 'V', a clearing on the edge of woods near Lichtenbeek on the north-eastern outskirts of Arnhem. This was the

arena for an heroic action that earned a Victoria Cross, and was probably witnessed by more people than any other deed that won an RAF award. As the stream of aircraft lumbered over the dropping zone, German anti-aircraft, machine-gun and small-arms fire engulfed

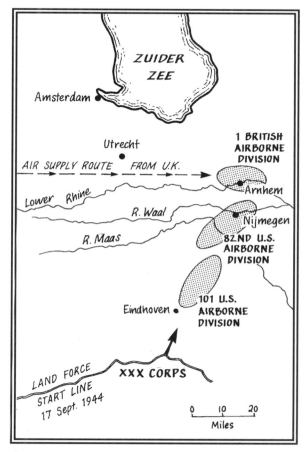

them from every angle. Five Dakotas and ten Stirlings were shot down in the course of the afternoon, but fortunately many were able to crash-land back over friendly territory or the crews had time to bale out. One Dakota was already on fire and gradually losing height when it began its run over DZ 'V'. Major General

Urquhart, commanding the troops below, later described what happened next:

'At the end of the run, the Dakota turned and made a second run to drop the remaining supplies. From foxholes and slit trenches and from the restricted spaces to which we were trying to attract the pilots: from blasted buildings and ditches and emplacements and rubble and earth, the eyes of hundreds and probably thousands of careworn soldiers gazed upwards through the battle haze. We were spellbound and speechless, and I daresay there is not a survivor of Arnhem who will ever forget, or want to forget, the courage we were privileged to witness in those terrible eight minutes ... We saw the machine crashing in flames as one of its wings collapsed, and we did not know that Lord had ordered his crew to abandon while making no effort to leave himself. There was one survivor.'

The survivor, Flying Officer H. A. King, was flung out of the stricken aeroplane as it broke up while he was helping two Royal Army Service Corps despatchers don their parachutes. The pilot, Flight Lieutenant David Lord of No. 271 Squadron, was posthumously awarded the Victoria Cross 'in recognition of most conspicuous bravery'. His citation described his decisions; first to continue to the DZ after being twice hit by flak, then, despite being singled out by the fire of all the guns around the DZ, he made a second run to drop two remaining containers. Finally, he ordered his crew to abandon the Dakota while he continued to battle with the controls of his crippled, burning aircraft. His citation concludes:

'By continuing his mission in a damaged and burning aircraft, descending to drop the supplies accurately, returning to the dropping zone a second time and, finally, remaining at the controls to give his crew a chance to escape, Flight Lieutenant Lord displayed supreme valour and self-sacrifice.'

The desperate tragedy of this sacrifice, and of all those other RAF and RASC colleagues who died in the drop over DZ 'V', was that the supplies were received not by the paratroops, but by the German defenders, who collected almost all of the vital loads. No message about the DZ had got back from Arnhem to HQ for relay to Nos.38 and 46 Groups, and there was no radio link between the troops on the ground and the aircraft overhead.

Well within support range, the Spitfires and Typhoons of 2nd TAF sat on their airfields awaiting the signal to mount flak suppression and close-air-support attacks. It never came because of a planning decision that 2nd TAF aircraft should not operate in the battle area when USAAF and UK-based RAF fighters were escorting the transports, so as to avoid collisions and losses to friendly fire. But on this occasion, partly because of a communication failure which produced a missed rendezvous with USAAF escort and flak suppressing fighters, and partly because of low cloud and thick haze, the transports had no escort. The German gunners were quick to realise that they had an unrestricted shoot. The absence of Allied air cover was also recognised by the Luftwaffe, which further disconcerted the British and Polish troops by mounting low-level strafing attacks by Bf 109s and Fw 190s.

Later on 19 September, information on the increasingly desperate ground situation reached HQ in England, together with news that XXX Corps was not achieving its planned progress. The 1st Airborne Division would therefore need resupplying for two more days at least. The disastrous mission to DZ 'V' would have to be reflown and further drops made. In the event, the resupply flights continued until 25 September. Enemy flak increased as the paratroops' defensive perimeter contracted. One DZ was overrun before the drop on 20 September, and another was attacked so heavily that few of the containers could be recovered.

On 21 September it was decided to reduce the mounting losses from flak by despatching the transports in four waves instead of a continuous stream. Unfortunately bad weather at fighter bases in Britain reduced the escorts for the first two waves and eliminated them completely from the last two. No message reached 2nd TAF, whose aircraft, according to plan, remained grounded. The transports were savaged by enemy fighters and flak. Sixty-one Stirlings and Dakotas were lost; 51 per cent of the day's transport force.

On 23 September, No. 575 Squadron, with Dakotas, was deployed to Brussels to work directly under No. 83 Group and 2nd TAF. This tighter control immediately produced a more satisfactory level of fighter escort. Also on that day, the last resupply mission was flown from England. Eight of 123 transports were lost to flak, ground marking was disrupted by enemy fire, visual signals were corrupted by German decoys and less than a third of the supplies reached British troops. The last drop, by No. 575 Squadron, was made on the afternoon of 25 September, and the evacuation of the remnants of the ground forces from Arnhem was completed by 0600 the following morning.

The total cost of 'Market Garden' to the RAF was 74 transport aircraft from Nos. 38 and 46 Groups, 32 fighter-bombers from 2nd TAF, 16 fighters from ADGB and 2 bombers from Bomber Command. The USAAF lost 52 transports, 86 fighters and 16 bombers. A total of 150 RAF aircrew, 116 RASC air despatchers and 228 glider pilots lost their lives. In addition, of 24 RAF ground radar men on the Light Warning Unit detachment to Arnhem, nine were killed, eleven wounded and taken prisoner, and four escaped.

The disastrous outcome of the Arnhem plan has been widely recorded. German army opposition was much stronger than expected, and the relieving XXX Corps did not reach the region before the remnants of the British Airborne Division and the Polish Parachute Brigade were compelled to withdraw after nine days of bitter fighting. Of some 10,000 men who were flown into Arnhem, more than 7,500 were killed, wounded, missing or taken prisoner.

The airlift had not been able to sustain the heavily outnumbered and outgunned airborne forces; nor had it even been intended that it should. But it helped to prolong resistance, and its aircrew matched the valour of their colleagues on the ground. The losses were not in vain. Many lessons were learned which were applied to the final large-scale airborne operation of the war, the Rhine crossing in March 1945.

# Phoenix Over Rangoon

*Painting by Mark Postlethwaite*
*Text by Michael Armitage*

FOR THE ALLIES, THE WAR IN THE FAR EAST HAD started as disastrously in Burma as it had across the whole region. When the Japanese invaded Burma only 37 British and American first-line combat aircraft, Brewster Buffaloes and Curtiss P-40s, were available to counter a Japanese air strength of about 400 machines. Reinforcements of Blenheim bombers and Hurricane fighters joined the tiny Allied force in the weeks that followed, but despite the very gallant efforts of the heavily outnumbered aircrew, the result was never in real doubt. By the end of March 1942 the Allied air force in Burma had been virtually wiped out, while on land the Japanese Army swiftly advanced through the country and soon stood close to the Indian border. Here, after very severe losses during the long retreat, the line was finally stabilised.

But the Japanese attacks had barely started, and the threat to India and to our command of the Indian Ocean, with its supply route to Egypt and North Africa, caused such reinforcements as could be spared to be rushed from the Middle East. One of the units so redeployed was No. 30 Squadron, which arrived in Colombo on 6 March 1942 with its Hurricane Mk. IIBs. It was a very timely reinforcement. On Easter Sunday, 5 April, a strong Japanese carrier task force was making its way north-west through the Indian Ocean and nearing Ceylon. About fifty Japanese Navy Type 99 bombers flew off and attacked shipping and the docks of Colombo; but, together with No. 258 Squadron and a handful of Fulmars of the Fleet Air Arm, the Hurricanes of No. 30 Squadron were waiting for them. The 36 defending aircraft managed to destroy 18 of the attackers for the loss of 15 Hurricanes and 4 Fulmars. Over the following four days, further Japanese raids were carried out, during which 15 of the attackers were shot down for the loss of another 8 Hurricanes and 3 Fulmars. For No. 30 Squadron it had

been a very bloody introduction to the Far Eastern theatre of war, and during the Japanese assault the Royal Navy suffered heavy losses, including the sinking of the aircraft carrier HMS *Hermes*.

For the Japanese, however, the loss of so many experienced pilots was also very serious. Three of their aircraft carriers were now forced to return to Japan to renew their complement of aircrew and aircraft, which meant that only two of the five carriers in the fleet were available to take part in the critical Battle of the Coral Sea. Meanwhile No. 30 Squadron was brought up to strength, and it remained in Ceylon in the air defence role until late January 1944, when it moved forward to Fazilpur in Arakan.

During the following four months No. 30 Squadron flew 931 operational sorties over Burma, most of them escorting the air supply sorties that played so vital a role in sustaining the troops of the 14th Army during their desperate battles in the jungle. On 24 May the squadron moved to Yellahanka near Bangalore to re-equip with P-47 Thunderbolts, returning to operations with these aircraft on 16 October.

Gradually the strength of the British forces in the region was rebuilt, and, despite the pressing demands of the other theatres of war, RAF reinforcements began to arrive. By June 1942 there were 26 squadrons, and by June 1944 South East Asia Air Command held something like 88 squadrons of the RAF, the Indian Air Force and the USAAF. With forces of this size, and with the Japanese badly stretched all across South East Asia, the Allies had taken the offensive. In Burma this included air attacks on Japanese targets, mainly, though not only, in support of Allied ground forces.

Some of the attacks were launched against more distant targets in Burma. These included heavy air assaults against targets in the Rangoon area on 3 and 4 November 1944, in Operation 'Eruption'. On those

two days, 49 Boeing Superfortresses and 29 Consolidated Liberators, escorted by 125 Lockheed Lightnings and Republic Thunderbolts, took part in the raids. Four of the Thunderbolts in those raids form the main subject of Mark Postlethwaite's painting.

The Republic P-47 Thunderbolt was the largest and heaviest single-engined single-seater built during the Second World War. It had been designed around the most powerful engine available at the time of its conception, the 2,000hp Pratt & Whitney R-2800 Double Wasp two-row radial. The prototype Thunderbolt first flew in May 1941, and the aircraft went into service in early 1943 with the US 8th Air Force, based in Britain. A development, the P-47D, soon followed the original P-47A and P-47B models, and it was this machine, known as the Thunderbolt II in RAF service, that equipped No. 30 Squadron in the Far East. The Thunderbolt had a top speed of 427mph at 30,078ft, a ceiling of 42,105ft and a range of over 1,400 miles with drop-tanks, a very valuable asset in the Burma theatre. It was armed with eight 0.5in machine-guns in the wings, and could carry a 2,000lb bomb load. These features made it a formidable aircraft in both the fighter and ground-attack roles. All told, over 15,000 Thunderbolts of all marks were built, 830 of them entering service with the RAF, with whom they served only in the Far East, where sixteen squadrons were so equipped. All of these were withdrawn soon after the end of the war.

In the raid of 4 November, depicted in the painting, a small force of Thunderbolt IIs belonging to No. 30 Squadron, each carrying two 137gal drop-tanks, made a rendezvous with Liberator bombers of Nos. 215, 355 and 356 Squadrons of the RAF. The fighters escorted the bombers to Rangoon, more than 400 miles from Cox's Bazaar, from where they had taken off. The bombers made an accurate attack on the heavy railway

workshop at Insein, just to the north of Rangoon. The Liberators are seen on their bombing run, flying on a south-easterly heading with bombs bursting on Insein in the northern outskirts of the city.

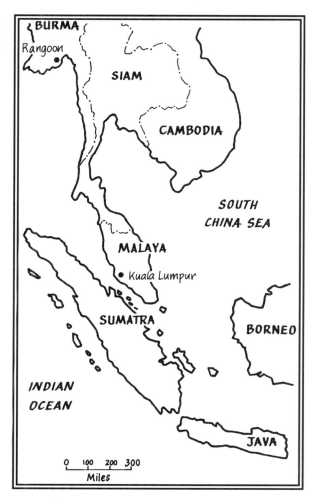

The Japanese had accurate height-finding radar, but co-ordination with their anti-aircraft artillery was known to be slow. During bombing attacks the Liberators therefore often made a sharp descent of several hun-

dred feet before starting their bombing run, leaving the flak bursting above them. During this raid the formation was attacked by a number of Japanese Nakajima Ki-44 Army Type 2 fighters, given the Allied codename 'Tojo'. These machines had a maximum speed of 383mph at 17,400ft, and carried two 7.7mm machine-guns firing through the propeller arc and one 0.5in machine-gun in each wing; they were therefore outclassed by the Thunderbolts.

In the painting the Thunderbolts have dropped their long-range tanks and are engaging the Japanese fighters. The aircraft RS-W of No. 30 Squadron is flown by Flight Lieutenant Harry Whidborne DFC, Red Leader, who shot down one of the Tojos. Another was damaged. Red 2 was flown by Pilot Officer Don Smith, Red 3 was flown by Flight Lieutenant Tom Pulford, and Red 4 by Flight Sergeant John Pyman.

Taking the results of the two raids on 2 and 4 November together, not only was Burma's only heavy railway workshop destroyed, but four Japanese aircraft were destroyed, five more probably destroyed and twelve more were claimed as damaged. Allied losses, none of which were caused by enemy action, were one Superfortress and three Thunderbolts. One of the Thunderbolts was a No. 30 Squadron machine which suffered mechanical failure. The pilot baled out, was picked up by the Japanese and survived the war as a POW.

*The artist writes:* This painting, like the Wapiti painting earlier in the book, was produced on behalf of the 30 Squadron Association for their Annual Reunion.

The good thing about working with a squadron association is that there is a ready supply of research material and eyewitnesses to help produce a totally accurate picture, and so it was with this one. The chairman of the association, who was always most helpful with research, had actually flown on the operation to be depicted, and so provided more than enough first-hand information from which to work.

The composition itself was very difficult, as I was tasked to show not just the Thunderbolts, but also the Liberators they were escorting, *plus* the Tojos they were intercepting, *plus* the docks they were attacking!

All of these had to be following the actual courses flown by the aircraft on the day, and it just so happened that the aircraft were over a very visible Rangoon at the time!

When the painting was completed, photos of it were sent around the world to the respective pilots involved. Eventually the answers came back, expressing much admiration but suggesting that I made Rangoon look more like a city and less like a small village! I subsequently embarked on a massive redevelopment scheme for my Rangoon 'village', and the final result can be seen here.

# 617 Squadron Sink the Tirpitz

*Painting by Gerald Coulson*
*Text by Tony Mason*

GERALD COULSON HERE PORTRAYS THE ACTION over Tromsö Fjord in Norway on Sunday morning, 12 November 1944. A Lancaster from No. 617 Squadron is releasing a 12,000lb Tallboy bomb on to the stricken German battleship *Tirpitz*, already hit by a previous bomber in the stream. *Tirpitz* is about to be removed from the German Naval Order of Battle for good, to the considerable relief of the Royal Navy.

The 50,000-ton *Tirpitz*, sistership of the *Bismarck*, was planned to be the second of eight battleships for the German navy in the years leading up to the Second World War. She was armed with eight 15in guns, twelve 5.9in guns, sixteen 105mm and sixteen 37mm anti-aircraft guns and 12 Oerlikon cannon. By the time she was moored in Tromsö Fjord she had been fitted with a further 40 20mm AA guns. She had been designed to carry no fewer than four Arado floatplanes, and despite being heavily armoured she had a maximum speed of 30kt. Launched at Wilhelmshaven in April 1939, *Tirpitz* became an immediate concern to the Royal Navy because of her potential threat to Allied shipping in the Atlantic and northern waters. Consequently, many RAF sorties were launched against the port facilities at Wilhelmshaven, though without success. In early 1942 she slipped northwards to Trondheim Fjord, where she was attacked four more times by RAF Bomber Command. Thirteen aircraft were lost without any hits being scored on the battleship.

In March 1942 *Tirpitz* escaped a torpedo attack by aircraft from HMS *Victorious* after the battleship had sought to intercept convoy PQ12 on its way to Murmansk. In July 1942 the mere possibility that *Tirpitz* was at sea, together with the pocket battleship *Von Scheer* and the cruiser *Hipper*, caused Britain's First Sea Lord, Sir Dudley Pound, to order the covering warships of convoy PQ17 to withdraw and the convoy to scatter.

Thereupon German aircraft and submarines sank 20 of the 32 hapless merchantmen.

As long as *Tirpitz* was able to lurk undamaged in the Norwegian Fjords a repetition of the PQ17 disaster remained an unpleasant possibility. As a single ship she comprised what naval strategists referred to as a 'fleet in being', and compelled the continuous presence in northern waters of at least one RN battleship and one Fleet aircraft carrier. Even then, there was doubt as to the ability of these forces to bring *Tirpitz* to a speedy end. That judgement was well founded in the light of the toll taken by *Tirpitz*' sistership *Bismarck* in May 1941 before, with great difficulty and only after being disabled, she was sunk by two British battleships.

In March 1943 *Tirpitz* moved further north, just south of the North Cape, to the inlet fjord of Kaa, north of Alta. She was now beyond the range of land-based British bombers, but still dangerously poised alongside the Allied Arctic convoy route. There she was attacked by British midget submarines and put out of action for several months, but by March 1944 she was once again operational and as a result came under attack by Fleet Air Arm Fairey Barracudas, which inflicted further heavy damage. Again the battleship was repaired, and yet again she moved out on sea trials. Further Fleet Air Arm attacks in August had only limited success, and cost eleven aircraft. It was time for the RAF to take over.

By 1944 Bomber Command's ability to reach, locate and destroy specific targets had greatly improved over its limited abilities of 1941. On 8 February 1944 a new bomb, the 12,000lb Tallboy, had been dropped for the first time by Lancasters of 617 Squadron, on an aero engine factory at Limoges. The bomb had been designed by Barnes Wallis and developed during 1943. Its perfect ballistic shape induced a very high terminal velocity, and it possessed the explosive force of a high-capacity blast bomb together with the penetrative power of an armour-

piercing weapon. Not surprisingly it was known as the 'earthquake' bomb. By September 1944 both Nos. 617 and 9 Squadrons of Bomber Command were equipped to deliver the Tallboy, and it was decided to use it against *Tirpitz*. As Kaa Fjord was beyond the combat radius of Lancasters based in Britain, arrangements were made for the bombers to use the Russian base at Yagodnik, near Archangel. On 15 September, 27 Lancasters drawn from both squadrons took off from Yagodnik, 21 carrying 12,000lb Tallboys and six with 'Johnny Walker' 4,000lb anti-shipping direct attack mines.

After several months' experience of concealment in the Norwegian fjords, the *Tirpitz* had perfected a comprehensive anti-aircraft defence. Early-warning radar stations and picket ships warned of imminent attack. The surrounding mountain slopes were heavily studded with guns and the steep, narrow sides of the fjord further complicated bombing runs. The ship was camouflaged by netting, and could be totally obscured within ten minutes by oily smoke generated from pots on the adjacent shorelines. Furthermore, the whole area was frequently obscured by low cloud.

Nevertheless, the combined force of seventeen Lancasters from No. 617 Squadron and ten from No. 9 Squadron took the battleship by surprise. Before the smokescreen could obscure the *Tirpitz* five Tallboys were dropped. Thereafter, and despite intense flak, the bomber stream continued the attack using the battleship's own gun flashes as the aiming point. Almost immediately afterwards, low cloud began to cover the fjord, and no photographic confirmation of the result of the attack could be obtained. Even five days later, marginal photographic evidence suggested that the ship had been hit, but the extent of the damage could not be determined.

Despite navigational problems in locating Yagodnik airfield on the outward journey, and heavy AA fire

during the attack itself, the only fatalities in the entire operation occurred when one of the Lancasters flew into high ground while returning from Yagodnik to the UK.

But still *Tirpitz* survived. As the smokescreen began to envelop the ship two hits were claimed, one by No. 9

Squadron and one by 617. Others were thought possible later in the attack. It was not known at the time that one Tallboy had inflicted severe damage on the battleship. A hole 32ft by 48ft had been ripped in her bow, flooding the forward compartments and rendering it too difficult this time to repair her for operations. The German high command therefore decided to use her guns as part of the coastal defences in Norway, and in October 1944 she limped down the Norwegian coast to Tromsö Fjord. Two

days later, on 18 October, she was spotted, together with a flak ship and three destroyers, by Firefly aircraft from HMS *Implacable*.

The extent of her damage was not known in Britain. It looked as though she had moved south, beyond the range of Russian forces then advancing across northern Finland, and she was thought to remain a threat to Allied convoys. Now, however, there was one vital change in the operational situation. The battleship's move had brought her just within Lancaster range from RAF bases in northern Scotland, and Nos. 9 and 617 Squadrons were tasked with finishing the job they had begun a month before.

On 29 October a joint force of nineteen Lancasters reached Tromsö Fjord, only to be thwarted by low cloud. The ship was struck again, suffering damage to her stern, but photographic reconnaissance disclosed that she remained afloat. Indeed, she accounted for another Lancaster, which, damaged by flak, crash-landed in Sweden without loss of life.

On 5 November another attack was aborted because of bad weather. From 26 November perpetual Arctic darkness would settle over Tromsö, precluding any further daylight attacks until early 1945. Darkness, of course, would not have impeded the *Tirpitz*, had she been seaworthy. The regional weather forecast for Sunday 12 November, however, was fine and clear.

In the early hours of 12 November, fourteen Lancasters of 9 Squadron and eighteen from No. 671 prepared for take-off from RAF Lossiemouth. They all carried Tallboys. The round trip to Tromsö was 2,252 miles. New Merlin 24 engines had been fitted to all of the Lancasters to increase their power, and each had a Wellington long-range fuel tank installed its fuselage and carried a Mosquito drop tank. To reduce weight still further, the mid-upper gun turret and the armour plating protecting the pilot were removed, and the ammunition stocks greatly reduced.

At 0300 the stream began to take off. One Lancaster of No. 9 Squadron was unable to get airborne because of icing, but the first aircraft, flown by Wing Commander J. B. Tait, already awarded the DSO and two bars and the DFC and bar, and leading No. 617 Squadron, arrived over the Fjord 5hr 40min later.

RAF electronic reconnaissance had previously identified the extent of German radar cover in the area. The Lancasters exploited a gap, flying at 1,500ft eastwards towards the Swedish border before turning north towards Tromsö. Despite this, their presence was detected at about 0715 UK time, but the Germans appear to have been uncertain about the bombers' objectives because of their heading well to the south of Tromsö. Consequently, *Tirpitz* did not request air cover until 0755.

The nearest air base was Bardufoss, less than 50 miles away from Tromsö and the home of the Luftwaffe's Jagdgeschwader 5, equipped with Focke-Wulf Fw 190s and commanded by Major Heinrich Ehrler, who already had 204 kills to his credit and had been decorated with the Knight's Cross with Swords and Oakleaves.

There was no co-ordinated air defence between the German navy and the Luftwaffe. Hitherto, the combination of camouflage, smokescreen and AA guns had been considered adequate protection for the *Tirpitz*. Now, however, after the crippling air attack in September, help was sought from the fighters.

The threat posed by the eighteen Fw 190s of JG 5 was very grave. With reduced armament and armour, flying at 185kt and with their manoeuvrability constrained by the 12,000lb Tallboys, the 31 Lancasters were exceptionally vulnerable in broad daylight, and in completely clear skies. Not for the first time, nor the

last, would an air operation be crucially affected by communications. The Fw 190s scrambled from Bardufoss to protect the last remaining German battleship, but they headed not for Tromsö but for Kaa Fjord, the previous hiding place of *Tirpitz*. The German unit had not been informed of the battleship's move south the previous month. Moreover, there was obviously no communication between the ground radars and the fighters, because they could not find either the battleship or the Lancasters.

Oblivious to the threat fast receding to the north, the bombers flew once more into the curtain of flak surrounding the battleship. This time, however, it was far less intense and accurate, perhaps reflecting the relatively short time the Germans had had to co-ordinate ship and shore batteries. No smokescreen was thrown up, either.

The *Tirpitz* was doomed. In less than ten minutes 28 Tallboys were dropped, several scoring direct hits or very near misses. Three minutes after the first hit at 0842, the battleship began to list heavily to port. At 0852 a gun turret was blown completely off as the magazine below it exploded, tearing a hole 120ft high from deck to keel. The ship slowly rolled through 140°, completely turning turtle with her superstructure embedded in the bottom of the fjord. One Lancaster was severely damaged by flak but, like its predecessor on 29 October, it was able to crash-land safely in Sweden. There were no other RAF casualties.

Although the entire attack was witnessed and photographed by a Lancaster of No. 432 Squadron, it was so concentrated that it was impossible to say exactly which aircraft, from which squadron, dropped the bomb that administered the *coup de grâce*. The first direct hit was probably achieved by Wing Commander Tait's Lancaster; the rest probably reflected the overall proportions of the attack, in which all eighteen Lancasters of No. 617 Squadron dropped their bombs, compared with ten dropped by No. 9 Squadron.

The result was not in doubt. *Tirpitz* was sunk, with the loss of almost 1,000 sailors from a crew of 1,600. She had never attacked an Allied ship, but she had been heavily responsible for the scattering and destruction of convoy PQ17, and had pinned down capital ships of the Royal Navy in northern waters during critical periods of the war when they would have been extremely valuable elsewhere. She had survived attack by Russian submarines, by the Royal Navy, the Fleet Air Arm and the RAF. She had cost the lives of many British airmen from the early days at Wilhelmshaven onwards. As the Secretary of State for Air observed, her destruction was a massive achievement by British aircraft and crews using a British bomb sight and a bomb which no other air force of the day could carry.

The sinking reinforced the lesson that a warship, no matter how well armed and armoured, could not survive without air cover against determined and well equipped bombers. It was not surprising that the luckless Major Ehrler of JG 5 was made the scapegoat for the loss. He was court-martialled and sentenced to three years' hard labour. Such was the parlous plight of the Luftwaffe by the end of 1944, however, that after four weeks he returned to combat and, flying an Me 262, was shot down over Berlin and killed on 4 April 1945.

Wing Commander Tait was recommended for the Victoria Cross, but instead was awarded a third bar to his DSO. Flight Lieutenant Knights, who had flown on all three of the *Tirpitz* attacks, was awarded the DSO, and Pilot Officer Evans was decorated with the DFC. Another memorable chapter had been added to the distinguished record of No. 617 Squadron, and another example of outstanding professionalism and valour added to the collective achievements of Bomber Command in the Second World War.

# Lancaster N-Nuts

*Painting by Norman Hoad*
*Text by Ron Dick*

NORMAN HOAD'S LANCASTERS ARE SHOWN OVER Germany in 1945, and the contrast with those early struggles could not be more complete. The shortcomings of 1939 have been overcome and, as the war enters its final stages, Bomber Command is at last in possession of the air weapon the strategists dreamed about; a heavy bomber force of awesome hitting power, capable of operating over its enemy's heartland by day or night in any weather without fear of crippling losses, and of destroying its selected targets with assurance. .

Air Chief Marshal Sir Arthur Harris led Bomber Command from February 1942 until the end of the war, and became one of the war's most memorable (and controversial) figures. Under him, the bomber force grew from one in which a force of 150 twins was considered a big raid to one which could, and often did, launch 1,000 or more four-engined aircraft at a time. In parallel, the development of navigation and bombing aids and techniques revolutionised the way the force operated and dramatically increased its effectiveness.

Bomber Command aircraft came to be fitted with radio and radar aids such as Gee, Gee-H, Oboe and $H_2S$. All had their limitations, but together they transformed the navigational capabilities of the bomber force. In addition, Pathfinder techniques were developed to lead the main force to its target with accurately placed flares and coloured markers, and experienced crews were used as 'Master Bombers' to stay in the target area and control the raid. Bomb-aimers' cameras and post-raid photographic reconnaissance ensured that Bomber Command's effectiveness was constantly monitored and improved.

In the struggle against the German defences, the Luftwaffe's control of its fighters was bedevilled by the metal-foil strips known as 'Window' and confused by diversionary raids and careful routeing. German radio transmissions were jammed and, by night, intruders harassed defending fighters. Worse still for the Luftwaffe, their basic capacity to defend deteriorated steadily after the D-Day invasion, and by 1945 they were no longer capable of seriously challenging the Allied air offensive. In the closing months of the war the German early-warning system gradually collapsed under the advance of the Allied armies, and the losses suffered by Luftwaffe fighter squadrons, particularly in daylight against the USAAF, meant that they no longer had sufficient pilots to fill their fighter cockpits, and most of those they had were inexperienced.

As the Luftwaffe declined, so the Allied air forces grew in strength, and daylight scenes like that represented by Norman Hoad's Lancasters became increasingly common over Germany. As the pre-eminent ' heavy', the Lancaster carried most of the weight of Bomber Command's relentless onslaught, being used in massive numbers to pound German targets by day and night with powerful effect. In 1945 no fewer than 56 squadrons were equipped with Lancasters, and the order of battle for April of that year shows a daily average of 1,087 Lancasters available for operations out of a total of 1,643 front-line aircraft, which also included 353 Halifaxes and 203 Mosquitos.

Superior though it was, the Lancaster was a fortunate accident, a veritable pheonix from the ashes of the twin-engined Avro Manchester's failure. Although the Manchester was in limited squadron service for some eighteen months from the end of 1940, its shortcomings, and most particularly those of its Rolls-Royce Vulture engines, had become all too apparent. The Avro design team had sketched out a modified Manchester with four Merlin engines early in 1940. This aircraft, the Manchester III, was the prototype for the Lancaster. It first flew in January 1941, and the Lancaster began squadron operations in March 1942.

From the outset the Lancaster inspired the affection of its crews. It was reliable, trustworthy and clearly the best of the Bomber Command heavies. Neither the Stirling nor the Halifax could match it for height and speed, and although it was not light on the controls, the Lancaster was described by most pilots as 'a dream to fly'. If it had an Achilles' heel, it was in its defensive armament. Three turrets were generally provided (nose, mid-upper and tail), but they were usually fitted with 0.303in machine-guns, and they were inadequate against attacks from below. This proved to be a dangerous weakness once the Luftwaffe introduced fighters with upward-firing cannon. Although a ventral turret had originally been included, its extra weight was thought too great a penalty and it was dispensed with, except on some aircraft in the Canadian squadrons.

Perhaps the Lancaster's most remarkable feature was its cavernous bomb bay, unbroken by bulkheads. With only minor modification this allowed an amazing variety of bomb loads to be carried, including the Barnes Wallis cylindrical bouncing bomb used on the famous raid against the Mohne and Eder Dams, the later 12,000lb Tallboy and the immense 22,000lb Grand Slam. No other Second World War aircraft was capable of carrying such large bombs or varied loads. Proof of the Lancaster's dominance in Bomber Command is seen in the statistics of the bomber offensive. In July 1943, for instance, it was noted that the Lancaster squadrons were dropping 132 tons of bombs for each aircraft lost. The figures for the Halifax and Stirling were 56 and 41 tons respectively. Not long afterwards both the Stirling and Halifax were withdrawn from operations against German targets, though

the Halifax rejoined the assault on Germany in 1944 when the Mk. III version became available.

By the end of the war the Lancaster had flown over 156,000 operational bomber sorties, more than the Halifax, Stirling and Wellington combined, and had dropped 608,000 of the 955,000 tons of bombs

dropped by Bomber Command. At an average of 2.2 per cent, the Lancaster's loss rates were consistently lower than those of any other bomber apart from the Mosquito. Some idea of the scale and ferocity of the bomber offensive can be derived from the fact that such an apparently low figure translated into the loss of nearly 3,700 aircraft during operations.

Most of the crushing weight of the bomber offensive was felt by Germany after the Allied invasion of

Normandy. Almost half of the total tonnage of bombs dropped by Bomber Command in five and a half years of war fell in the final nine months. The bombing rose to a climactic effort during March 1945, nearly 68,000 tons of bombs falling on German targets in that month alone, most of them from Lancaster bomb bays. It was more than the Command had dropped in its first three years. Particularly remarkable were two huge daylight raids against the Ruhr. On 11 March 1,079 aircraft, including 750 Lancasters, attacked Essen, and on the following day 1,108 aircraft, 748 of them Lancasters, struck Dortmund. These mighty blows paralysed both cities until the end of the war, for the loss of just five Lancasters. Sir Arthur Harris still felt that this was the best use for his bomber force, and he remained unenthusiastic about the official target – the oil industry.

In spite of his announced lack of conviction regarding the importance of oil as a target, Sir Arthur devoted rather more than a quarter of Bomber Command's total effort in the closing months of the war to attacking oil plants. (About a third was sent against cities). In March that involved major attacks on no fewer than 35 oil installations, twenty of them in daylight by forces of 100 or more Lancasters. Altogether, Lancasters flew some 12,000 operational sorties in March, 6,600 of them by day. Their losses for the month totalled 186 aircraft (1.6 per cent), but only 42 of those were in daylight (0.65 per cent). It is a sobering comment on the scale of the battle that the loss of 186 Lancasters in one month (the equivalent of more than nine squadrons) could be seen as evidence that the German defences were failing and that Bomber

Command's operational troubles had been left behind.

In returning to daylight operations, Bomber Command never attempted to match the massive and highly organised close formations of the US 8th Air Force. As Norman Hoad's picture shows, it was not unusual for Lancasters to be seen proceeding to their targets in loose 'gaggles'. The fact that Lancasters could not operate much above 20,000ft, and that they were inadequately armed is in itself an indication of the degree of air superiority existing for the Allies over Germany in the latter stages of the war. The change in relative strengths was marked, and RAF crews were surprised to find that daylight operations were now usually less hazardous than those at night.

RAF aircraft used a number of different techniques for their daylight bombing in 'gaggles'. At the most basic level, when skies were clear and visibility good, crews were given the responsibility of finding their own way to the target and bombing individually. Slightly worse conditions could see the main force being given the assistance of Pathfinders, who could mark the target and perhaps provide a Master Bomber to give directions. Alternatively, main force aircraft could bomb on a Gee fix, or after a timed run from such a fix. Finally, formations of up to eighteen aircraft could be led by a Pathfinder aircraft using Oboe or Gee-H. In this case, the main force aircraft bombed either when the leader dropped his bombs or on his signal. Simply described, the techniques sound less than precise, but as used by Bomber Command they were remarkably effective.

The last major raid on a German city occurred on the night of 14 April 1945, when 500 Lancasters and 12 Mosquitoes attacked Berlin. During the war's remaining days, Bomber Command concentrated mainly on such targets as naval facilities and railway yards. Lancasters flew their last bombing sorties on 25 April, when their principal target was Hitler's 'Eagle's Nest' and the neighbouring SS barracks at Berchtesgaden. The raid was ordered because there was a suspicion that surviving Nazi fanatics intended to make their last stand in the Bavarian Alps. A force of 359 Lancasters and 16 Mosquitoes went to Berchtesgaden in daylight and took considerable satisfaction in pounding their principal enemy's famous redoubt, whether he and his colleagues were there or not. The 'Eagle's Nest' itself, 9,300ft up, was in cloud and escaped, but the retreats of Goering and Bormann were demolished, as was the Berghof, where Hitler had been in the habit of receiving those on whom he wished to work his political will, including Neville Chamberlain in 1938. The last bombs had been dropped, two Lancasters were lost, and the bomber offensive was over.

*The artist writes:* Norman Hoad's talent as an aviation artist has long been recognised, and it should be no surprise that he has a skill in capturing the essence of Second World War in the air. He took part in the final phase of the air assault on Germany, and flew the Lancaster in the foreground of this painting on a number of operations. Air Vice-Marshal N. E. Hoad, CVO CBE AFC* was commissioned as an officer in the RAF in May 1943 and joined 61 Squadron as a Lancaster pilot in 1944. In the course of his operational tour he regularly flew Lancaster ED860/QR-N, known as 'N-Nuts'. It was among Bomber Command's most celebrated aircraft, a formidable survivor which finished the war with 130 missions and two enemy night fighters to its credit.

Norman Hoad was the captain of 'N-Nuts' for an attack by 189 Lancasters of No.5 Group on Königsberg at the end of August 1944. The raid was carried out at extreme range. Low cloud covered the aiming point initially, but patience and some close control by the master bomber made this one of the most accurate and successful 5 Group raids of the war. It was not achieved without cost. Fighter opposition was surprisingly heavy, and 15 Lancasters were lost. A number of others were severely damaged, among them 'N-Nuts', which was temporarily withdrawn from the front line for repairs.

Norman Hoad's crew were allocated another Lancaster for their remaining missions, and it was in this aircraft that they attacked Brunswick on 14 October 1944, when 233 Lancasters from 5 Group hit their target hard. The attack was so heavily concentrated and destructive that the Brunswick authorities reported the size of the raid as being at least 1,000 aircraft. This time opposition was light, and only one aircraft was lost, but it was Norman Hoad's. He was on his 21st operation when he survived the experience of being shot down and became a prisoner of war.

Norman Hoad remained in the RAF after the war, and retired as an Air Vice-Marshal in 1978. While still in the Service he built up a considerable reputation as an aviation artist, and his paintings are rightly prized by collectors all over the world. His evocative painting of 'N-Nuts' and her sisters was completed as a personal remembrance of daylight operations in 1944, and now serves as a record of a typical Lancaster 'gaggle' over Germany in the closing months of the Second World War, painted by one who was there.

# Operation 'Manna'

### Painting by John Young
### Text by Michael Armitage

THE CREWS OF THE THREE AVRO LANCASTERS IN John Young's painting must have been pinching themselves to make sure they were not dreaming. For very nearly five years, aircraft of the RAF had been crossing the North Sea into Holland to attack targets in German-occupied western Europe, and each time they did so they were met by an intense barrage of flak. Yet here they were, in May 1945, flying into Holland over silent German anti-aircraft guns while bitter fighting was still going on around Berlin, in East Prussia and Bavaria, and while Allied forces were still advancing towards Hamburg. These Lancasters were taking part in Operation 'Manna'.

It was well named. A modern equivalent of the Biblical bread from heaven, it was about all manner of life-saving supplies being dropped over Holland at the end of April and during the first week of May, 1945. Operation 'Manna' was the Allied response to a particularly desperate shortage of food in the western part of Holland, the three provinces still held by units of German Army Group H. The four eastern provinces had already been liberated by the advancing Canadian First Army and the British Second Army, but the German troops now isolated in the west of country were not only holding out, but they had been ordered by Hitler himself to carry out a 'scorched earth' policy, leaving nothing of value for the Allies to capture.

Food had been in very short supply throughout Holland during the war, but the situation for the western provinces lurched into desperate crisis on 17 April 1945, when the German occupying forces first evacuated the Wieringermeerpolder of its 7,000 inhabitants and then blew up the main dyke, flooding 20,000 hectares of arable land and inundating 512 farms so as to put a serious obstacle in the path of the Allied advance. This area had been the granary of Holland, and the flooding was a disaster for the Dutch popula-

tion. Already this region of the country was without gas, light, fuel or transport, and the daily ration of foodstuff for the heard-pressed civilian population had been progressively reduced until, during March, it amounted to only two slices of poor bread, two potatoes and half of a sugar beet per person. This meant a daily intake of only about 525 calories. In April the daily calorie intake fell again, this time to around 400 per person. In other words the hapless inhabitants were subsisting at starvation levels.

It was clear to the German administration in Holland that the end of the war could not be very far off, and meanwhile the Allies had warned the Germans that they would be held accountable for any Dutch deaths resulting from their failure to feed the civilian population. As a result, Dr Seyss-Inquart, the German governor of occupied Holland, disobeyed Hitler's 'scorched earth' order and initiated a series of secret meetings to alleviate the situation. The eventual outcome was a meeting between Seyss-Inquart and leaders of the Dutch resistance movement, and then a further meeting arranged by the German Army between Dutch representatives and representatives of the Allied forces.

These approaches were communicated to Churchill and Roosevelt, with the result that General Eisenhower, the Supreme Allied Commander, was given full powers to negotiate arrangements with the Germans to supply food to the beleaguered Dutch population. Local ceasefires were agreed, and arrangements were made between the Allied and the German forces to establish drop zones into which food supplies could be delivered by Allied aircraft. At first there were to be only four: Duindigt racecourse near the Hague, Ypenburg and Valkenburg airfields, and the airport at Waalhave, near Rotterdam. Later there would be ten such drop zones. It was agreed that the drops could start on 27

April, and that they would take place between 8am and 7pm.

In Britain, American bombers and Lancasters of RAF Bomber Command were prepared for this remarkable mission, and No. 115 Squadron was tasked to carry out food-dropping trials using a technique perfected by Major R. P. Martin, a South African flight commander in the squadron.

Following the success of the trials, volunteers worked in the snow on RAF airfields during the night of 26 April to load 600 tons of food into 253 Lancasters. The food was packed into discarded cement sacks, then slung on hastily manufactured canvas slings in the bomb bays so that the cargo could be released accurately over the designated drop zones. Each aircraft carried 3,280 man/day rations consisting of flour, chocolate, egg powder, tea and other goods that had long disappeared from Dutch larders. Many of the aircrews and the officers and men involved in loading the aircraft added to the cargo from their own somewhat limited supplies of cigarettes, chocolate and other small items.

After a last-minute delay caused by the sensitivity of the mission and the problems of reliable communications between active opponents in the continuing war, Eisenhower sent a message to Seyss-Inquart on the evening of 27 April, saying that the drops would begin the following day. But the bad weather that was adding to the plight of the Dutch now also hampered the air operation. Approval to launch the aircraft was cancelled no fewer than six times before, on Sunday 29 April, the first flights finally set off.

Weather conditions were still marginal, and over the North Sea a freak blizzard caused the Lancasters to fly as low as 150ft above the waves as they made their way to the dropping zones. Not surprisingly, there was

considerable unease both on the Allied side and on the German side about the whole operation. Would the German air defences seize this unique opportunity to inflict crippling losses on the aircraft of Bomber Command? The flight paths were known, the drop zones

NORTH SEA

Amsterdam

The Hague
Rotterdam
Arnhem

Antwerp
Dusseldorf

Brussels
Maastricht
Valkenburg
Aachen
Liége

▨ Initial main dropping areas

were clearly marked with white crosses on the ground and lead-in lights of red and green. Perhaps it was a trap.

From the German point of view, the Allied operation might turn out to be a cover for a mass drop of parachute troops. Both sides were ready for trouble. The Lancaster crews manned their combat positions as they flew into Holland, while at the agreed drop zones the

Germans had not only deployed concentrations of anti-aircraft guns, but had also placed disguised members of the Gestapo and the Sicherheit Dienst among the Dutch civilians waiting for the supplies, in case the drops included weapons for the Dutch resistance movement.

To the relief of all concerned, and not least to the immense satisfaction of the Dutch population, the operation went according to plan. The bombers on the first mission arrived over the drop zones at about 1330 on 29 April and successfully dropped all of their supplies to the waiting Dutch. Although on the second day of Operation 'Manna' some Allied aircraft were fired on, almost certainly in error, the German anti-aircraft guns were withdrawn from the drop zones, and the operation then continued smoothly for the following week.

John Young's painting shows three Lancasters, probably Mk. Is, flying into Holland over one of the coastal estuaries near the Hook of Holland, about 20 miles south of Rotterdam. The earlier bad weather seems to have cleared up, and the aircraft are therefore two or three days into the operation, perhaps on 1 or 2 May 1945. As agreed with the German authorities, the bombers are coasting in at low level, 200ft or so above the flat landscape of the local countryside, and although the crews will no doubt be much more relaxed than on the first day of Operation 'Manna', the Lancasters' guns will all be manned and the gunners will very soon be able to see below them some of the thousands of Dutch people who have left their houses to witness the sight of war machines delivering not bombs, but food. All told, about 500 aircraft of Bomber Command and 300 more from the US 8th Air Force unloaded 7,458 tons of supplies over Holland. Little of the food was lost.

About 95 per cent of all the supplies dropped was duly taken to central warehouses, from where it was carefully distributed by the German-controlled Dutch administration. Although the air drop was a very considerable relief to the starving Dutch population, on its own it was not enough and other, more substantial, supply arrangements were made meanwhile by the Allies. In yet another extraordinary meeting, this time on 30 April, senior Allied officers met with Prince Bernhardt of the Netherlands, who had been flown in from Britain, and Dr Seyss-Inquart to agree the importation of another 1,600 tons of food supplies from the Allies each day; 700 tons would be sent in by rail, 300 by road and 600 by barges along the Dutch canals. More air drops were made in the meantime, and the whole supply effort continued under these conditions of local truce until the German surrender on Saturday 5 May, when it became a more routine though no less essential affair in the immediate aftermath of war.

*The artist writes:* As a teenager of the 1940s I went to sleep to the sound of hundreds of Lancasters flying to their mighty air battles, and the simple sketches of childhood turned to more serious painting as time went by. Lancasters were always a popular subject at exhibitions, but aircrew and their families favoured more peaceful renderings of their favourite aircraft and I developed a series of 'coming safe home' subjects. Operation Manna was an excellent alternative for those who enjoyed the thought of the bomber on a mercy mission, with the added enhancement of daylight. It was this train of thought which led to the commissioning of this work for the RAF Museum 1994 calendar — a chance to portray low-level flying and my favourite Dutch machines —the ones with four-bladed props!

# Final Action

*Painting by Jim Mitchell
Text by Peter Cooksley*

THERE WERE GREAT INTERVALS OF TIME AND distance between first the flight and the final RAF sortie of the Spitfire. The former took place at Eastleigh, Southampton, most probably on 6 March 1936 (some claim that it happened on the previous day), and was made in the temperate skies of Hampshire. In contrast, the concluding action by Spitfires was flown on a hot and sultry Malayan afternoon fourteen years later, during the last day of the year. Much had by then changed, and although the aircraft which made the type's final sortie were not the last variant, the amount of development that had taken place is illustrated by the fact that there had been proposals that the later, Griffon-engined marks should even have a new name, Victor.

The first indication that Supermarine's chief designer, R. J. Mitchell, had produced a thoroughbred was probably voiced by test pilot 'Mutt' Summers immediately after the maiden flight, when he clambered from the cockpit of the prototype and said to those gathered round: 'I don't want anything touched'. It was rare for a pilot to be so impressed by his initial experience of a new aircraft, although this did not mean that the first Spitfire was perfection from the outset; merely that there were no major snags and that no alterations to the controls were necessary before the next trial.

This was a testimony to 'R.J.'s' aestheticism as much as his abilities as an engineer, for, apart from the teething troubles suffered by most pieces of machinery, the original design (which might have been called the Shrew), had been developed with little use of wind tunnel testing. Apart from spin-ning trials, the only part of the aeroplane which had been tested in this way was the radiator installation.

After Mitchell's untimely death in 1937, his work was continued by Joseph Smith. The Type 379 Spitfire XIV was powered by a two-speed, two-stage Rolls-Royce Griffon 65 which was so flexible that no high- or low-altitude versions were deemed necessary, and the mark's performance, assisted by engine boost, enabled it to be used to counter the V1, a notoriously difficult target to intercept. The Mk. XIV also introduced the new rear-view hood for the pilot, combined with a cut-down rear fuselage. But it appeared relatively late in the European conflict and was built in relatively small numbers, only 225 being produced in a mixed batch of Mk. VIIIs and Mk. XIVs. Main deliveries went to the Far East.

The Mk. XIV was an interim improvement for the planned 'Super Spitfire', on which development work began towards the close of 1943 to exploit advances in aerodynamics. The Spitfire thus evolved was designated the Mk. XVIII. It was fitting, therefore, that a number of these should be first issued in January 1947 to No. 60 Squadron, RAF, then operating from Seletar, Singapore. This unit had great experience in such climes, having been associated with India, a fact commemorated by its badge, which depicted the head of a makhor, a hoofed creature found in the region of the Khyber Pass. It had been based at Lahore, Agartala, Chittagong and, finally, Kemajoran, where Spitfire XIVs and XVIIIs replaced the Republic Thunderbolt IIs it had operated since July 1945.

The Spitfire XVIII had no prototype in the accepted sense. Instead, the first production aircraft, SM843, was pressed into use for manufacturer's trials, being employed in this manner from 8 June 1945. To the casual observer, perhaps the most notable feature was the five-bladed Rotol/Jablo propeller. Structurally there were few differences between the Mk. XVIII 'Super Spitfire' and its immediate predecessor, though less obvious changes were the strengthened wings, a sturdier undercarriage to cope with the fuel tanks now carried in the rear fuselage, and the fitting of G45 oblique cameras behind the cockpits of fighter reconnaissance (FR) models. There was also provision for external drop tanks, and trials with these on SM843 came in for particular criticism when it was dived to the limiting speed of 400mph. A report claimed that the aircraft became 'unpleasant to fly', and it was suggested that a limit of 320mph be imposed. Despite such problems, the first Spitfire XVIII, SM844, was delivered to the RAF on 28 May 1945 and was later sent to 28 Squadron in Hong Kong.

Although No. 60 Squadron had never flown Spitfires before, the new mark proved popular with pilots, perhaps particularly so after their experience with the heavy United States Thunderbolts, and was the first Griffon-engined version to be considered for large-scale production. It had the 'C'-type wing, housing two 20mm cannon and twin .50-calibre machine-guns and able to carry 1,000lb of bombs and rockets. Deeper double radiator fairings were introduced, and operations in the thin air at high altitude demanded the aforementioned five-bladed airscrew with its large spinner and wooden, plastic-sheathed blades with brass leading edges. This, mounted ahead of a two-stage supercharger, gave the Mk. XVIII an inordinately long nose. Moreover, the use of such a propeller seemed likely to pose problems regarding high tip speeds and ground clearance, but these were solved by shortening the blades. A completely redesigned fin and rudder of increased area was also fitted.

The postwar period when No. 60 Squadron re-equipped was increasingly dominated from 1948 by the Malayan Emergency, and the problems of dealing with it were increased by the fact that the strength of the RAF, both in the Peninsula and Singapore, had been greatly reduced. Even so, the choice of Singapore as the main air headquarters was a wise one, as the RAF was soon to be deeply involved, mainly in making attacks against guerrilla bases and carrying out reconnaissance as part of Operation 'Firedog'. Army participation took the form of a drive by four battalions during mid-November 1949 against the 600 rebels hidden in the dense jungle. This was supported as necessary by the RAF's two operational Spitfire squadrons in the area, Nos. 60 and 28 (also flying Mk. XVIIIs), together with the photographic reconnaissance Spitfires of No. 81 Squadron, these being the first to be involved in the operation when ordered to Taiping to assist in reconnoitring the area. Meanwhile, Nos. 28 and 60 Squadrons were sent to Kuala Lumpur, from whence sorties were initiated to locate and attack guerrilla hideouts. However, it was already clear that the days of operational piston-engined aircraft were numbered. The RAF's fighter squadrons were re-equipping with Gloster Meteor and de Havilland Vampire jets, new examples of the latter having a maximum speed some 100mph greater than that of the Spitfires.

The explosive staccato note of four Rolls-Royce Griffon motors shattered the peace of the heavy afternoon, bright with sunshine, as four of 60 Squadron's machines started up. Their rhythmic roar set the surrounding jungle alive with a cacophony of sound from startled wild creatures which only died away as the Spitfires taxied out, each in a cloud of choking, fine, red dust, to take off and begin to climb. As they did so the sun caught the distinctive black and yellow stripes round their noses, behind the coloured spinners. Three of these were blue but the fourth was red, a recognition feature of NH850 'Z', flown by the unit's commanding officer, Squadron Leader (later Group Captain) W. G. Duncan Smith, DSO and bar, DFC and two bars, who led the formation. The other lead aircraft, NH849, was flown by Flight Lieutenant 'Dickie' Keogh. Both men wore sunglasses rather than conventional goggles, the better to protect their eyes from the glare of the sultry afternoon. Each of the two lead aircraft carried a single 500lb bomb under its fuselage, but their other armament differed. While Keogh's Spitfire was armed with only four 60lb rockets, Smith's had six of similar calibre.

Having climbed to 8,000ft, the four machines passed over occasional Malayan villages set in jungle clearings, their destination being one such settlement in the Kota Tinggi area of Johore, near which lay Communist positions. These were bombed in diving attacks before specific positions were pounded by rocket fire and then strafed by the Spitfires' machine-guns and cannon.

There were no celebrations, formalities or ceremonial procedures to greet the four on their return to base. The airscrews jerked to a stop, the wheels were chocked and the hot and weary pilots climbed from their cockpits. It was just another job completed 'successfully', according to the official report. No one knew that, with this December action, Spitfires had performed their final mission. However, the aircraft whose name had become world famous was not to vanish forthwith from Malayan skies. The reconnaissance versions with No. 81 Squadron were to be set the task of mapping the entire country to assist ground operations within 50 miles of their base. An era was drawing to a close.

The ending of the Second World War meant that the operational life of the Spitfire XVIII was brief; production was cut back and many orders were cancelled. Most of the 300 built went to India and the Far East, the majority going straight into storage. The two recorded participants in the historic final sortie were typical examples, NH849 having been sent to India on 25 February 1946 and taken on charge by No. 60 Squadron in February 1950. Likewise, NH850 had come from India, going in April 1950 to the squadron that was to use it against Malayan terrorists. Neither of the machines depicted were to last much longer, both being struck off charge on 8 March 1951. They deserved a better fate.

But the Spitfire's final offensive role did not go unmarked. Some time later, in a ceremony in Singapore, Ronnie Harker, chief test pilot of Rolls-Royce, and Vickers-Armstrongs test pilot Jeffrey Quill presented No. 60 Squadron with a beautiful silver commemorative model of a Spitfire on behalf of the two companies. It was appropriately inscribed with the words *Nunc Dimittis* – 'Lord, now lettest thou thy servant depart in peace'.

*The artist writes:* Although I have painted many variants of the Spitfire, 'Final Action' shows a much later mark of the aircraft which is bulky and much larger than the earlier versions. When researching this painting, minute detail was made available to me, such as the fact that Spitfire NH850 carried two fewer rockets than its companion, and that both pilots wore sunglasses rather than regulation goggles because of the low angle of the Malaysian afternoon sun. As always, accuracy in the painting is vital.

# Jungle Drop

*Painting by Maurice Gardner*
*Text by Michael Armitage*

ONE OF THE MOST DIFFICULT CAMPAIGNS, AND certainly the longest, in which the RAF took part during the years after the Second World War was that in Malaya, from June 1948 until July 1960.

During the war, communist guerrillas in Malaya had been supported and supplied by the British in their fight against the Japanese occupying forces. But once the war was over these same guerrillas, denied their aim of forming a communist government, took to the jungle once again and launched a terrorist campaign to destabilise the country. The undeclared war that followed was called 'The Emergency', and it began with the murder of planters in isolated areas during 1948. The insurgency reached its height in 1951, by which time Britain, with local and Commonwealth support, took special measures to deal with the several thousands of terrorists at loose in the jungle.

These measures eventually included the deployment of about 67,000 police, 300,000 Home Guards and 26 infantry battalions or their equivalents. British, Ghurka, Malayan, Fijian, African, Australian and New Zealand units all at one time or another took part in the campaign, which was conducted mainly by small infantry units living and fighting in the dense jungle.

In order to cut the terrorists off from the villages from which they were able to draw supplies, nearly 462,000 Chinese Malays were moved by the government into 509 settlements protected by local Home Guards and surrounded by barbed wire fences and guard posts. Once this resettlement programme had been completed, operations against the insurgents began in earnest, with troops spreading out through the jungle and pursuing the terrorists on their own terms. Terrorist activity reached a peak during June 1951, 606 incidents being recorded in that month. Thereafter the security forces gradually cleared whole stretches of the jungle-covered countryside, reducing the number of

incidents as they did so and eliminating 7,500 terrorists by the middle of 1954. From then on the security forces were operating against a hard core of remaining insurgents, and the campaign became one of sustained attrition. By the end of 1954, although about 3,000 terrorists were still at large, the number of incidents had fallen to only 65 a month. During 1957, as the campaign wound down, another 200 or so terrorists were accounted for, and for the first time since the start of the Emergency no incidents were reported. Nor were there any fatalities among the security forces or the civilian population.

Throughout the twelve-year campaign the RAF, together with Royal Australian Air Force and Royal New Zealand Air Force units, carried out numerous bombing attacks on suspected guerrilla camps, and many other missions were flown using rockets, bombs and cannon fire in direct support of our troops on the ground as they closed with terrorist units. These activities were carried out by squadrons of the Far East Air Force (FEAF) based in Malaya and on Singapore Island, strongly supported by aircraft detached from squadrons based in the UK and the Middle East. At the height of the Emergency, FEAF held two bomber squadrons, two light bomber squadrons, two fighter squadrons and two squadrons of fighter-bombers. The aircraft operated by these units included Spitfires, Mosquitoes, Hornets, Vampires, Venoms, Lancasters, Lincolns, Canberras and even Sunderland flying boats. At various times as the Emergency continued, aircraft from no fewer than twenty squadrons from outside FEAF also took part in attacks on the terrorists, again flying a wide variety of aircraft including, on occasion, Valiants and Vulcans from the V-bomber force.

However, by far the most important contribution made by air power to the eventual and complete success of the campaign was that of the transport aircraft and

helicopters. When the campaign began, the available transport force was made up of Nos. 48, 52 and 110 Squadrons, all flying Douglas Dakotas out of Changi. In December 1949, No. 41 Squadron RNZAF joined the force, followed by No. 38 Squadron RAAF in June 1950. These transport aircraft made an invaluable contribution to the success of operations on the ground by extending the mobility of the security forces. Troops could be flown quickly and at short notice to meet the changing security situation in different parts of Malaya. Airlifts of this kind, initially using Dakotas and then Vickers-Armstrongs Valettas and, later, the helicopters that were to join FEAF, were to become an everyday part of Army and air force activity throughout the Emergency.

The Dakotas also introduced the techniques of supplying ground patrols by means of air drops, an operation involving packs that weighed some 270lb each, using 18ft and 24ft diameter parachutes. Later a 28ft disposable parachute was brought into service. By February 1952, Vickers Valettas like the one depicted in Maurice Gardner's painting had arrived in theatre, and these now took part in their first 'drop'. It was to be the first of many thousands.

The Valettas released single bags of supplies from about 100ft above the dropping zone, flying as slowly as possible to ensure accuracy. This required the flaps to be partly extended, and the aircraft had to be flown in such a direction that the way out of the dropping area was 'downhill'. Many of the drops had to be made in the Central Highlands of Malaya, among hills that sometimes rise to 6,000ft. The lack of accurate maps, the broken terrain and the cloud which often came down to cover the high ground completely could make these operations extremely hazardous. Several Valetta crews were lost, either because they had been caught out by bad weather in badly-mapped terrain, or

because they had suffered engine failure at low level over the jungle.

The Valetta was designed to an Air Ministry Specification of 1946 as a military variant of the Viking airliner. The prototype made its maiden flight on 30 June 1947, and the aircraft entered service as the Valetta C.1

with 240 Operational Conversion Unit in 1948. It had a crew of four and capacity for 34 troops or 20 paratroops with full kit. The Valetta was powered by two 1,975hp Bristol Hercules 230 engines, which gave it a top speed of 258mph at 10,000ft and a rate of climb of 1,275ft/min. Its maximum range was 1,410 miles, or 530 miles when carrying a full load of paratroops.

Although the Valetta turned out to be less reliable than the Dakota in service, it had a slightly better rate of climb than its predecessor and carried a 50 per cent

greater payload. All three FEAF transport squadrons, Nos. 48, 52 and 110, were soon equipped with Valettas, and they were also issued to the Far East Communication Squadron. By 1953 the security forces in Malaya had built a series of hill forts in the remoter parts of the country to serve as operational bases, and air supply of these forts and of troops on extended patrols in the jungle became an essential part of anti-terrorist operations. From July 1953 to March 1954, for example, two battalions of infantry operated continuously in southern Kedah, while a further four battalions of security force troops were deployed in north-west Pahang. Both operations were supplied throughout entirely by air. Some idea of the scale of these and other operations may be gained from the fact that, during 1954 alone, 2,080 such supply missions were flown and almost 6.8 million pounds of supplies were dropped.

In the painting, Flight Lieutenant (now Squadron Leader, Retired) Alan Smith is at the controls of a Valetta of 48 Squadron. His navigator is Flying Officer Harry Marshall, and Master Signaller Hutton is the Signaller dispatcher. Two Army dispatchers from 55 Company, RASC, are busy ejecting a supply bag for an anti-terrorist patrol at the side of a river just to the east of Ipoh. A parachute from an earlier run over the drop zone can be seen hanging in the trees at the edge of the dropping area, as can a balloon used to mark the patrol's position. The smoke was another aid to help aircraft locate patrols in the dense jungle.

It is not going too far to say that, without the support of the air transport units, the anti-terrorist campaign in Malaya would have lasted far longer than it did, and it might well have failed altogether. Even when the terrorists were thrown on to the defensive, in the early 1950s, there was an essential need for the security forces to operate in inhospitable parts of the peninsula, independent of conventional supply lines. And even after the need for air support of ground forces by bombers and fighter-bombers had diminished, the demand for regular and reliable air supply continued. The Valettas were an essential part of that effort throughout most of a conflict that has now passed into history, but which helped to ensure the post-colonial freedom of Malaya.

*The artist writes:* The working title for this painting was simply Jungle Drop, and it was created following a request by Squadron Leader Alan Smith, who wanted a painting of this subject to add to his personal collection. The scene depicts Squadron Leader Smith at the controls of his Vickers Valetta, and is a good illustration of the type of resupply work he was performing during the Malayan emergency. He was able to furnish all the details necessary to complete the work from his personal records; in particular the smoke and balloon indicators.

# Corporate Prelude

*Painting by Philip West*
*Text by Michael Gething*

DESIGNED AND BUILT IN THE 1950S AND 1960S, primarily to carry nuclear weapons, the Avro Vulcan, second of the three V-bombers, was used 'in anger' only in the twilight of its service with the RAF, and then only in a conventional role.

In April 1982, No. 101 Squadron was on the point of disbandment, leaving only Nos. 44 and 50 Squadrons, flying the last Vulcan B.2s in RAF service. One of the options for striking back at the Argentine invaders of the Falkland Islands was the use of offensive airpower. The problem faced by the planners was that of range; the Falklands lie about 4,000 miles from the nearest possible land base, Wideawake Airfield on Ascension Island. Air Chief Marshal Sir Michael Beetham, the Chief of the Air Staff, was adamant that the Vulcans would do the job.

It was decided that No. 44 Squadron would provide the Falklands bomber force, but a great deal of preparatory work was needed before the Vulcans could take on this unexpected task. The aircrews were placed on standby and, on Good Friday 1982, the engineers at Waddington were instructed to restore the air-to-air refuelling (AAR) capability on ten aircraft and prepare the Vulcans for dropping conventional high-explosive bombs. While the bomb load would cause no major problems, the AAR capability had been unused for several years and the refuelling probes had been removed. Engineering parties scoured the globe in a frantic search for long-discarded probes. Eventually enough were located and delivered to Waddington, where ten aircraft were re-fitted, tested and declared serviceable for AAR operations.

Two weeks after Easter 1982 the Waddington engineers under then-Squadron Leader Roger Pye were asked to find a way of fitting the Vulcans with the Westinghouse AN/ALQ-101-10 electronic countermeasures (ECM) jamming pod, known as the Dash Ten pod, which was in service with RAF Germany's Buccaneer fleet. Again history played its part. Before the Polaris submarine-launched nuclear missile became the UK's deterrent weapon, it had been intended that RAF Vulcans would fulfil the role, armed with US Skybolt missiles carried on underwing pylons. Before Skybolt was cancelled in 1962, early production Vulcan B.2s were built with hardpoints for these pylons, and the hardpoints were found to exist on nine of the ten aircraft being prepared for operations. They would be used to carry the Dash Ten pod. The problem was that the pylons themselves did not exist, because they had not been produced before the cancellation of the Skybolt programme. It was left to Squadron Leader Pye to manufacture something suitable from materials to hand. The ingenuity of the engineering staff was taxed but, in the end, a locally-made pylon was produced, two being custom-built for each aircraft. One would carry the ECM pod, while the other eventually took a pair of AGM-45 Shrike anti-radar missiles (ARMs), courtesy of the US Navy.

The aircrew began their training in AAR techniques on 14 April, catching up on thirteen years without the capability in just thirteen days. To assist, each crew was assigned an AAR instructor from the Victor tanker force. He would remain with the crew for operations, flying in the copilot's seat, except during the operational part of the mission. Changing crew members in the cramped cockpit of a Vulcan from a 'live' ejection seat was no easy matter. By the time the Vulcans deployed to Ascension Island each crew had completed three daylight refuellings (known as 'prods') and two night prods.

From 20 April the Vulcan crews were busy refreshing their low-level-flying and conventional bombing techniques. By the time their AAR and other training was completed, the aircraft being prepared for the actual raids, to be codenamed 'Black Buck', were ready for

operations. On the afternoon of 28 April three Vulcans left RAF Waddington for Ascension Island in the South Atlantic.

The five 'Black Buck' missions flown by the Vulcans of No. 44 Squadron (out of seven planned) were the longest-range bombing missions in the history of air warfare to that date. Each mission was flown by a single aircraft, although a flying reserve took off with each formation. In the event, only two aircraft flew the missions: XM607 was used for three, and XM597 for two.

The first raid, 'Black Buck 1', took off from Ascension on the afternoon of 30 April 1982. The two Vulcan B.2s, XM598 (prime) and XM607 (reserve), were each armed with 21 1,000lb HE bombs with Mk. 497 fuzes. They were accompanied by eleven Victor K.2 tankers from Nos. 55 and 57 Squadrons. As reserve, XM607 took off last, but shortly afterwards the prime aircraft was declared unserviceable and XM607 became the mission aircraft.

Captained by Flight Lieutenant Martin Withers, the crew of XM607 comprised Flying Officer Peter Taylor (copilot), Flight Lieutenant Bob Wright (navigator/radar), Flight Lieutenant Gordon Graham (navigator/plotter), Flight Lieutenant Hugh Prior (Airborne Electronics Officer, AEO) and Flight Lieutenant Richard Russell (the AARI from the tanker force). After what seemed an eternity according to Flight Lieutenant Prior, but was only seconds, Flight Lieutenant Withers announced on the intercom: 'Looks like we've got ourselves a job of work, fellahs!'

The formation split into waves, Victors refuelling Victors and the Vulcan, with the aim of giving each air-

craft sufficient fuel to return to Ascension or, as a last resort, to divert to Rio de Janeiro. The further south the formation flew, the fewer its numbers, and with only two Victors and the Vulcan remaining, the final Victor-Victor refuelling took place. While taking on fuel from Victor XL189 of No. 55 Squadron, flown by Squadron Leader Bob Tucker and his crew, the other Victor's probe contact became unlocked. While the aircraft attempted to re-engage, the receiver's probe was damaged and it could no longer take on fuel. This meant that the two tankers would have to reverse roles, XL189 taking back fuel in order to see the Vulcan down to its last refuelling bracket.

Although they were flying at the most fuel-efficient altitude, consumption proved higher than planned. Thus, at the final refuelling, the tanker signalled 'break-off' before the Vulcan's tanker was fully topped-up. As radio silence was being maintained, Withers and his crew were not to know until they had landed at Ascension after the raid that Bob Tucker and his crew had taken a joint decision to pass on more fuel that they could really spare. They had insufficient fuel on board to return to Ascension. Fortunately, such an eventuality had been foreseen, and another Victor found Tucker's aircraft and refuelled it, making a safe return possible. For enabling the Vulcan to complete its mission, at the risk of running out of fuel himself, Squadron Leader Tucker was later awarded the Air Force Cross.

Meanwhile, on board XM607, Martin Withers and his crew were unaware of Tucker's circumstances and were not happy with their own. They had insufficient fuel to divert to Rio or to make the planned rendezvous with the return tanker. Nevertheless, flying at 31,000ft until they were just short of Argentine radar cover, they then dropped to 300ft to fly beneath the Argentine cover on the Falklands.

Before the descent, copilot Taylor reclaimed his seat from the AARI for the bombing run. At 40nm from its target the Vulcan climbed to 10,000ft and turned on to a heading of 235°, aiming for the airfield at Port Stanley. The straight-in run over the airfield, using the $H_2S$ radar, was described as a textbook attack. The Carousel INS had put the aircraft directly on track, crossing the runway at an angle, as planned. Although the release of the 21 bombs took only five seconds, it seemed like an eternity to the crew.

Fortunately, the target was not heavily defended by anti-aircraft fire. A brief illumination from the Skyguard radar, directing 35mm anti-aircraft guns, was dealt with by the Dash Ten pod and transmissions stopped. The bomber straddled the target, and the one crater on the runway, probably made by the third or fourth bomb, effectively closed the airfield to high-performance Argentine aircraft. Most of the other 20 bombs fell on open ground on each side of the runway, but a hangar and a parked Pucara aircraft were damaged.

After bomb release, the Vulcan returned to economical cruising altitude, although it should have remained at 300ft, where it would still have stood a good chance of evading the enemy radar cover. Luck, aided by the use of tactical air navigation and direction finding equipment between the Victor, Vulcan and a patrolling Nimrod, made possible a final refuelling. Although a leak developed, sufficient fuel was taken on board to enable XM607 to make a safe recovery to Ascension Island 15³/₄hr after take-off. For this vital flight, fraught with many difficulties and several potential hazards, Flight Lieutenant Withers was awarded the Distinguished Flying Cross.

For the second 'Black Buck' raid, XM607 was again used, captained by Squadron Leader R. J. Reeve, and it was also used on the final raid, 'Black Buck 7'. The other aircraft used on the series A raids was XM597. 'Black Buck 3' was cancelled owing to bad en-route weather, and 'Black Buck 4' was aborted when a Victor went unserviceable before the penultimate refuelling. 'Black Buck 5' was an anti-radar sortie, the Vulcan being armed this time with four AGM-45 Shrike ARMs.

'Black Buck 6', flown on the night of 2/3 June 1982 and captained by Squadron Leader Neil McDougall, was another Shrike mission. Two of the four missiles were launched, but to no real effect because the radar on to which the missiles were homing was switched off. However, the return flight proved interesting. On the final homeward-bound refuelling

the Vulcan's probe shattered before sufficient fuel had been transferred to continue the flight to Ascension. The only alternative was to divert to Rio. Before landing, it was necessary to jettison the two remaining missiles, but one hung up and could not be released. The Vulcan landed at Rio and, after the crew disembarked, they covered the offending missile with their anoraks to prevent local photographers obtaining 'incriminating evidence'. Had the Brazilian authorities so wished, they could have impounded the aircraft and its crew for carrying an offensive weapon into their airspace.

Two independent sources have confirmed what happened next. After a while a Brazilian armaments officer appeared and, in broken English, insisted on inspecting the shrouded missile. Reluctantly the crew removed their anoraks, revealing the Shrike. The Brazilian officer then produced a book from his pocket. One crew member insisted it was a *Jane's Pocket Book of Missiles*. The Brazilian then deliberately turned up the page describing the Sidewinder short-range air-to-air missile, which the Vulcan could have carried as a last-ditch defence against any Argentine fighter attack (and would therefore not be so provocative to the Brazilians). He pointed to the page showing the Sidewinder, then pointed at the Shrike. 'Is Sidewinder, *sî*,' he said. Appreciating his diplomacy (or was it total ineptitude?), the RAF crew did not dispute his findings.

From this point the story differs. One source suggests that the missile was impounded by the Brazilians, the other is emphatic that within twenty-four hours an RAF Hercules arrived at Rio and the embarrassing missile was quietly removed. Either way, after seven days XM597 was on her way back to the UK via Ascension Island, the Brazilians having extracted an assurance from the RAF that this particular aircraft would play no further part in Operation 'Corporate'. Squadron Leader McDougall was awarded the Distinguished Flying

Cross for his pioneering missile attacks (or could it have been for his diplomacy?).

The final raid, 'Black Buck 7', was carried out on 12 June 1982, two days before the surrender of Argentine forces in the Falklands. It was directed against equipment and personnel at Port Stanley, rather than the runway. At this stage the RAF was expecting to be taking over the facilities on the base very soon. The arguments over whether or not the 'Black Buck' raids applied any real leverage to the reoccupation of the Falklands will probably continue for many years. At the time, the one bomb crater in the runway was considered effective enough, since it prevented Argentine Mirages, Skyhawks and Super Etendards from using Port Stanley as a forward operating base, and they continued to fly combat missions from mainland Argentina, at the extreme limit of their operating radius. Had they had more time over their target, the Royal Navy task force, the outcome of Operation 'Corporate' might well have been different.

As for the Vulcan, the last bomber unit, No. 44 Squadron, disbanded at the end of 1982. However, six examples, converted for AAR as the Vulcan K.2, remained in service with No. 50 Squadron until March 1984. *Ave*, Vulcan.

*The artist writes:* I had just purchased a book covering the Falklands air war and the now famous Black Buck raids, and this gave me the idea for the painting. I then built a kit of the Vulcan, and from this spent many hours sketching, finally coming up with the image I liked; the Vulcan has a unique shape, and at the same time the painting offers something original. Research is vital in creating a factually based painting, and having some good friends in the RAF helps immensely. Aesthetically, the mighty Vulcan is a beautiful aircraft. It makes painting an attractive picture that much easier.

# Action at San Carlos Water

*Painting by Geoff Lea*
*Text by Michael Gething*

IT IS NOT GENERALLY REALISED THAT RAF PILOTS were serving with all three Naval Air Squadrons flying the British Aerospace Sea Harrier FRS.1 fighters deployed for Operation 'Corporate'. Some seven pilots served as exchange officers with their Fleet Air Arm (FAA) colleagues during the conflict, taking their share of combat air patrols and ground-attack missions.

Beginning with the P.1127, the grandfather of Harrier, this family of vertical/short-take-off and landing (V/STOL) aircraft had been a star turn at airshows around the world. Many critics of the type dismissed its unique qualities as a combat aircraft, claiming that it would never survive in combat, or that it would not be capable of anything but 'party tricks'. The air and ground crew involved knew differently and, 'when the blast of war' blew in their ears, they and their Sea Harriers (and, later, Harrier GR.3s) did, indeed, 'imitate the action of the tiger' to quote the Bard of Avon.

As the only fixed-wing combat aircraft deployed with the Task Force until the arrival of the RAF's Harrier GR.3s, the Sea Harrier was called upon to act in all of its designated roles; as a fighter, a reconnaissance aircraft and a ground-attack fighter. In the early stages of the conflict, Argentine Mirage III fighters were deployed as escorts to the attacking aircraft. But, after the first Vulcan raid on Port Stanley airfield on 1 May 1982, they were retained in the Argentine mainland to defend against potential Vulcan raids there. As a result the Argentine Canberras, Daggers, Pucaras and Skyhawks were left to fly their attack missions unescorted, which left them at the mercy of the Sea Harrier Combat Air Patrols (CAPs).

However, before the RAF contribution to Sea Harrier operations over the Falklands is examined, the scene must be set. When HMS *Hermes* sailed from Portsmouth on 2 April 1982 eight aircraft were embarked, assigned to 800 Naval Air Squadron (NAS).

By 5 April a further four had been deployed on board. Some of the extra aircraft had been diverted from 899 NAS (the FAA training unit, equivalent to the RAF's OCU), from MoD(PE) trials, or they had been delivered direct. Flight Lieutenant E. H. Ball was already on the strength of 800 NAS, while Flight Lieutenants D. H. S. Morgan and R. Penfold were transferred in from 899 NAS. For Operation 'Corporate' they were all part of an expanded 800 NAS, commanded by Commander A. D. ' Andy' Auld, RN.

On board HMS *Invincible*, 801 NAS, commanded by Lieutenant Commander N. D. 'Sharky' Ward, with four of its Sea Harriers supplemented by four 899 NAS aircraft, sailed on 5 April. Flight Lieutenant I. Mortimer, already on the strength, was joined by Flight Lieutenant P. S. Barton from 899 NAS.

With 899 NAS depleted, a new unit, 809 NAS, commanded by Lieutenant Commander Tim Gedge, was re-formed at Yeovilton on 8 April to provide replacement aircraft and pilots to 800 and 801 NAS. Experienced aircrew were drafted in from a variety of staff and exchange postings, including two experienced RAF Germany pilots, Flight Lieutenants S. Brown and J. Leeming, while all remaining 899 NAS ground crew were transferred into 809 NAS. Five aircraft came from the storage unit at RAF St Athan, two from the Sea Harrier Support Unit and one direct from British Aerospace, under accelerated delivery.

These aircraft were eventually ferried to Ascension Island to join SS *Atlantic Conveyor*, already carrying Harrier GR.3s and Chinook and Wessex helicopters. The ship departed on 7 May 1982, arriving within V/STOL range of HMS *Hermes* on 18 May. Later that day four Sea Harriers, including those flown by Brown and Leeming, deployed to *Hermes*, becoming part of 800 NAS. On the same day one Sea Harrier was deployed to *Invincible*, the final three going across the

next day. This immediate transfer of Sea Harriers (and also RAF Harrier GR.3s) to the two carriers proved to be very fortunate, as on 25 May the *Atlantic Conveyor* was struck by an AM.39 Exocet missile fired by an Argentine Super Etendard, and later sank.

Back in the UK, only three Sea Harriers of those remaining undelivered were available. One was with the Aeroplane and Armament Experimental Establishment at Boscombe Down for further development flying, while the other two were transferred to an embryo 899 NAS. In June 1982, among other pilots transferred to the Yeovilton-based element of 809 NAS for training, using the two 899 NAS aircraft, were four more RAF pilots: Squadron Leaders R. Thomas and J. A. West and Flight Lieutenants P. J. Collins and D. R. Gibbons. These pilots did not see action during the conflict. Although Thomas and Gibbons left 809 NAS in July and October respectively, Collins and West remained with 809 NAS for its post-conflict deployment on HMS *Illustrious* until the unit disbanded once more on 17 December 1982.

So much for the 'infiltration' of the FAA by the RAF. As the shooting war began in earnest, all three RAF pilots of 800 NAS took part in the nine-aircraft strike against Port Stanley airfield on 1 May, in the wake of the first 'Black Buck' raid. This mission was reported with the now-famous quote from BBC reporter Brian Hanrahan, who observed: 'I counted them all out, and I counted them all back'.

The aircraft of Ball and Morgan were armed with BL755 cluster-bomb units (CBUs), and that of Penfold with delayed-action 1,000lb HE 'iron' bombs. Penfold was to place two of his bombs on the runway, scabbing it, while the others' CBUs fragmented over the airfield. The only damage sustained on this first raid occurred when a 20mm HE anti-aircraft round exploded as it

passed through the fin of Morgan's aircraft, leaving smaller holes in the tailplane. He was also forced to break an AAA gun-laying radar lock-on by jinking and dumping chaff, carried loose in the Sea Harrier's airbrake. The aircraft was rapidly returned to service by the ship's battle damage repair team.

Geoff Lea's painting depicts a Sea Harrier on CAP deflecting a Dagger (the local name for the Israeli-built Mirage V, or Nesher) of the *Fuerza Aerea Argentina* from an attack on a Royal Navy LPD assault ship and a tank landing ship (LST). Although this particular action was not known to have been flown by an RAF pilot, it is typical of the many missions they did fly.

Armed with two AIM-9L Sidewinder infra-red guided, short-range air-to-air missiles (SRAAMs) and a pair of 30mm Aden cannon, and carrying two 100gal

drop-tanks, Sea Harriers from both squadrons (or all three, if one acknowledges a continued identify for 809 NAS after transferring its aircraft to the carriers) flew many armed reconnaissances and CAPs in defence of the Task Force.

The first RAF kill by a Sea Harrier, and, incidentally, the first air-to-air victory, fell to Paul Barton of 801 NAS at about 1910Z (1910 GMT) on 1 May 1982. Attacking a pair of Mirage IIIEs, Barton and his RN wingman finally manoeuvred in behind them and, coming in just below one at a range of about a mile, launched a Sidewinder. The missile exploded, causing the Mirage to disintegrate, although its pilot ejected. Barton's wingman damaged the second Mirage with another Sidewinder, but it escaped, only to be shot down by 'friendly fire' close to Stanley.

Later that day, Bertie Penfold of 800 NAS scored the RAF's second kill of the conflict when he launched an AIM-9L at a Dagger from a range of some three miles astern. The Dagger exploded, killing the Argentine pilot. On 21 May John Leeming of 809 NAS, operating as part of 800 NAS, engaged an A-4 Skyhawk with 30mm cannon fire from above and behind, aiming just aft of the cockpit. The aircraft disintegrated and fell into Falkland Sound.

On 23 May Dave Morgan and Leeming encountered a trio of Puma helicopters escorted by an A.109 helicopter gunship. They made a pass over the helicopters, and one Puma pilot lost control and crashed. Both Morgan and Leeming then engaged the A.109 with cannon fire, causing the heavily-armed helicopter to explode. After a few minutes, as the Sea Harriers came around again, Morgan caught another of the Pumas on the ground and damaged it with his remaining 30mm rounds. This helicopter was later destroyed by 801 NAS aircraft.

The first RAF loss, thankfully not fatal, occurred on 1 June when Ian Mortimer of 801 NAS was hit by an Argentine Roland surface-to-air missile. He was flying at about 10,000ft, some seven miles south of Port Stanley. The Roland hit his rear fuselage and Mortimer was able to eject safely. He was subsequently rescued by a RN Sea King in the early hours of 2 June.

Although many CAP, strike and reconnaissance sorties were flown, the next RAF kill did not occur until 8 June, at about 1945Z. Having taken off from *Hermes* just under an hour earlier, Morgan and his RN wingman were almost ready to return when they noticed that a landing craft was about to be attacked by four A-4B Skyhawks. With the advantage of height, the Harriers dived on the Skyhawks. Morgan fired an AIM-9L at one aircraft, which exploded. Turning, he launched his second missile, which caused a second Skyhawk to break in two. His attack with cannon against a third aircraft was frustrated by problems with his head-up display, and although he missed, the visual cues generated allowed his wingman to down the Skyhawk with a Sidewinder. The fourth Skyhawk jettisoned its tanks and remaining bombs and made off. This action produced the final air-to-air kills of the conflict, the RAF having been in at both the first and last kills.

It has not been the author's intention to ignore the role of the Fleet Air Arm. Rather, he has concentrated on the RAF contribution to the Sea Harrier's Falklands battles.

# *Wessex over Northern Ireland*

*Painting by Michael Rondot*
*Text by Ken Delve*

MICHAEL RONDOT OFFERS AN UNUSUAL APPROACH to a little recorded subject in this painting, a close-up, head-on study of a pair of distinctive Wessex helicopters over Northern Ireland. Hugging the ground contours to avoid detection and maintain the element of surprise on arrival, they are alert for trouble as the crew search for the Dropping Zone. The troops in the cabin adjust their equipment, ready to deploy into position as soon as the wheels touch down.

Hugging the ground contours to avoid detection, the Wessex helicopters in Michael Rondot's painting are alert for trouble as they search for the dropping zonae (DZ). The soldiers in the cabin adjust their equipment, ready to deploy into position as soon as the 'chopper' touches down. The ability fly into and out of small spaces, including urban areas, gives military and security forces an enormous degree of flexibility and mobility, an essential requirement in counter-terrorist internal security operations.

In July 1957, No. 275 Squadron, whose home base was Thornaby, detached a flight of three Bristol Sycamore HR.14s to RAF Aldergrove in Northern Ireland to act as a Search and Rescue (SAR) Flight. This was a logical move at the time, as the various RAF flying units had the same requirements for SAR cover as did their compatriots on the UK mainland. The major limitation was simply a lack of helicopters, as, since the successful employment of helicopters in Malaya in the late 1940s, there had been an increasing demand for their services. During the Malayan Emergency the helicopter had come of age and acquired a wide range of roles, particularly casualty evacuation (CASEVAC) and liaison duties, but with an increasing utility in all manner of tactical roles.

Northern Ireland soon proved an ideal location for the integration of helicopters into the tactical role of the Army and their involvement in internal security (IS) operations. Malaya and Cyprus (the anti-EOKA terrorist operations) provided the foundation of tactics and operational principles, and over the next 30 years the situation in Northern Ireland established beyond doubt the essential place of such aircraft in this role.

Northern Ireland's geography makes life very easy for the terrorist and very difficult for the security forces. The countryside consists of small fields with an abundance of hedges, valleys, farms and other such hideaways. With low-key security policies the initiative will always rest with the terrorist, and anything that can be done to help redress the balance is very valuable. Helicopters help by providing both a rapid reaction capability in the event of trouble and offering an excellent means of surveillance.

In April 1959 the three Sycamores of the Aldergrove SAR Flight became No. 118 Squadron, originally with a planned limited life, since the general shortage of helicopters and the increasing number of operational theatres caused much juggling of resources. However, the squadron was so heavily tasked by the authorities that political pressure was brought to bear to extend their stay. It was even suggested that the unit should be expanded to enable it to undertake forward deployments and so work even more closely with the security forces, the Royal Ulster Constabulary (RUC) being very keen on the idea. September 1960 saw an agreement to extend the unit's life, but this was short-lived, and when in September 1962 the IRA announced an end to violence, the opportunity was taken to disband No. 118 Squadron and re-allocate its aircraft. This did not, however, mean an end to helicopter employment in the area, but rather the intention to make use of the new SRT Force which had meanwhile been formed in mainland Britain. Unfortunately, the first such deployment turned into something of a farce when only five Whirlwinds of the planned twelve helicopters (six Belvederes and six Whirl-

winds) were present in November 1962 for Exercise 'Winged Coachman'.

Nevertheless, the principle of bringing in helicopters as and when needed remained in place until 1970. There was now to be a seven-year lull until 14 August 1969, when units of the British Army were deployed on peacekeeping duties in the province. Over the following months the situation continued to deteriorate, and the scale of terrorist activity rose.

The decision was then taken to deploy a Flight of, on average, six Westland Wessex HC.2 helicopters of No. 72 Squadron, whose home base was Odiham, as a semi-permanent detachment at Aldergrove. This was the start of a commitment that continues to the present day, the Wessex proving to be a reliable and dependable workhorse for such duties. Designed as a tactical transport/ ground assault helicopter, the Wessex first entered service with the UK's armed forces in the Royal Navy in 1961, and the HC.2 version equipped No. 38 Squadron, RAF, three years later. The Wessex's speed and its ability to carry up to sixteen persons in addition to its three crew members has made it an ideal aircraft for use in the IS role in Northern Ireland, where its distinctive hump-nosed shape is a familiar sight.

The range of roles performed by the various helicopters, including those flown by the Army Air Corps, has been very impressive, encompassing mobility, the insertion of ground forces, monitoring, the observation of demonstrations and other gatherings (often being used to identify ringleaders), and the resupply of isolated security posts deep in 'bandit' territory which it would be difficult and potentially hazardous to resupply by land convoy.

When an incident has taken place, such as an explosion or even the discovery of a suspicious vehicle,

a helicopter can be called in to search the area for potential booby traps before risking a ground force. This aerial surveillance is perhaps the single most important role of the Northern Ireland-based aircraft. Helicopters also undertake a wide range of communications and liaison duties, such as moving VIPs from place to place at min-

imum risk. Last, but by no means least, is the vital CASEVAC role, transporting injured soldiers and civilians to medical care. Many lives would have been lost but for the rapid aerial transport of seriously wounded personnel.

Over the years a number of helicopters have been hit by groundfire, but little damage has been caused. On 12 February 1978, however, an AAC Gazelle was shot down near Newry and the crew killed. Generally speaking, the helicopters have proved to be remarkably resis-

tant to groundfire, although there was always concern that the IRA would acquire shoulder-launched heat-seeking missiles such as the SA-7, which would have given them a much better chance of bringing down the helicopters which they so despised.

On 12 November 1981 the Wessex squadron moved its HQ to Aldergrove to become fully established in Northern Ireland, and since that date it has been a vital asset in Ulster. The helicopter is such a flexible aircraft that it can perform a very wide variety of roles, and during its time in Northern Ireland it has performed superbly well in all that it has been asked to do. Certain aspects, especially those concerned with Special Forces, will remain under wraps for some years yet, but its potential in the quiet insertion and recovery of such forces is obvious. The more usual duties have been those outlined above. Very few demonstrations or other Republican gatherings took place without there being a helicopter nearby, using various imaging sensors to gather intelligence and monitor potential trouble. Such routine work is the essence of any anti-terrorist campaign, and in the days before helicopters the acquisition of such intelligence was both harder and more dangerous. Even though a type of peace has at last returned to the Province, a peace that all hope will become permanent, the security forces need to remain alert and ready for any reversion to terrorist activities by either side.

The helicopter has been one of the great success stories of air power in the past 40 years, and its prospects for the future are excellent. In many operational theatres it has proved a vital adjunct to the missions flown by its fixed-wing cousins. In the IS scenario its value is beyond measure.

# Tornado Airfield Attack

_Painting by Norman Hoad_
_Text by Ken Delve_

IN ANY WAR, THE FIRST PRIORITY OF ANY AIR FORCE is to gain air superiority, and the Gulf War of 1991 was no exception. The Iraqi Air Force, although lacking in quality, was numerically strong, and rendering it impotent was of primary importance. Various measures were taken by the Coalition forces to achieve this, notably attacks on Iraqi airfields by Tornado GR.1s of the RAF.

Some idea of the size of the target airfields facing the Allies in Iraq can be gained from the one in Norman Hoad's painting. The main runway extends roughly far left to right, with a second runway crossing it. But the runways are not the target. The Tornado has released its weapon over the taxiways and the dispersal areas on the far side of the airfield. The dispersals on the near side will no doubt be targeted in a later raid, so that the hardened aircraft shelters in which Iraqi aircraft are housed will be isolated from the taxiways. Later on in the campaign to deny Iraqi airpower, special weapons will be used to penetrate the massive concrete shelters, destroying not only the shelters themselves, but also the aircraft and equipment inside them.

The Tornado GR.1 was uniquely suitable for this mission. Designed at the height of the Cold War as a long-range interdictor, it had to be able to survive in the hostile environment created by the integrated Warsaw Pact defence system of fighters, surface-to-air missiles (SAMs), and anti-aircraft artillery. The solution adopted was to penetrate and attack from ultra-low level at night, or in bad weather, using a first-pass blind-attack capability. Ultra-low-level penetration minimises the chances of the attackers being detected by radar, maximises interception problems for the defending fighters, and negates the medium- and high-altitude SAM systems at a stroke. At the same time, it shrinks the engagement envelopes of the short-range, low-altitude SAMs and AAA. To increase survivability still further, Skyshadow ECM and BOZ-107 chaff and flare pods are routinely carried.

The ability to carry out low-level attacks at night depends on two things. The first is terrain-following radar, which allows Tornado to fly at a preset altitude down to 200ft, automatically avoiding all obstacles. The other is ground-mapping radar coupled with a super-accurate navigation kit. Once planned, mission details are recorded on a tape cassette which is fed into the on-board computer. The crew can then fly a planned time line, with extremely accurate indications of whether they are early or late. This is combined with a readout of how far off track they are. As if this is not enough, the navigation kit can be updated en route using radar-significant check-points. The outstanding accuracy achieved in this way allows accurate attacks to be made without the target ever being seen.

The other essential attribute of Tornado GR.1 is its smooth ride at high speeds and low altitudes. This is largely due to its variable-sweep wing, which is of small area and, at maximum sweep, low aspect ratio, giving a low gust response.

Tornado's weaponry was equally well suited to the task of airfield attack. Two Hunting JP233 dispensers could be carried beneath the fuselage, each containing 30 SG357 cratering submunitions and 215 HB876 area-denial mines. These are dispensed simultaneously, and descend under small parachutes. The submunitions penetrate and break up concrete surfaces such as runways and taxiways, while the mines hinder repair operations. After the munitions are released, the JP233 dispensers are automatically jettisoned.

More than a dozen main operating bases in southern and western Iraq were targeted by the RAF Tornado force. This was a formidable undertaking; some were more than twice the size of London Heathrow Airport, with two long runways and literally miles of taxiways. The number of cuts needed to render even one of these bases inoperable was formidable, and it was clearly impossible to halt Iraqi air operations completely with the means available. A policy of maximum harassment was therefore adopted, in part by cutting the access between hardened shelter complexes and the main taxiways.

In all, 40 Tornado GR.1s were deployed in three composite squadrons, with personnel drawn from regular units in the UK and Germany. The first squadron, drawn from Nos. IX, XV, 17, 27, 31 and 617 squadrons, was based at Bahrain International Airport (RAF Muharraq in years gone by). The second, comprising crews from Nos. 2, IX, 14, 16, 20 and 617 squadrons, deployed to Tabuk in the north-west of Saudi Arabia. Finally, elements of Nos. IX, 14, 17 and 31 squadrons settled in at Dhahran, on the Gulf coast, where six reconnaissance Tornado GR.1As were also based.

The first Tornado missions were launched at 0100 local time on 17 January 1991. These consisted of four Tornadoes from Dharhan and eight from Muharraq, all carrying two JP233 dispensers and two large drop tanks of either 1,500- or 2,250-litre capacity. The latter brought the all-up weight to 30.5 tons, making the air-

craft sluggish, although the Tornado's fly-by-wire control system ensured that stick forces remained the same as always. The target was Tallil airfield, near Basrah.

The laden Tornados climbed to medium altitude and headed towards Iraqi-occupied territory. Around them were hundreds of aircraft, all heading in the same direction and all with their navigation lights on. Ahead were their tankers; Victors and VC10s. Locating them, the Tornadoes topped-up their tanks and descended to low altitude. Flying in Card-four formations, with 2-3nm between aircraft, they switched off their naviga-

tion lights as the border was neared and engaged automatic terrain-following flight for an altitude of 200ft. 'Hard Ride' was selected on the Tornadoes' control system to ensure that they followed the ground contours as closely as possible, and then, to use an expression current at that time, they went 'sausage-side'.

Cruising across the desert at 200ft in thick, velvety blackness, the crews seemed to be alone, but of course they were not. Filling the sky over southern Iraq was a vast aerial armada of F-4G Wild Weasel defence-suppression aircraft, F-15C Eagle fighters flying escort, EF-111 Raven electronic warfare aircraft and many other attackers, all heading for other targets. As they approached the target, afterburner was used to accelerate to 600kt and cancelled when that speed was reached. Speed decayed only slowly at full military power, and there was little point in overflying the target with after-

burner flames betraying their exact whereabouts to the waiting Iraqi gunners. Each Tornado crew, navigating independently, made course corrections to bring their aircraft on to its final attack heading. These differed; each aircraft had a specific target on the airfield to attack, and, in any case, it would have been tactically

unsound to have all aircraft approach from the same direction.

Little was visible outside the cockpit. Wing Commander Jerry Witts, commanding 31 Squadron at Dhahran, described the scene:

'We ran in at it, and I couldn't see a thing. My navigator had it [the target] on the radar and the autopilot was doing the work. I threw all the switches and we let the thing [JP233] go.

'It takes a few seconds. It was like going over a cobbled road very quickly. It seemed very important to me to stay very low, because if anyone did start shooting that's where I wanted to be. All of a sudden we were up at about 800ft and I was fighting like a dingbat to keep the plane down and get away as fast as we possibly could.'

The defences were taken by surprise, and little opposition was encountered initially. Once alerted, however, the Iraqis reacted furiously, lighting up the whole sky with tracer from anti-aircraft guns interspersed with the glare from SAMs. It was not aimed fire; the high speed and low altitude of the attacking Tornadoes ruled that out, but it was a ferocious barrage through which the later attackers were forced to fly.

On the western side of Saudi Arabia the Tabuk Tornadoes were also in action. Four, also armed with JP233s, set off to attack Al Assad Air Base, supported by two Tornadoes each carrying three Alarm anti-radar missiles. Four Alarms were successfully launched, and the main force, arriving five minutes later, attacked unscathed. Another four-ship formation successfully raided Al Taqaddum. All Tornados engaged on the night of 16/17 January returned safely.

War does not end with the dawn, and on the following day a raid was launched against the air base of Al Rumaylah. As daylight allowed the Iraqi gunners to aim visually, an overflying attack with JP233 was not viable. Instead, four Tornadoes from Muharraq carried 1,000lb bombs, using a toss-attack profile to loft them at the target from several miles back. Owing to technical problems, one Tornado was late taking off. As the other three pulled up to the bomb release point one was hit and caught fire, forcing the crew to eject.

On the following night, 17/18 January, Tornadoes were again out in force against Iraqi airfields. The defenders had learned from previous experience. Whereas on the first night most AAA fire had been high-angle, it was now on a much flatter trajectory which posed an increased hazard to the low-flyers. First off from Muharraq were four JP233-armed aircraft on a deep penetration to Ubaydah bin al Jarrah, followed two hours later by a further four heading for Shaibah, near Basrah. All eight aircraft hit their targets, but shortly after leaving Shaibah one aircraft went down, the only combat loss of the war on a JP233 mission. One of the al Jarrah raiders also sustained damage, but this was from birdstrike and not from enemy action.

The Tabuk contingent sent eight aircraft back to Al Assad during the evening of 17 January, at the same time launching a four-ship Alarm attack on the huge airfield at H3. The latter was followed a few hours later by three JP233-armed Tornadoes preceded by four Alarm aircraft, but this time the Iraqi defenders were ready and waiting, and put up such a solid barrage of AAA that the runway attack was called off.

Such attacks continued for a day or two longer, interspersed with toss-bombing missions. A variation on this theme took place on the night of 19/20 January, when eight Tornadoes from Muharraq visited Tallil Air Base. Four delivered toss attacks against the airfield defences, using airburst-fuzed 1,000-pounders, shortly before the remainder ran in with JP233s. During this raid a Tornado was hit by a SAM and its crew were forced to eject.

After four nights, air opposition had been neutralised, for the loss of four Tornadoes. Eight Iraqi main operating bases had been closed, while several others were severely restricted. Air superiority was assured and, shortly after, the Tornado force was switched to medium-level operations and directed against a wider variety of targets.

*The artist writes:* Both the Lancaster N-Nuts painting and this Tornado strike scene depict two phases in the development of air power as the dominant arm in modern warfare. The Lancaster had to rely on massed numbers to achieve effectiveness, whereas the Tornado, with precision guided munitions, can deliver a weapon load with such accuracy that large numbers are unnecessary. Both, along with the now defunct 'V' Bombers, mark critical and progressive steps in the attainment of the means to destroy an enemy's ability to wage war.

# Tipping In AND Doors Closed

*Painting by Mark Postleth-*
*waite*
*Text by Peter Jacobs*

AT 0200 (BAGHDAD TIME) ON 2 AUGUST 1990, Iraq invaded Kuwait. Within a matter of a few days the country was occupied and Iraqi forces appeared ready to move into Saudi Arabia. The invasion brought an immediate international response and United Nations condemnation, resulting in the movement of Allied forces into the area to protect Saudi Arabia under Operation 'Desert Shield'. Britain responded by sending Tornado F.3s and GR.1s, with support aircraft and personnel, into theatre. By the end of August an experienced composite unit of Tornado GR.1s, including seven crews from the famous No. 617 ' Dambuster' Squadron based at RAF Marham, had arrived at Bahrain International Airport on Bahrain Island in the Persian Gulf, previously known as RAF Muharraq, ready to counter any advance by Iraqi forces into Saudi Arabia.

Throughout the remainder of 1990 intense diplomatic efforts were made to persuade Iraq to withdraw its forces from Kuwait, but despite United Nations resolutions applying increasing economic and political pressure, Iraq refused to comply. During this time a second Tornado GR.1 unit had been formed at Tabuk and the strength of the unit at Muharraq increased. While diplomatic negotiations continued, the Allied forces in Saudi Arabia and other associated Gulf states continued to grow. The initial build-up had been concerned with the prevention of an invasion of Saudi Arabia, but it had become obvious by the end of the year that the Allies needed to establish an offensive option to demonstrate their intent to recover Kuwait. When the United Nations' deadline for Iraqi forces to withdraw from Kuwait by 15 January 1991 was passed, the UN authorised the use of military force under Operation 'Desert Storm'.

The preparatory planning for the first 'Desert Storm' missions had been conducted by a few selected

crews for a number of months. The task that had been assigned to the Tornado GR.1 crews was Offensive Counter Air, which meant denying the Iraqi Air Force the use of its large and well-constructed airfields. This task would initially be carried out by RAF Tornado GR.1s, using the JP233 anti-airfield weapon, which required delivery from low level across the airfield, a difficult and most dangerous task, though absolutely vital to the early stages of the campaign.

In the early hours of 17 January, the UN deadline having passed, the first Allied air strikes went into action, intent on crippling the Iraqi air defence, command and control system and the nuclear and chemical warfare threat. Included in these first attacks were RAF Tornado GR.1s on long-range missions to attack two of the most important Iraqi airfields, Shaibah and Al Jarrah. As the air offensive increased, the Tornado GR.1s made many more determined day and night attacks on targets deep in Iraq.

With the collapse of the Iraqi air defence network and the consequent reduction in the surface-to-air missile threat, it was no longer essential for attacks to be carried out at low level. After the first week of operations the decision was made to abandon the low-level attacks and to start carrying out attacks at medium level, from about 20,000ft. This required changes in weapons and tactics. The Tornado GR.1s were able to carry out medium-level attacks because American aircraft could 'jam' electronically, or attack, the radars associated with the missile batteries. Additionally, medium-level attacks took the Tornados beyond the range of most of the Iraqi anti-aircraft guns. The weapon loads also changed, typically comprising up to eight 1,000lb free-fall bombs.

Although these vital differences in attack methods meant that the Tornado loss rate would be reduced, the crews now faced the problem of accurate weapon deliv-

ery. The GR.1 had been designed for high-speed, low-level missions, not for medium-level, free-fall bombing attacks. The aircraft's sophisticated computers were not designed to calculate bombing solutions from medium level, with the associated problems of wind effects, so more traditional bombing methods had to be used, relying more on the skill of the crew to achieve accurate results. With the change in tactics and weapons came a change in targets. Gradually the array of targets grew to cover oil storage facilities, power stations and ammunition dumps.

On 12 February 1991 six RAF Tornado GR.1s from Muharraq were detailed to carry out a daylight attack against a military installation in Southern Iraq. Flying as Number Three of the formation in Tornado ZD717 'C' was Flight Lieutenant Paul Wharmby and his navigator, Flight Lieutenant Steve Kennedy, from No. 617 'Dambuster' Squadron, flying their eleventh operational sortie. Also taking part in the mission were American defence-suppression F-4G 'Wild Weasels', armed with anti-radiation missiles, tasked with destroying the enemy surface-to-air missile sites around the target area. The plan for this particular mission reflected the many training missions that had previously been carried out in the build-up to Desert Storm.

Following an intense briefing, the six Tornados took off from Muharraq and headed towards the rendezvous with the VC10K air-to-air refuelling tanker. Owing to an unserviceability in its sophisticated electronic warfare equipment, Number Six soon had to return to Muharraq, but the five remaining Tornados continued to the rendezvous with the tanker. Having refuelled to full, the Tornados left friendly airspace and continued across the Iraqi border into hostile territory.

The route over Iraq had been planned with the benefit of excellent intelligence, and it carefully avoided known defences. However, the location of mobile mis-sile and gun systems was harder to monitor, so there was the occasional worry about whether or not these defences would be encountered. As they approached the target the Tornados detected several enemy missile systems within the target area. Although the Iraqi early warning network had largely been put out of action, the anti-radar missiles of the defence-suppression F-4G 'Wild Weasels' had certainly let them know what was about to happen. Steve Kennedy recalls:

'I remember seeing indications of an enemy system on our radar warning receiver and almost immediately seeing the sky above us "criss-crossed" with smoke trails as the American Wild Weasels launched their anti-radiation missiles.'

Each Tornado was carrying five 1,000lb free-fall bombs, and the attack was to be carried out using a 45° dive from medium level, a method which would increase the accuracy of the attack. However, it did mean that the nearer an aircraft got to the ground, the more susceptible it was to the enemy's anti-aircraft fire. Steve Kennedy adds:

'As we approached the target things seemed to get quieter, but after we had tipped-in for the attack the puffs of smoke of the enemy's AAA started to appear in front of us; after releasing the bombs, whilst in the dive recovery, it seemed to be bursting around our ears.'

The Tornado flown by Paul Wharmby and Steve Kennedy was the last to carry out a dive attack, since by the time Numbers Four and Five were ready to start their dives there was a carpet of AAA beneath them, so they carried out a level bombing attack from medium level. Having delivered their attacks, the Tornadoes made their way back to friendly airspace without further incident. Steve Kennedy concludes: 'It was always a relief to get back across the border, and Paul could not resist doing an aileron roll each time to celebrate the fact!'

All of the Tornados returned safely to Muharraq after a mission lasting just over four hours. Although the aircraft and crew returned safely on this occasion, Tornado ZD717 'C' failed to return from a mission just two days later, when it was shot down by surface-to-air missiles during a laser-guided-bomb (LGB) attack against Al Taqaddum airfield. Its pilot, Flight Lieutenant Rupert Clark, managed to eject and was taken prisoner, but navigator Flight Lieutenant Steve Hicks was killed.

The use of free-fall 1,000lb bombs was not the most accurate of bombing methods. Although it proved adequate against large and non-hardened targets, free-fall bombing was not effective against either smaller or hardened targets. The solution to this problem was the LGB, which was basically a 1,000lb bomb with a seeker head and steering vanes. The technique relied on a second aircraft to illuminate the target with a laser beam, and the accuracy of delivery was simply devastating. From then on, almost every mission flown by the Muharraq Tornados involved the use of LGBs.

Paul Wharmby and Steve Kennedy completed a further seven operational sorties before the Gulf Conflict ceasefire came into effect on 28 February. While the air victory in Desert Storm was primarily due to the vast American effort, the RAF contribution, and in particular the contribution of the Tornado GR.1 crews in the delivery of specialist weapons, was significant in ensuring a quick campaign. The end of the Gulf Conflict of 1991 did not, however, mean the end of RAF involvement in the area.

Despite his humiliating defeat, Saddam Hussein continued to wield strong control within Iraq. A Kurdish rebellion launched in March 1991 was met with fierce opposition by the Iraqi army, and as a result a multinational force was assembled to give humanitarian assistance to the Kurds. The air supply task was terminated in July when a no-fly zone was established under Operation 'Warden', banning Iraqi aircraft from flying north of the 36th Parallel. Meanwhile, the 'Marsh' Arabs in Southern Iraq sought independence from the repressive Baghdad regime, and their revolt was countered by an Iraqi air offensive. This was considered contrary to the terms of the UN resolutions, and a second no-fly zone was imposed south of the 32nd Parallel, under Operation 'Jural'. Continued Iraqi movements towards the Kuwait border during late 1994, and the uninterrupted rule of Iraq by Saddam Hussein, have meant that a strong UN military presence remains in the area to the present day.

The paintings 'Tipping In' and 'Doors Closed', by Mark Postlethwaite, show Tornado GR.1 ZD717 'C', flown by Flight Lieutenants Paul Wharmby and Steve Kennedy of 617 Squadron, carrying out its attack against a military installation in Southern Iraq on 12 February 1991. The term 'tipping in' refers to the aircraft starting its dive attack, while 'doors closed' was the codeword sent by the crew to indicate that the Tornado had left the target.

Special thanks are due to my colleague, Squadron Leader Steve Kennedy, for his assistance with this account.

*The artist writes:* For people of my generation, the Gulf War was immensely significant. For the first time in our lives we watched as friends and others of our age went off to fight a war. It was a strange time; many of us stayed glued to the TV, hoping to stay in touch with what was happening out there, just as if it had been some kind of global soap opera. This war, more than any, was a visual war. With the blanket TV coverage we were constantly bombarded with some incredible images of what the modern high-tech war was like.

I knew that I had to try to capture some of this on canvas. I was quickly commissioned to paint a Tornado in action in the Gulf, and some weeks later it was arranged for me to visit 617 Squadron at Marham to gather the necessary references. It was here that I really first recognised the Tornado as a classic warplane. Gone was the sleek, clinical and shiny speed machine, in its place was a heavily-laden, dirty, battleweary warrior that had come of age in the history of air fighting.

With the tremendous help of 617 pilot Flight Lieutenant Paul Wharmby, a veteran of 18 missions over Iraq and also a talented artist himself, I set to work to produce the two paintings shown here. Both depict a single raid that 'Wam' was involved in, on a target near Baghdad. Working from his personal recollections and documents, I was able to build up a fairly accurate picture of the moment when he rolled his aircraft, ZD717 'C', into the dive for the attack. This became the painting 'Tipping In'. Following this, I wanted to show a slightly more flattering angle on the Tornado, and came up with the other painting, 'Doors Closed'. This shows his aircraft climbing away from the target at maximum dry power and with the Tornado swing-wing set for enhanced manoeuvrability. The title 'Doors Closed' came from the radio message that was sent to confirm that the bombs had been dropped.

# Coup de Grâce

*Painting by Michael Rondot*
*Text by Ken Delve*

MAINTAINING TIGHT FORMATION, A PAIR OF Sepecat Jaguars bank at low level away from the Iraqi warship they have just attacked. The pilot of the lead aircraft snatches a quick look back to the target to get a fleeting visual assessment of whether their attack was a success, and the blazing and listing vessel testifies to the accuracy and power of the Jaguar in the low-level attack operation, for which the 25-year-old aircraft design is still well suited.

Desert-pink SEPECAT Jaguars became a frequent sight on world newsreels during the early months of 1991, as the aircraft flew numerous daylight missions against Iraqi targets in and around Kuwait. The involvement of Coltishall's Jaguars in the Gulf crisis had begun the previous August. Within days of the 2 August invasion of Kuwait by Iraqi forces, a number of RAF units were alerted for rapid deployment to the region. At Coltishall in Norfolk the word to prepare came on 8 August, and the station went into a practised routine of getting its operational aircraft ready to move, along with all the ground support and personnel that a modern combat unit requires.

While the boxes were being packed, the aircraft were undergoing a quick repaint using Alkali Removable Temporary Finish (ARTF), which proved to be anything from a dusky brown to a distinct shade of pink. The station's units were classified as NATO mobile squadrons, so rapid deployment was an aspect with which they were familiar. In the years since the Gulf crisis they have been almost constantly engaged on United Nations air enforcement and peacekeeping duties.

Orders to deploy came on 10 August, and the following day the first batch of Jaguars took off for the Gulf, flying via Cyprus with air-to-air refuelling support provided by Victor tankers. By 13 August they had arrived at Thumrait in the Oman. The situation was very tense, as it was still generally expected that the Iraqi forces would continue their advance into Saudi Arabia or the Gulf States. The Omani host squadrons, themselves Jaguar operators, helped the transition to local conditions; flying at low level over the desert was a whole new ball game to pilots who were used to the terrain of Europe. Operating in temperatures in excess of 45° meant that new procedures had to be adopted by aircrew and groundcrew alike. Many a bare hand was scorched through careless touching of the aircrafts' metal skins. On the operational side it was anticipated that the Jaguars would be operating in the area of Kuwait, some 500 miles north of their present location, so detailed AAR plans had to be made. After the initial rush to arrive at a workable routine, the immediate threat of invasion receded and the detachment was able to re-evaluate the situation and take stock of what had been achieved to date. However, for the pilots the most important priority remained that of becoming familiar with operating at ultra low level over the desert.

The major problem with ultra-low-level flying over the desert, that is to say below 100ft, is the lack of visual clues. In the Operational Low Flying (OLF) environment the pilot achieves his mean operating height through visual reference, although in some aircraft a low height warner is fitted to provide a visual and/or audio warning if the aircraft descends below a given preset altitude. While this is very useful, it refers only to the terrain immediately below the aircraft, and not to any obstacle ahead. An experienced pilot can operate in the OLF environment with few problems, although the requirement of simply avoiding the ground and various obstacles forms a high proportion of his workload. The other problem with the desert is that of optical illusions. These are present to a greater or lesser degree in all low-level environments, but in the desert, with poor contrast, extreme sunlight or low sun angles, they become

even more hazardous. The difference between skimming just over a 'hidden' sand dune or colliding with it is not very great, and most desert aviators have come close on occasions. On 13 November 1990, Flight Lieutenant Keith Collishaw in GR.1A XX754 was killed in just such circumstances during a low-level training exercise over Kuwait.

The twelve-aircraft Jaguar Detachment (JagDet) moved to Muharraq, Bahrain, bringing the aircraft much closer to the operational theatre, although they were still 250 miles from Kuwait and AAR would therefore be essential for most sorties. The self-defence fit of the aircraft was enhanced by the addition of over-wing AIM-9L Sidewinder rails; the ability to carry a pair of these highly effective short-range air-to-air missiles gave a much appreciated capability. Survivability in the overall high threat environment, Iraqi forces being well equipped with anti-aircraft missiles and guns, was provided by a Westinghouse AN/ALQ-101(V)-10 jamming pod, a pair of flare dispensers under the rear fuselage and the standard Phima pod to dispense chaff. The Jaguars also received modifications and upgrades to a variety of their systems, including giving the Adour engines a 'tweak' to increase their thrust.

Although the detachment had spent most of its work-up concentrating on low-level attack profiles, the decision was taken to adopt medium-level deliveries as the primary option. This meant a rapid rethink on tactics and weapons, none of the RAF's standard weapons being suitable. The Canadian unguided CRV-7 rocket projectile was adopted, carried in an LAU-50033/A pod containing nineteen rockets. A standard load for each aircraft was two pods. Medium-level operations also meant that the RAF's normal cluster-bomb weapon, the BL755, was unusable; the solution was to adopt the American CBU-87 Rockeye II, which had a medium-

level mode. It proved to be a very effective area weapon against troops, soft-skinned vehicles, open-air ammunition dumps and other targets.

Day one of the conflict saw the Jaguars attack targets in Kuwait, followed the next day by targets in Southern Iraq. After these early missions the reactions of some of the pilots were identical to those of their forebears of 50 years before: 'It's the first time I've seen tracer and stuff coming at me. It certainly concentrates the mind a little. It was the longest minute of my life,' and 'It's quite impressive actually, watching it all go off. But after that I was more concerned with running away bravely.'

Towards the end of January the Jaguars were tasked against the Silkworm anti-ship missiles that the Iraqis had installed along the coast near Kuwait City to counter the expected US Marine amphibious landing. A strong amphibious assault force was present in the Gulf, and had undertaken numerous rehearsals to encourage the Iraqi commanders to believe that such an assault would form an essential element of any Coalition advance into Kuwait.

To clear the Gulf of Iraqi warships, most of which were small fast attack craft and coastal patrol vessels, Coalition aircraft, and especially helicopters, undertook many anti-shipping missions like the one depicted in Michael Rondot's painting. The Jaguars used CRV-7 in this role with some success. On one mission the attackers set up an almost 'academic range pattern' as they made passes over the enemy vessels. At least six, possibly seven, Polnochny landing craft were sunk or damaged by the Desert Cats. Wing Commander Bill Pixton recalls one such attack:

'The AWACS was telling us that the picture was clear, so there were no enemy aircraft in the area. We almost set up an academic range pattern on the ship, we did two passes rockets and four passes guns each, when

normally we would never consider re-attacking in a high-threat environment. The crew was seen to have abandoned the ship, the vessel being left ablaze and dead in the water as the Jaguars returned to base.'

As the ground assault rolled on, so the attacks against the Republican Guard formations in the Basra area were intensified to prevent these units from acting as a cohesive reinforcement or rallying point. The front-line Iraqi forces crumbled, and Coalition air power kept up the pressure by attacking lines of communication. Bridge busting, including pontoon bridges, became a regular feature of the offensive missions. Although the Coalition had achieved a degree of air superiority verging on air supremacy, this did not completely negate the ground-to-air threat, both from SAMs and, more dangerously, from the enormous amount of AAA of a wide range of calibres.

By combining aircraft into 'packages', with Suppression of Enemy Air Defences (SEAD) assets such as the F-4G Wild Weasel and EF-111 Raven going along whenever such protection was required, the danger was certainly lessened. However, it could not be eliminated, and against most targets the Jaguars would approach at medium level, dive to acquire the aiming point, drop their weapons and pull out before entering the most dense AAA zone, chiefly made up of smaller-calibre weapons, most of which were ineffective above 5,000ft. The tactic would vary according to the type of target and, hence, the type of weapon to be delivered, and the assessed level of the air defence threat. The RAF Jaguars were not the only ones in action, a detachment of French air force Jaguars operating from Al Ahsa airfield. They were heavily engaged against targets in Kuwait, and were able to use their laser-guided AS.30L missiles to good effect.

The RAF's Desert Cats proved their worth by flying 611 combat sorties without loss, a total of almost

1,000hr operational time. During these sorties they expended 750 1,000lb bombs, 395 CBU-87s, 32 pods of CRV-7 and 9,600 rounds of 30mm ammunition. Postwar Battle Damage Assessment has proved unable to determine the effectiveness, on a sortie-by-sortie basis, of all of the munitions expenditure by Coalition aircraft, but there is no doubt about the enormous overall impact of air power in the campaign. The ground forces successfully reoccupied Kuwait, but their way was very much cleared by the awesome firepower of Allied air power. JagDet played its full part in that mission.